YANKEE Magazine's
Practical Problem Solver

1,001 Ingenious Solutions to Everyday Dilemmas

by Earl Proulx
America's Favorite Handyman
and the editors of YANKEE magazine

YANKEE BOOKS

Printed in the United States of America on acid-free ∞,
recycled ♻ paper

Library of Congress Cataloging-in-Publication Data
Proulx, Earl.
     Yankee magazine's practical problem solver : 1,001
ingenious solutions to everyday dilemmas / by Earl Proulx
and the editors of Yankee magazine.
        p.   cm.
    Includes index.
    ISBN 0–89909–375–2 hardcover
    1. Home economics.   2. Dwellings—Maintenance and
repair.
    I. Yankee (Dublin, N.H.)   II. Title.
TX158.P77   1998
640—dc21   97–43248

Distributed in the book trade by St. Martin's Press

2 4 6 8 10 9 7 5 3 1 hardcover

YANKEE Magazine's
Practical Problem Solver

YANKEE BOOKS STAFF

Managing Editor: Jeff Bredenberg

Cover Designer: David Q. Pryor

YANKEE PUBLISHING STAFF

Publishing Director: Jamie Trowbridge

Book Editor: Sharon Smith

Contributing Writers: Linda Buchanan Allen, Lori Baird, Gordon Bock, Joan Cleveland, Jim Collins, Stephanie Graziadio, Connie Hatch, Dougald MacDonald, Michelle Seaton, Don Weafer

Editorial Consultants: Boyd Allen III, Barbara Bailey, Cathleen Baird, Elizabeth B. Buchanan, Russell C. Buchanan, Carolyn Burns, Debby Carroll, Tom Cavalieri, Susan Chop, Ashley Christie-Blogin, Andy Collins, Ann-Marie Cunniff, Maggie DelGallo, Richard Edmunds, Adelaide Eshbach, Abigail Faulkner, Robert Fico, David Frankel, Peter Gagnon, Susan Gagnon, Madelyn Gray, Sandra Harding, Mike Heffernan, Anne Hogg, Phillip Hogg, Cary Hughes, Mari Jones, Susan Joyce, Barbara Kops, Kristen Laine, Suzanne Linehan, Deedy Marble, Michigan State University Extension Service, Steve Mikulka, Terry Moore, Dave Nelson, Ed Nowack, Mary Owens, Martha Paul, Rose Rawlings, Stan Rosenfeld, Heston Scheffey, Dave Scott, Nancy Seaton, Stephen E. Sickles, Steve Smith, Paula Solomon, Donna Starito, State of Connecticut Department of Consumer Protection, Kathi Travers

Book Designer: Jill Shaffer

Illustrators: Anna Dewdney, Jill Shaffer

Indexer: Nanette Bendyna

Fact Checkers: Robina Gangemi, Robin Honig

Copy Editor: Barbara Jatkola

Proofreaders: Faith Hanson, Barbara Jatkola

Computer Keyboarder: Sheryl Fletcher

Editorial Assistant: Nancy Trafford

Contents

OUTSIDE THE HOUSE 71

Animal Pests 73

Bats • Bees • Birds • Blackflies • Cutworms • Deer •
Moles • Mosquitoes • Raccoons • Skunks • Slugs •
Spiders • Squash Bugs • Squirrels • Termites • Ticks •
Woodchucks

Yard and Garden 87

Lawns • Fruits and Vegetables • Herb Gardens • Flower
Gardens • Garden Tools • Trees and Shrubs • Fences

EVERYDAY LIVING 105

Cooking 107

Fruits and Vegetables • Dairy Products • Meat, Fish,
and Poultry • Rice and Potatoes • Other Foods • Baking
Tricks • Emergency Rescues • Meal Stretchers •
Leftovers • Eating Dilemmas • Feeding a Sick Person •
Gifts of Food

Buying Wisely 123

Groceries • Medicines • Clothing • Sports and Hobby
Equipment • Books and Magazines • Personal Services •
Appliances and Furniture • Shopping Strategies • Factory
Outlets • Buying Secondhand • Yard Sales

The Home Workshop 144

Organization • Space Savers • Fatigue • Protecting and
Maintaining Tools • Everyday Frustrations

Household Repairs 156

Walls • Doors • Windows • Floors • Ceilings • Plumbing
and Heating • Roofs • Decks

Cars and Other Vehicles 170

Fuel Efficiency • Locks and Keys • Windshields and
Wipers • The Exterior • Tires and Wheels • Overheating •
Heaters and Air Conditioners • Tough Starts • Parking

Introduction

All I asked was a simple question. The rough sketches for this book had just come in, and I asked if, in the illustration on page 241, the driveway to Earl's house should be steeper. Yes, it should, Earl said, and he told me he'd bring me a picture that I could show the artist.

Next thing I knew, I was looking at an aerial photo that showed exactly what the artist needed to see: how Earl had sited his house and built his driveway to cut down the amount of shoveling he'd need to do every winter.

"And you see those stacks?" Earl was telling me. I peered again and saw four or five dark areas that looked like wooden tepees. "That's how I stack my wood," he explained. "Never falls over."

That's what you get with Earl: always a little something extra, whether it's a novel idea for a household repair or a suggestion for a better way to stack your firewood. Yankee employees, who first met Earl when he was head of the company's maintenance department, have known for years that when they can't figure out how to solve a household problem, the answer is always the same: Ask Earl.

Jamie Trowbridge, *Yankee* Magazine's publishing director, tells the story of taking his kitchen stove apart one evening to clean up after a mouse infestation. He scrubbed the stove inside and out, but even after he experimented with different detergents, a hint of the mouse smell persisted. By that time, it was fairly late, and he had to get things straightened out before his toddlers got into the mess the next morning. What to do? He called Earl, who provided a simple but effective solution to the problem. Others—both staffers and the readers who have met Earl through his monthly *Yankee* Magazine column, "Plain Talk"—have called on him for advice on everything from termites in the basement to tarnish on the silverware. Nine times out of ten, Earl will have an answer based on his own seventy-plus years of experience. And when he doesn't, he'll research the problem. Or he'll think it through and come up with a solution that makes perfect sense—but is so ingenious that no one else would have thought of it. Earl's fix for Jamie's stinky stove, for example, was to rub vanilla extract over the metal where the mice had lived, and that did the trick.

That's why, when it came time to pull this book together, there was no question about where to begin: Just ask Earl! So, once again, we did. And he, along with nearly a dozen other writers and editors, came through with great fixes for squeaky floors and leaky roofs, torn camping gear and ripped convertible roofs, bursting closets and bulging ceilings. And then they went beyond household repairs and explained how you can use an ironing board as a portable gift wrap station or an emergency hotel room desk, how you can get a stubborn car battery going again, and why you should always carry dental floss on vacation. They even suggested ways you can manage medical problems that might otherwise slow you down, and they came up with techniques for tactfully coping with friends who are chronically late. They concentrated on the practical, the down-to-earth, the ingenious—the kinds of simple but wonderful ideas you can use every day of your life.

After all, to Earl and all the other contributors to this book, there are no problems, only challenges—all of which can be solved with a little Yankee ingenuity.

Just ask Earl.

—Sharon Smith
Editor

Inside the House

Back when I worked for my father, people didn't specialize as much as they do today. When you worked for someone then, you did anything he asked, whether it was carpentry, plumbing, masonry, or simple cleaning. Every spring, the people my father worked for would hire him to open up their lakefront cottages and get them ready for summer. And opening them up meant everything from getting the water running to making sure the motorboats were ready to go to cleaning inside the camps.

One of my jobs was to clean the windows. Many of those cottages had large lead glass windows, and I had a devil of a

time cleaning the corners of each pane. My mother provided the solution to this problem. She let me borrow an old meat skewer and told me to wrap my cleaning cloth around that. The pointed tip of the skewer allowed the cloth to tuck tightly into each corner and helped me to clean the windows as well as the owners could ask.

I made sure I learned something from everyone I worked with when I was young. Usually this meant watching my father and his men in action, but more than once it was my mother who gave me the right solution to a problem. And you know, a lot of the ideas in the following pages are the kinds of things my mother might have suggested. In "Household Organization," you'll find all kinds of ideas for dealing with limited space. (Let's face it, doesn't everybody think the space she's working with is limited?) "Clutter Cutters" is packed with tricks for sorting the treasures from the trash—the kinds of things you can really use when you're trying to minimize the mess. "Cleaning" offers terrific ideas for getting the grime off the kitchen floor or the chocolate stains out of your best blouse, and "Odors" has suggestions for everything from smelly closets to stinky garbage disposals. Finally, when you've sorted, cleaned, and deodorized everything in sight, look to "Home Decorating" for tips on coming up with inexpensive desks and sewing tables, instant window curtains, and inventive ways to display all those knickknacks that were too precious to throw out.

HOUSEHOLD ORGANIZATION
Making Space in Your Place

THE KITCHEN

Put Lazy Susan to Work

❏ If your refrigerator is jammed with so many jars, bottles, and wrapped packages that you can never find what you're looking for, install a one- or two-tier plastic lazy Susan on one of the shelves. Use it for ketchup, pickles, mustard, salad dressing, and so forth. Lazy Susans are available in kitchen supply stores.

Honey, I Shrunk the Fridge!

❏ The bad news is, your kitchen's tiny. The good news is, your refrigerator isn't stuffed. Consider installing a half-size refrigerator in place of the full-size one. This will give you some extra room to add cabinets, shelves, racks, and/or a counter above the smaller fridge.

Put Your Cabinets on a Diet

❏ One way to deal with kitchen cabinets that seem to be bursting from their hinges is to repackage some of the foods you buy and store. Cereals, for instance, come in boxes that are large and bulky and are only about three-quarters full (packed by weight, not volume, as they say). If you repackage such items (and other dry goods such as flour, sugar, beans, and rice) in sealable plastic bags or small, stackable airtight containers,

> ☑ **PROBLEM PREVENTED**
>
> ## Kitchen Flambé
>
> Cooking oils are highly flammable, so store them away from the stove. Put them in a pantry cupboard or a cabinet on the other side of the kitchen.

Household Organization

you'll save considerable space in your cabinets and get rid of bulky packaging material. Your foods also will last longer without attracting pests.

Up Against the Wall!

❏ Another way to deal with overstuffed kitchen cabinets is to take advantage of available wall space in your kitchen. Move your staples—flour, dried beans, sugar, macaroni—from inside your cabinets to open shelves. You can pick up inexpensive, ready-to-hang shelves at almost any home center—or save money by purchasing some lumber and shelf brackets and building your own. If you repackage and store your staples in airtight containers such as inexpensive glass canning jars, you'll be killing three birds with one stone: First, you'll clear out your kitchen cabinets. Second, with your staples in full view, you'll always know what and how much you have. Third, canning jars on shelves look terrific and add decorative charm to the kitchen.

 DOLLAR STRETCHER

Your Pantry Shouldn't Be Paltry

Creating a backup pantry area for canned goods and other nonrefrigerated staples will allow you to stock up when nonperishables go on sale and also save you that extra dash to the supermarket. (A cupboard in the mudroom or basement serves the purpose well.) Organize the items on shelves by category—say, soups, spaghetti sauces and pasta, canned vegetables, and so forth. This saves time, as you'll know right where to reach for an item.

Give a Kid Some Space!

❏ Having a preschooler rummage through kitchen cabinets looking for sippy cups and plastic plates can mean broken dishes on the floor or cuts and bruises on your child. So give your child his own kitchen cabinet. Choose one down low, close to the floor. Fill it with his stuff—plastic cups, plates, and cutlery, as well as snack foods that your child is allowed to get on his own.

Baby, Where Are the Bottles?

❏ Tired of rummaging through cabinets and drawers for bottles or other utensils for that nighttime feeding? Try designating one kitchen cabinet for baby's things: bottles and nipples, feeding spoons, even formula and baby food if there's room. That way, everything you need is in one place, no matter what time you need it (or how sleepy you are).

BEDROOMS

The Family Jewels

❑ Are you constantly rummaging through a box of assorted earrings only to come up one short? Try storing pierced earrings on clean window screening for easy access. Cut the screening to whatever size you need, then cover the edges with masking tape to prevent scratching. Simply put the posts of each pair of earrings through the front of the screen and clasp them behind. Hang the screen on small hooks on the back of a door.

❑ If you're tired of untangling bracelet or necklace chains every time you go to put one on, hang them up. Press pushpins into a corkboard and hang the jewelry from the pins, drape necklaces over a picture frame, or attach a tie rack to the back of your closet door and drape your necklaces over the individual hooks.

Trunk-ated

❑ Living in an area that requires you to wear sweaters three-quarters of the year means you want them to be accessible (not in the attic). If you don't have room to store them in your dresser all year round, keep them in a trunk in your bedroom (or wherever you have space) during the warmer months. Depending on the room, the trunk can double as a coffee table, end table, or nightstand. If the trunk is not lined with cedar, toss in a few cedar blocks or balls to keep the moths away from your best pullovers.

Storage on Wheels

❑ If you need extra storage space in a bedroom, try purchasing a couple of boxes on wheels, made espe-

TIME SAVER

Don't Stack and Carry

You can save time putting away clean dishes by storing your dishes and flatware in cabinets and drawers next to your dishwasher or dish rack. In one step, you can put them right where they belong instead of piling them on the kitchen counter and then carrying them to their proper spot.

cially to fit under the bed. You can store off-season clothing or other items in these and still have them accessible. Many catalogs carry these boxes, as do specialty shops that sell storage items.

Go with the Airflow

❑ Don't have room for a guest bed or the budget for a sleep sofa? At an outdoor-equipment store, buy an inflatable air mattress (the kind you can fill by reversing the vacuum cleaner airflow) for guests. Once it's inflated, cover the mattress with conventional bedding and set it up on the floor. After the guests leave, deflate the mattress and store it in a closet or under your bed. This approach works best if your guests are young and agile enough that they won't mind sleeping on the floor; it's not recommended for elderly houseguests.

CLOSETS

Mop Up

You'll get the hang of adding storage space if you install an extra rod in a closet crammed with jackets and slacks. This is also good for kids' clothes.

❑ If brooms and mops are falling on top of one another in the broom closet, attach a wall-mount grip to the

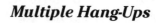

back of the closet door (or to one of the walls) and hang them there. You can buy the grip at a discount store or hardware store.

❑ If you don't have a broom closet, attach a wall-mount grip to the back of the basement door and hang your brooms and mops there.

Multiple Hang-Ups

❑ If you don't have enough room for all your short clothing items in the closet, buy another rod and hang it partway down the wall. That way, you'll have two rods instead of one and double the space for shorts, shirts, short skirts, and so forth.

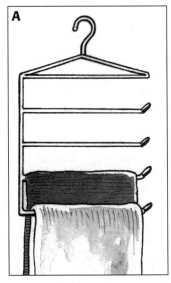
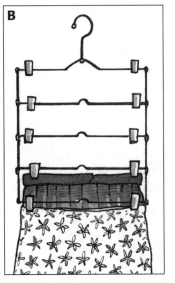

*Beat the crowding
with hangers designed
especially to store
multiple pants (A)
and skirts (B).*

❏ Need help for an overcrowded closet? Try investing in one of the vertical pant or skirt hangers sold in discount stores. These allow you to hang five or six garments from each hanger so you can get more pieces into that bulging closet.

Shelve It

❏ If you need more storage space in a small closet, set up a system of bins or baskets on closet shelves. It's easy to toss items into the open containers when you're picking up—and much easier to find them later.

Hit the Ceiling

❏ If you need more shelf space in a closet, check the height of the ceiling inside your closet. It may be high enough that you can install an extra level of shelves.

Take 'Em to the Cleaner

❏ If you don't have enough space to store off-season clothes, take them to the dry cleaner. Many dry cleaning establishments will store off-season clothes, some for just the cost of having the clothes cleaned. The service is particularly likely to be available in urban areas.

Hang Your Hat Here

❏ You can't figure out where to put hats; there's just not room in your closet. To solve the problem, hang a wooden pegboard on the inside or outside of your closet door. Or hang the pegboard on the wall of a room so that the hats hanging on the pegs add a decorative touch.

✔ PROBLEM PREVENTED

Keep Little Fingers out of Cleaning Supply Closets

Cleaning supplies are poisonous. Whether children live in your house or just visit there, make sure you keep all cleaning agents in cabinets with child-proof locks. (You can buy these locks at hardware stores or stores that sell baby supplies.)

Scheme with Colors

❏ Keeping track of which sheets fit on which bed can be a hassle. Give each bed in your home a different color scheme or pattern (green stripes, Victorian flowers, solid blue, and so on) and store each group of bed linens as a set, folded together. When you're ready to put clean sheets on a bed, you won't have to hunt for the right ones.

LAUNDRY

Cut Your Washing in Half

❏ Laundry can pile up quickly if you wash towels after every use, but sharing them isn't very sanitary. To reduce the washing chores (and your water and energy use) without spreading cold and flu germs, assign a particular color to each member of the family, then give each person a full set of towels in his color. Or assign a separate towel rack to each person. Collect and wash all the washcloths and towels once a week.

It's a Wash

❏ If you have a small load of delicate wash to put in your washing machine and you don't want to lose any of it, put it all in a bag. You can use an old zippered pillow cover for this purpose or buy a small mesh laundry bag—designed specifically for this kind of use—in the baby section of a department store.

Don't Spare the Rod

❑ Need a space-saving way to hang wet clothes to dry? Hang an extra shower curtain rod down the middle of your shower, parallel to the rod on which the curtain hangs. (The rod stays in place, but out of your way, so you don't have to set it up and take it down every time you use it.) This is an especially good way to drip-dry blouses, dresses, and shirts on hangers.

Behind the curtain is a great spot for drip-drying laundry. Add an extra shower curtain rod just for this purpose.

LIVING ROOMS AND FAMILY ROOMS

Bookshelves Aren't Just for Books

❑ You don't have enough drawers or cabinets for the things you want to reach easily, and you have more trinkets than your coffee table will hold. What to do with all the odds and ends? Display them in a bookcase. Put your sewing gear in a small basket and place it on one shelf; cluster a few small vases there; add candlesticks and perhaps some family photos. You'll be able to show off your prized knickknacks and add interest to the bookshelves at the same time.

What's in the Coffee Table?

❑ How can you create extra storage in your living room or family room? Use a low blanket chest or sea chest as a coffee table. Inside, you can keep toys, games, table linens, or anything else that you want accessible but out of sight.

Sink It

❑ Don't have room for an entertainment center? Try putting your stereo system or TV in a dry sink. You can probably pick one up fairly inexpensively at a yard sale or used furniture store. There's usually room for your VCR or stereo components in the main compartment,

We Made Our Own Music Box

My husband is a music buff. He also is a pack rat. He has records, CDs, cassette tapes—even reel-to-reel tapes—that he just can't part with. Not wanting to fill our home with CD towers and cassette cases, I searched for furniture that would hold these recordings unobtrusively. My favorite find was an old firewood box with a hinged top. It now sits in our dining room, sandwiched between two other antiques—but its secret contents are hundreds and hundreds of cassette tapes.

—LINDA BUCHANAN ALLEN
Exeter, New Hampshire

CDs or tapes can go in the side drawers, and the TV can sit on top. (You'll have to drill holes for wires in the back of the dry sink, so don't choose a precious antique.)

FOR CHILDREN

Get a Bureau They Can Sleep On

❏ If your child's bedroom is too small for a bureau or you need extra space for toys, try switching to a platform bed, which has drawers built right into the frame, beneath the mattress. These beds are especially good for children because they are usually lower than standard beds and the drawers are easily accessible.

Hang In There

❏ Can't see your kids' rooms for the toys? Get all those dolls and trucks off the floor and onto the walls. Most hardware and home stores sell inexpensive ready-to-hang shelving. Or buy some lumber and shelf brackets and build your own shelves. They don't need to be very wide; eight inches is probably enough. If your children are very small, hang the shelves low enough that they can reach them without climbing. But if kids are older and you can trust them not to climb, start at the ceiling (for toys they don't often play with) and work your way down the wall. Shelves allow your children to display their prized toys and dolls *and* keep their rooms clean.

❑ Shelves can help you create order out of chaos even when it comes to the smallest toys—blocks, action figures, and tiny trucks. Carry the shelving concept one step further by sliding small plastic bins (available at any discount store) onto the toy shelves. That way, you (and your children) can reach toys easily and toss them back in for quick cleanup. Designate a bin for puzzles, one for plastic figures, one for blocks, one for crafts, and so forth.

Handy Hand-Me-Downs

❑ What can you do with clothes one child has outgrown while you're waiting for the next child to wear them? Organize the clothes by size and season (for instance, 2T, winter). Then box them (heavy filing boxes work well) and label the boxes. Give each box a number, with the smallest sizes getting the lowest numbers. Store the boxes in sequence in a closet, under a bed, or in the attic.

THE HOME OFFICE

Paper Mountains

❑ The average household generates reams of paperwork, and much of it must be filed for future reference. But home filing systems often break down when more than one person maintains them because different people have very different ideas about how to label the same document. To make sure files don't disappear, determine who in the household usually handles each class of documents and make sure only that person files them. (Ideally, designate a separate file cabinet— or at least separate file drawers—for each person.) For example, one spouse might handle the taxes and bills, while the other might track the kids' school papers and the car or home maintenance records.

The X Files

❑ Problems may arise when a person who filed a needed document isn't available to find it. To get around this dilemma, color-code your files. Assign each class of documents—bills, taxes, auto repairs, and the like—to a specific color hanging file. If the standard colors sold in office supply stores don't give you enough choices to cover all your filing categories, you can get really organized by mixing and matching labels of different colors. Tape a color key to the side of each file cabinet for quick reference.

Facts on File

❑ Are your purchase receipts, warranties, instructions, and maintenance records scattered all over the house? Bring some order to the chaos by setting up a file for each major purchase you make—everything from the new toaster oven to the riding lawn mower. Toss the receipt from the purchase into the folder, along with the warranty and any instructions. As you take the item back later for repairs and routine maintenance, tuck those receipts in the file, too. That way, when you need to know when a particular part (say, a muffler on a not-so-old car) was last replaced or whether it's still under warranty, all the information you need will be in one place.

Tickled Pink

❑ Even if you keep a calendar for appointments, you may find yourself forgetting other important dates. And how do you keep track of the scraps of printed information you'll need for them? Take a tip from journalists and salespeople and maintain a "tickler file" for your personal life. These are files, organized by date, into which you can put, for example, a newspaper clipping on an upcoming garden lecture or the background material for your meeting with the school principal. When the appropriate date rolls around, you'll have the material handy.

❏ There are many ways to organize a tickler file, including fancy calendars and software programs for home computers. Here's a simpler method, which uses hanging files or a large, freestanding accordion file (available at office supply stores). Create 12 large folders, each labeled for one month of the year. Then create 4 or 5 separate files—for Week 1, Week 2, and so forth. File items for the current month in the appropriate weekly files. File items for the more distant future in the monthly folders. As each new month approaches, redistribute the items to the weekly files. Check the files every few days to tickle your memory.

The One-Touch Solution

❏ It's easy to fall into the trap of building stacks of paper all over your home or office. How does this happen? You open a piece of mail or clip a newspaper article and put it in a pile to wait for some future action. Pretty soon, there are little piles everywhere. To escape the paper trap, make it a personal rule to touch a piece of paper only once. When you first look at any piece of paper, always take the next step immediately: Throw it away, file it properly, respond, or pass it on. You can still build a "to read" file, but you should have only one, and when you take something out, you shouldn't put it back. Take the next step as soon as

TIME SAVER

If It's Tuesday, It Must Be Band Practice

I t takes a highly organized family to keep track of Johnny's soccer practice, Suzy's clarinet lesson, and Mom's dental appointment— and to prevent all kinds of scheduling conflicts. To organize a wide array of busy schedules, set up a calendar in a central location and make it a point to mark all the family's commitments on it. (You might even try using a different color ink for each member of the family.) Use only one calendar; entering events on more than one only adds to the confusion. Post the calendar where everyone can see it and add to it—perhaps on a corkboard on the family room wall, on the inside of the door to a convenient kitchen cabinet, or in a drawer next to the phone you use most frequently.

And Then There Was That Painting of Great-Grandma . . .

If your most valuable possessions are stolen or damaged, insurance should cover the loss. But remembering—let alone proving—what you lost can be frustrating at best. How can you protect yourself in case the worst should happen? Set up a personal property inventory *now*. List each item you own that's either valuable or unusual. Include the original purchase price if it's available. Accompany the list with photos of each room, showing those possessions. Store the list and photos in a safe-deposit box or at the home of a trusted neighbor. Then remember to update the list—and the photos—as necessary.

you're done reading so you won't have to touch it again.

The Claims Alone Could Give You a Headache

❑ Medical bills and insurance claims are often complicated and confusing, and they can pile up fast. If you're having trouble keeping track of which insurance claims have been submitted and what's been paid to whom, start a running chart of expenses and claims so that you know at a glance where things stand. Your chart should have six columns: name of patient; date of visit; provider of service; date and amount submitted to insurance company; date and amount insurance company paid; net paid to provider. If you update the chart on a regular basis, at least you'll minimize the headaches.

Marked Bills

❑ You're tearing your hair out trying to keep track of bills. To get a handle on things, designate a desk or kitchen drawer for all incoming bills. As soon as one arrives, open it, note the date payment is due, and write that date on the front of the envelope. Then put the marked bill in the bill drawer with the others, held together by a rubber band. The ones due soonest should be at the top of the pile. That way, you can tell at a glance which payments are due and when.

INCOMING MAIL

The Two-Minute Mail Sort

❑ Nothing seems to stop the mail from piling up. To get the mess under control, buy a couple of baskets and place them relatively near the door you use most often. As soon as the mail comes in the house, sort through it and toss all the catalogs in one basket. Label bills and keep them separate from the rest of the mail. If you don't have time to deal with everything else right away, drop it in the other basket until you can sort it out. That way, at least it all *looks* organized. (Weed old catalogs out of the basket at least once a season.)

❑ An alternative is to place a trash can or paper recycling bin between your mailbox and the house (or between the mail slot and your home office). Throw away the obvious junk before it even gets inside.

Baskets Are "In"

❑ If everyone's mail and other papers seem to be hopelessly mixed together, assign a basket to each person in the household. Keep the baskets somewhere convenient. You may even want to use a variety of shapes and sizes and hang them on the wall so they can help decorate as well as organize. Put each person's mail, school papers, and other odds and ends in his "in" basket each day. Then he can deal with it at a convenient time, and paper isn't scattered all over the place.

GARAGES AND ATTICS

Gear, Gear Everywhere

❑ Keeping sports equipment organized so you can find it when you need it is a chore, especially in small homes or apartments. One solution—and a good way to get more space out of a garage—is to string clothesline across an open space and hang gear from it. If you tie overhand knots every 10 to 20 inches to create loops in the rope, you can use climbers' cara-

---

☑ PROBLEM PREVENTED

Weighty Decisions in the Attic

Unless your attic was constructed specifically for use as a living space, the floor probably was not built to hold a lot of weight. If you don't want to be awakened some night by a heavy trunk crashing through to the bedroom below, store heavy items around the perimeter of the attic, which has more support. This is particularly important for filing cabinets, boxes of books, magazines, and furniture. Arrange lighter items inside the perimeter. Try not to pack the attic full of stuff (now there's a challenge!), as the floor could have weak spots, and a full attic can be a fire hazard.

---

biners to clip almost anything to the loops. This is also a good place to dry wet equipment when you get back from an outing. Carabiners are sold at climbing stores, of course, and at most outdoor-equipment and sporting goods outlets. Marine supply stores have similar clips.

Tool Time

❏ Are your lawn and gardening tools scattered around the garage and difficult to find when you need them? Hang them on clips or racks (available at hardware or home improvement stores) attached to the garage walls. Alternatively, place nails or dowels in solid walls or use pegboards. The objective is to hang your tools up out of harm's way and in clear view. Some people even paint outlines of the tools on the walls to remind them and others where to put each tool—and to tell at a glance if a tool is missing.

Keep your tools in line—literally. Paint an outline around each tool hanging on the garage wall (A), and you'll know instantly if one's disappeared (B).

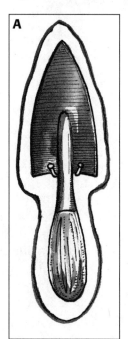
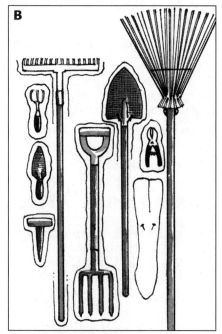

The Solution Is Over Your Head

❏ Often floor space in a garage or shop must be kept open, leaving few options for storing lumber or pip-

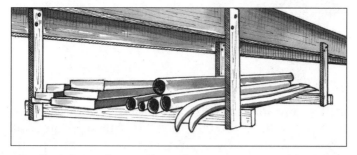

Attach two-by-fours to the rafters, then connect them with crosspieces. Voilà! You've created the perfect overhead storage spot.

ing—let alone skis, sailboard masts, or canoe paddles. If your garage has wooden ceiling rafters, it's easy to build an overhead rack with two-by-fours or other simple lumber. Nail or bolt pairs of one- to two-foot pieces of lumber to the rafters, pointing straight down from the ceiling. Then attach crosspieces to them to make a level platform. Slide the skis, paddles, or pipes onto this platform to put them away. Make sure to position the rack so it won't bump your head or your car.

Furniture for the Future

❑ You have furniture that you aren't using and want to store, but you're not sure where to keep it. Put it in the attic rather than the basement. An attic stays drier than a basement. Cover the furniture with a drop cloth to keep dust off but allow the piece to "breathe" (plastic traps moisture). And keep the attic windows about one-third open all year round for ventilation.

THE REST OF YOUR LIFE

The Key Issue

❑ If you have a handful of neighbors' house keys and want to identify them without jeopardizing security, put each on a different, distinctive key ring *without* a name written on it. (For instance, you might use a color code—a green plastic key ring for one neighbor, a red one for another.) Then store the keys apart from your own keys.

Car Keys: The Auto(matic) Response

❑ If you find yourself searching for the car keys every time you leave the house, try putting a small basket by the main entryway or screwing a hook into the door frame. Get into the habit of putting your keys there as soon as you come in the door.

Upstairs, Downstairs

❏ It's convenient to leave items on the stairs to be carried up or down on your next trip, but sometimes all those odds and ends can be a pretty unmanageable armful. (It also can be dangerous to leave lots of small items where people may trip over them.) To make things less cumbersome, keep one basket at the top of the stairs and another at the bottom. Then you can carry several items at once without dropping them. You may even want to invest in one of those baskets designed specifically to fit on the stairs. Available at some discount stores and gift shops that sell baskets, they're attractive as well as functional.

Going up? To minimize clutter, place a special basket at the bottom of the stairs and drop into it everything you want to take along on your next trip up.

It's in the Bag

❏ When you're in your car, it seems inevitable that at one time or another you'll need some small household item that you don't have. To get a handle on this problem, make up an "emergency" bag (a cosmetic bag or sealable plastic bag will do just fine) with items such as a pen, a pad of paper, safety pins, a few paper napkins, Band-Aids, and tissues. Keep the bag in your glove compartment.

❏ You always forget to take one or two items to certain friends or family members whom you visit regularly. You can chalk it up to a faulty memory and live with the aggravation, or you can set aside a separate tote bag for each person. As you come across things you intend to take to that person, toss them in the bag. Then you'll be unlikely to forget all those photos, magazines, and other odds and ends at the last minute.

Sentimental Journey

❑ When you empty a house—say, after the death of an elderly loved one or when you are ready to move from your own home—what do you do with the small, sentimental items you don't want to throw away? Don't feel as if you have to decide about everything immediately. Just box the items and label the boxes. You can sort through and dispose of things later, when you are ready.

I Can't See without My Glasses!

❑ Looking for lost glasses is not only inconvenient; it's also difficult if you can't see well. Instead of putting your glasses down wherever you take them off, establish a system. If you need them first thing in the morning, always put them on your nightstand (or in the nightstand drawer). If you wear them mostly for office work or reading, keep them in your briefcase or desk drawer.

❑ If you wear glasses mainly for driving, keep them in your purse or on a shelf or table near the front door. Or mount a basket or wooden candle box on the wall next to the door. Keep your glasses right there; you can grab them on your way out and replace them on your way back into the house. This works well for keeping track of sunglasses, too.

Just Feel Your Way to the Swimming Pool

❑ Need to wear your eyeglasses until just before you step in the swimming pool but don't want to leave them where they're likely to get broken? At a discount store, pick up an inexpensive eyeglasses case that has a strap on the back (the kind that's designed to hook onto a belt). Hang the case from the pool fence and pop your glasses in it just before you dive in.

PROBLEM PREVENTED

Bad News for China

Wrapping your china in old newspaper for storage may seem like an inexpensive and convenient idea, but it will damage the glaze. Newspaper ink rubs off on china and is nearly impossible to remove. Instead, try using plain newsprint (without ink on it), which is available from moving companies or art supply stores.

CLUTTER CUTTERS
Sorting Through and Clearing Out

WHAT TO TOSS

Trash or Treasure?

❑ Having trouble parting with your junk because you think some of it might actually be valuable? If you have even the slightest inkling that an item—a painting, a piece of furniture, or a piece of jewelry—might have more than sentimental value, have it appraised so you'll know once and for all.

❑ A terrific way to find out the value of your possessions is to get the opinion of someone at the top of the field. Christie's, the famed New York auction house, offers appraisals to anyone. All you need to do is send in a photograph of the item, along with a clear and complete description of it (markings, signatures, stamps, and the like). Christie's has about 25 regional offices that perform this service, or you can send your information to New York. To get the phone number for Christie's in New York and find out more, call information at (212) 555-1212. Or ask your librarian how you can contact other large auction houses to learn about similar services that they may offer.

The Poodle Skirt Could Probably Go . . .

❑ If you're having trouble deciding whether to toss an old piece of clothing, try to remember whether you've worn it in the past two years. If you haven't, you probably never will.

Kitchen Cabinets: Another Can of Beans

❏ If your kitchen cabinets are bursting at the seams, gather up all the canned foods you haven't used (and probably won't use in the near future) and donate them to a local food bank. (Just be sure the canned goods aren't more than a year old; if they are, discard them.) And don't wait for the holidays. Many food banks and charitable organizations are overwhelmed with donations during the holidays but may be desperately in need at other times of the year.

Just Say No to Old Drugs

❏ Looking to gain space in the medicine cabinet? Check the dates on those old prescription bottles and over-the-counter medicines. Although in most instances old medications won't harm you if you accidentally take them, they can be dangerous if a child swallows them. Generally, the best approach is to flush the outdated medicines down the toilet and throw away the bottles. Chemotherapy drugs and large amounts of prescription drugs can hurt septic systems, however, so your best bet is to seal the containers well so children and pets can't get at them, then throw them away.

Clear Those Closets

❏ Can't seem to cut the clutter in your closets? Here's one strategy: When you buy a new piece of clothing, get rid of an old one. When you buy a new pair of socks to replace a ratty old pair, get rid of the old pair right away. When you buy new sneakers, toss out the old ones.

File It under "Efficiency"

❏ Is your desk or file cabinet bulging with three-year-old credit card and utility bills? One fairly painless way

---

And You Think *You're* Short on Closet Space

You think *you* have problems staying organized? The first Europeans who came to this country built homes with no closets! Most of what the early colonists had they hung on pegs or stored in chests. (Of course, their collections of clothing, kitchen gadgets, and G.I. Joes didn't exactly take up a lot of space.)

to minimize the overload is to go through the files every month or so and throw out old bills and files you don't need to keep. Then rotate important bills and files from the last quarter to "deep" storage. That could mean a box under the bed or on a high shelf. Only current files belong in your desk drawer.

❏ Those who aren't into details may prefer the mass move approach: Let those bills and receipts pile up in

How Long Should I Keep It? Part I

Many people are reluctant to part with documents, old bank statements, and the like. In some cases, such hesitation is appropriate. Certain records should be saved indefinitely—stored in a safe-deposit box, with copies in other locations. Others, however, can be cleaned out regularly. Here are some ideas on what to save and for how long.

RECORDS	HOW LONG TO KEEP
Automobiles	
Payment book	Until car is paid in full.
Purchase-and-sales agreements	Until car is sold or traded.
Record of gasoline purchases	If car is used for business, keep records for three years to substantiate tax returns.
Repair records and receipts for parts	Until car is sold or traded. If car is used for business, keep records for three years to substantiate tax returns.
Title	Until car is sold or traded.
Bank Business	
Passbook	For three years, to substantiate income claims on tax returns.
Statements	Three years.
Employment	
Paycheck stubs	Check them annually against W-2 forms, then discard.
Pension records from prior employer	Indefinitely.

files in a desk drawer or filing cabinet for a year. Then start an annual New Year's Day tradition of cleaning out the old year's files and plunking them in a box (or boxes) labeled with the appropriate year. Stash the box in an out-of-the-way spot until you're comfortable tossing all the records for that year. If you have the space for it, this approach is great because it avoids the tedious task of culling through every piece of paper in your old files.

RECORDS	HOW LONG TO KEEP
Home	
Deed	Until property is sold.
Home insurance policy	Until property is sold.
Lease or rental agreement	Until you move and any claims are settled. Also keep—for the same period—a set of pictures showing move-in condition of property.
Mortgage papers	Until property is sold.
Purchase-and-sales agreement	Indefinitely.
Receipts and records from improvements to all homes you own	Three years after you sell your last home. (IRS tracks your lifetime gain or loss through all properties.)
Title insurance policy	Until property is sold.
Receipts	
Cash receipts for major purchases	Until item is sold. You might need them to substantiate purchases for household insurance inventories.
Charge account and credit card slips	One year for general purposes; indefinitely if needed as proofs of purchase. Store with tax return if needed to substantiate deductions.
Check registers and canceled checks	Three years. Put checks needed to substantiate tax deductions with a copy of the appropriate return.

*I Knew That Story on Elvis
Would Come in Handy...*

❑ Many people have stacks of old magazines cluttering the home office, attic, or basement. If this is a problem for you, ditch the stacks! This is particularly true of publications you used to save for their reference value. Although it may have made sense to save these magazines in the past, times have changed. Computer magazines, for instance, are out-of-date within six months to a year. *Consumer Reports* and other similar magazines are now quickly obsolete because of today's shorter product cycles. Travel publications are dated within a year or two. More important, technology has made much better ref-

How Long Should I Keep It? Part II

Once you've sorted through the old bankbooks, auto records, employment records, home-related information, and miscellaneous receipts, what's left?

RECORDS	HOW LONG TO KEEP
Credit records	Until debt is paid or for up to three years afterward if needed to substantiate tax returns.
Insurance policies	As long as the policies are in force. Keep copies of all active policies, along with a list of policy numbers, insured persons and property, beneficiaries, and issuing companies and agents.
Medical bills	Three years if needed to support tax returns.
Tax returns and supporting materials	Six years. The IRS must initiate most audits within three years of a return's filing. However, it can wait six years or more if income is substantially underreported or a return is deemed fraudulent.
Traffic violation and accident records	Six years.
Warranties and guarantees	Until warranties expire. Save with purchase receipts attached.

erences available. Home computers allow access to nearly infinite research resources through on-line services. Your local library probably offers access to these services, as well as the magazines you used to save, either on-line or on microfilm.

NEW HOMES FOR CASTOFFS

Sew It Away

❑ When you want to find a good home for clothing (or any fabric) that you'd like to discard, ask a friend who enjoys quilting if she'd like to look through it. She may find some fabric she'd like to use in a quilt. If the clothing is wool, you could try offering it to a friend who braids rugs.

Wanted: Good Home for Aging Armchair

❑ To find a home for a single item that you'd like to sell or give away, call your local newspaper. Many newspapers, especially those in small towns, offer free advertisements to customers trying to give away items or sell them for $50 or less.

❑ Another source of cheap advertising for items you want to dispose of is the bulletin board at a local grocery store or Laundromat. Many of these places have community bulletin boards designed, in part, for this purpose. Try posting a notice there, describing the item honestly and including your phone number. You may want to list a nominal price for the item rather than saying it's free. That sometimes brings a better response.

HAZARDOUS MATERIALS

Call for Help

❑ It was bad enough cleaning out the garage back in the days when that meant many trips to the dump. Nowadays the process can be much trickier. When tossed in with the rest of your household trash, substances such as paint thinner, solvents, corrosives, and most automotive fluids can be very harmful to both the environment and the person whose responsibility it

What Those Funny (recycling) Symbols Really Mean

We see them almost every-where these days, but what do they mean? And even though they're all called recycling symbols, which ones really mean you can actually recycle the product?

 Polyethylene tereph-thalate. Plastic soda bottles and spice bottles are made from this resin, the most commonly recycled plastic. (Remove plastic screw-on lids from the bottles; they are not recyclable in most communities.)

 High-density poly-ethylene. Nearly all plastic milk, bleach, and detergent bottles are made from this plastic. So are some dairy containers, such as those that hold yogurt and cottage cheese. (Many recycling centers require that you remove paper labels, as well as lids and rings from around the bottle tops.)

 Polyvinyl chloride (PVC). Credit cards, garden hoses, shower curtains, and sham-poo bottles are all made from PVC. Since this plastic is not widely recycled, avoid it when you can.

 Low-density polyeth-ylene. Plastic sand-wich bags are made from this plastic, as is shrink-wrap, such as the kind found on compact discs and food products. It is not commonly recycled.

 Polypropylene. Some of the products made from this plas-tic include lids, caps, and long underwear. It's not widely recycled.

 Polystyrene (also known by its trade name, Styrofoam). Fast-food containers and coffee cups are often made from this material, al-though some large chains have stopped using it because it doesn't biodegrade. These days, it's being recycled into building insulation.

 The "other" cate-gory. Items that carry this symbol are made from a combination of different plastics or a plastic that can't be recycled.

 This sign denotes that the item was manufactured from recycled products.

is to handle that trash. So how do you get rid of these odds and ends that have been accumulating in the garage? Many communities have periodic household hazardous waste collection days. To find out whether your community does, call your local town hall or fire department. (To reach the fire department, call the number listed in the phone book under your town's name. Don't use 911—it's meant for emergencies only.)

Aerosols: The Pressure Is On

❏ If aerosol paint (and other chemical) cans get punctured at your local dump or landfill, those chemicals will spill and leach into the ground, damaging the soil and groundwater. That rules out tossing them in the household trash, so how *do* you dispose of them? Here's one way: Take any nonhazardous aerosol materials outside and spray the contents into an empty box or paper bag. When the paint or other substance is dry, you can dispose of the box or bag, as well as the cans, with your household trash.

Every Litter Bit Helps

❏ Looking for a safe way to dispose of small amounts of paint or wood preservative? Pour the material over some clay kitty litter—allow roughly three parts litter to one part liquid—and let it dry out. Be sure to use *clay* litter and not the kind with clumping or deodorizing chemicals. (The clay litter is the least expensive, too.)

Paint Away

❏ One way to dispose of a small amount of paint is to spread it on some lumber you plan to throw away or pour it, a thin layer at a time, into a cardboard box, adding another layer after the previous one dries. Then you can simply toss out the lumber or cardboard box.

Button, Button, Who's Got the Button?

❏ "Button" batteries, the kind that go into watches and cameras, are small enough that it's tempting to toss

Uses for Empty Yogurt Containers

Stop! Don't throw out that collection of empty yogurt containers. You say you need a reason to hold on to them? Here are a dozen.

1. To hold nails and screws in your home workshop

2. As molds for homemade Popsicles

3. To carry your powdered laundry detergent to the Laundromat

4. To organize needles and pins in your sewing kit

5. To organize paper clips and thumbtacks in your home office

6. As chillers for your picnic lunch (freeze water in them, replace the lids, then put them in plastic freezer bags)

7. As containers for pocket change (an effective alternative to one big pile on top of the bureau)

8. As seed starters

9. To hold baking soda or potpourri in the back of your closet

10. To hold leftovers (you can heat them in the microwave, too)

11. As sand castle molds for the beach

12. To hold water to clean your brushes while you paint pictures

them in with the rest of the trash. But these items may contain lithium, mercury, or silver—none of which is good for the environment or for people—so they shouldn't land in a landfill. To dispose of one of these batteries, take it to a jewelry store, a watch repair shop, or a camera store and ask the shop to recycle the battery. Although such shops are not required by law to accept batteries, many will be glad to comply.

A Pointed Lesson

❑ Finding a way to safely dispose of dangerous materials such as broken glass, razor blades, and sewing needles is very important, especially if you live in a neighborhood with lots of kids or pets. Here's the solution: Toss all these materials into a metal can, such as a coffee can. Cover the can with the original lid or cut a piece of cardboard to fit the top and seal it with duct tape. Make sure the can is labeled clearly so the person who handles your trash can tell what it is, then set it out with the rest of the trash.

YARD SALES

If Only I Had More Junk . . .

❏ If you'd like to have a yard sale but feel you just don't have enough stuff to sell (or a large enough yard to accommodate a sale), consider putting together a group sale with some friends, relatives, or coworkers. Ideally, plan the sale several months ahead of time so that everyone has time to collect items. Hold the sale at the home in the "best" neighborhood, and when you advertise it ahead of time, be sure to specify that it's a group sale. You'll attract more shoppers—and more affluent ones—to the event.

For the Junior Capitalist

❏ One terrific way to clean out your kids' toy chests—and give them a lesson in the finer points of capitalism—is to help them organize a kids-only yard sale. Gather together a bunch of old toys, clean them up,

---

ONE PERSON'S SOLUTION

Everything in Its Place

Every year, I have a yard sale with some friends from my neighborhood, so I've become somewhat of an expert. I keep a big box marked "Yard Sale" in my basement. Throughout the year, when I find something I think I can sell, I clean it up, put a price on it, and place it in the box. That way, everything's all ready when it's time for the sale. I also put in the box the brown paper bags I get from the grocery store. They're handy to wrap and carry items.

—SUSAN GAGNON
Hopkinton, New Hampshire

and set a date. If your child doesn't have enough toys for a sale, consider a joint enterprise with one of his playmates. A couple of days before the event, hang some signs around the neighborhood and notify your child's playmates.

Timing Is Everything

❏ A particularly good time to hold a yard sale is on the Friday and Saturday of Memorial Day weekend. Yes, do start on Friday! Traditionally, that weekend is a time when many folks open up their summer homes, and your incomplete sets of dishes or old pots and pans may look especially attractive to someone who's outfitting the kitchen in a cottage.

The Price Is Right

❏ Writing up dozens of price tags and attaching them to yard sale items will take hours and hours of your time. To avoid this hassle, don't bother to price every single piece. Instead, set items out on tables, arranged by price.

A Few Things to Save

If accumulated clutter has you ready to empty your whole home, wait! There are some items that you may want to hold on to.

• **Packing materials.** Save the boxes and packing materials that your more expensive appliances (TV, toaster, computer, CD player) came in. They're vital if you need to send the appliance out for repair. And if you move, the original boxes are always the safest way to transport items. Finally, if there comes a time that you want to sell the appliance, it'll fetch considerably more money if it's in the original carton. In the meantime, use those cartons to store other items.

• **Directions and special tools.** If you own any furniture or appliances that came with assembly tools and directions, be sure to keep the tools and directions in a safe place. If you move, you'll be glad you did. (If you decide to take the items to the dump, tape the directions and tools to the piece so that if someone else can use it, he'll know how to take it apart and put it back together.)

❏ Alternatively, use different-colored stickers to designate prices. Use orange dots for $1, blue dots for $2, and so on. (You can find the stickers at any office supply store.) Make one or two large signs showing your pricing scheme and hang them where shoppers can see them.

If You Have a Yard Sale, Will They Come?

❏ It almost goes without saying that advertising—in the local paper, on community bulletin boards, and with large, clear signs directing people to the site—is the best way to attract people to your yard sale. But what else can you do to entice folks? Put something eye-catching in the front yard or at the corner of your street to lure them in. Balloons or a large stuffed animal will be a real attention getter; one veteran yard sale host stands a six-foot Gumby doll in the front yard.

❏ In addition to those responding to your ads, you'll want to attract casual passersby to stop at your yard sale. One way to do that is to set out items grouped by type—clothing, kitchen appliances, dishes, toys and games, comic books. That way, a person who's particularly interested in one category is more likely to feel that your sale is worth a stop.

A Get-Rich-Not-So-Quick Scheme

❏ Most folks don't have yard sales to make a lot of money; the goal is usually to get rid of junk. But how can you increase the likelihood that folks will buy your stuff? One strategy is to knock the price down on an item in which someone is obviously interested. If, say, you notice someone holding a knickknack that you've marked at $2, say to her, "I'll let you have that for a dollar."

Leftovers

❏ Yard sales are great for cleaning out closets—and the garage and attic. But what do you do with the stuff that doesn't sell? First, as the afternoon wears on, mark everything down drastically. Second, at the end of the day, take the leftovers to the dump or recycling center. Do *not* let them back in the house!

CLEANING
Dirty Business

ALL-PURPOSE CLEANERS

Save the Planet and *Clean the House*

❑ You may find that you're sensitive to or simply prefer not to use chemical cleaners around the house. Here's an all-purpose household cleaner that you can make yourself. In a bucket, combine ¼ cup baking soda and 1 quart warm water. Use this cleaner for bathroom fixtures, countertops, tabletops—almost anything. Apply with a sponge, then rinse with fresh water.

❑ Alternatively, add enough vinegar to some salt to make a paste, spread it on a damp sponge, and use it as a gentle but effective scouring powder.

❑ Straight baking soda on a damp sponge also is an effective scouring powder (and a deodorizer, too).

Germ Warfare

❑ Everyone knows cleanliness is important in the home—especially in the kitchen, where foods are prepared, and the bathroom. But how can you make sure sinks and counters in those rooms are disinfected? One way is to wash them with a mixture of ½ cup borax (available at hardware stores) and 1 gallon hot water. Wear rubber gloves while you sponge down these areas, then rinse them well.

❑ Another excellent disinfectant is rubbing alcohol. Make sure the product you buy is at least a 70 percent solution. (It will be marked clearly on the label.) Do not dilute it further, but sponge it on and let it dry. Make sure the area you're working in has plenty of ventilation, and wear rubber gloves—rubbing alcohol will dry your skin. Don't wipe the alcohol off before it dries, or it will not disinfect.

SPONGES

Clean Pinups

❏ Dirty kitchen sponges attract cockroaches and are a breeding ground for germs. Keep sponges clean by putting them in the dishwasher, on the top rack, once a week or so. Use clothespins to secure them to the rack.

A Good, Hot Bath

❏ If you don't have a dishwasher and still want to clean and disinfect your sponges, put them in a clean bucket or your sink with some boiling water and a tablespoon or two of bleach. Let them sit for a couple of minutes, then squeeze them out and rinse them.

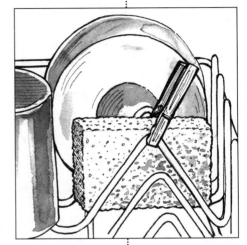

Make your dishwasher a sponge washer. Secure dirty sponges in place with clothespins.

CRYSTAL AND GLASS

Come Clean

❏ To clean cut glass, dampen it first with water, then sprinkle it with a little baking soda. Work the mixture in with a soft, damp cloth, then rinse well with water and dry.

❏ You can eliminate some stains and scratches on glass by rubbing them with a little toothpaste (not the gel type) on a soft, damp cloth. Rinse well, then dry with a soft cloth.

POTS AND PANS

Cream of Clean

❏ Here's how to clean and polish your dingy aluminum pots and pans. Fill each with water and add 2 tablespoons cream of tartar (available in the spice section of any grocery store). Boil for five to ten minutes, then wash and dry as usual.

Chock-Full of Vinegar

❏ To clean an aluminum coffeepot and remove lime and mineral deposits, fill the pot with equal parts white vinegar and water. Boil the mixture until the deposits are gone, then wash well.

Put the Stainless Back in Your Steel

❏ When your stainless steel gets dull and streaky, clean it with a little white vinegar on a soft, clean cloth. Apple cider vinegar works in a pinch, too.

Enameled Pots: Snow White

❏ White enameled cookware is beautiful until it gets stained. Then it just looks grungy. Here's how to remove those stains and keep your cookware looking brand-new. Fill each pot with hot water and add 2 tablespoons household bleach. Let the pots sit until the stains are gone. (If you get impatient, you can speed up the process by adding more bleach.) Then wash well with hot, soapy water and rinse.

SILVER

Un-Tarnish Your Image

❏ Clean and polish tarnished silver by putting 2 tablespoons baking soda in a bowl and adding warm water, one drop at a time, until a thin paste forms. Spread the paste on the silver with a soft, clean cloth. Let it sit for a few minutes, then rinse and dry well. Finish by polishing with a soft cloth.

Skip the Elbow Grease

❏ Looking for a method of cleaning silver that doesn't require a lot of elbow grease? Place the silver in a large pot with a small sheet of aluminum foil. Add enough water to cover the silver (it's important to keep the silver covered with water), then add 1 teaspoon baking soda and 1 teaspoon salt. Boil the water for two to three minutes, then remove the silver. (Be careful; it'll be hot.) Rinse it well, then dry it with a soft, clean cloth.

Label Reading 101: What's in Your Cleaning Product?

Take a walk down the cleaning aisle of your local grocery store and read the labels. What exactly are you getting when you buy an all-purpose cleaner? What's the best product to cut grease? Here are some clues to choosing the right cleaner for the right job.

Acids are terrific for removing hard-water spots from aluminum, brass, bronze, and copper, as well as rust stains from iron. Vinegar and lemon juice are safe, mild acids. Stronger acids, such as oxalic, hydrochloric, and sulfuric acids, are often the active ingredients in rust removers and toilet bowl cleaners. Because strong acids can cause severe burns, always read the labels, keep them out of the reach of children and pets, and use them with caution.

Alkalies remove dirt without much rubbing and are terrific for cutting grease. Don't use an alkali on oil-based paint (which it will dry out) or aluminum (which it will darken). Baking soda is a mild alkali. Stronger alkalies are found in ammonia and in cleaners such as borax and TSP. The most caustic alkalies, used in drain and oven cleaners, include lye. Any product that contains lye should be used with extreme caution because it can severely burn or damage skin.

Bleaches clean and whiten. Chlorine bleach—which doesn't actually contain chlorine—is the most common variety used in household cleaning products.

Detergents, including laundry detergents, are cleaners with ingredients that loosen dirt so it can be washed away. Detergents labeled either "heavy-duty" or "all-purpose" contain phosphates and are good grease cutters. Since phosphates can be harmful to the environment, many manufacturers have stopped making detergents with them.

Sanitizers are chemicals that destroy bacteria. They're common in bathroom and kitchen cleaners.

Spirit solvents, similar to the chemicals used in dry-cleaning fluid, remove oily dirt. They're common in wood polish.

Just One Touch and It's . . . Tarnished?

❑ If your silver tarnishes quickly after you polish it, the problem may be those rubber gloves you're wearing. Try wearing cotton gloves while polishing your silver.

COPPER AND BRASS

Like a Shiny New Penny

❑ Sure, your copper-bottom cookware looked terrific the day you took it out of the box, but now, years later, it's stained, gray, and dull. To clean it, put 3 to 4 tablespoons salt in a small bowl. Add white vinegar or lemon juice, a few drops at a time, to make a paste. Dip a damp sponge in the paste and then rub it on the copper. You shouldn't have to scrub too much. If you don't notice a difference immediately, add a little more vinegar. (This homemade polish may scratch the metal, so although it's perfectly appropriate for copper-bottom pots, it's not a good idea to use it on your $1,200 cookware.)

ONE PERSON'S SOLUTION

Don't Talk Dirty

I work at home and spend a lot of time on the telephone, interviewing people and taking notes. My phone gets really dirty from day-to-day use and from being nicked with a pen every so often. I know that alcohol works well to clean the plastic on a computer, so one day I tried it on my phone. I dabbed a little on a cotton ball, and it worked like a charm—especially on the ballpoint pen stains.

—MICHELLE SEATON
Medford, Massachusetts

Take a Shine to Brass

❏ You can clean dingy brass with a paste of lemon juice and cream of tartar (available in the spice section of any grocery store). Apply it to the brass and let it sit for about five minutes. Wash with warm water, then polish with a clean, soft cloth.

Olive to Polish Brass

❏ If the brass fixtures in your home seem to tarnish quickly, rub them with a little olive oil after you polish them. The oil provides a coating that protects the brass from moisture, the primary cause of tarnish. (This works well for kick plates and decorative objects, but it's not a great idea for doorknobs or anything else you need to grab hold of.)

GOLD JEWELRY

All That Glitters . . .

❏ You've already spent a fortune on the gold; don't spend more on expensive polish. Wash gold in warm, soapy water, then dry it with a clean cotton cloth. Finish by polishing it with a chamois cloth.

Take Care of Those Cavities

❏ If soap and water don't quite do the job, or if the piece you're cleaning has a lot of nooks and crannies, clean the gold with a very soft toothbrush, some toothpaste (not the gel type), and a little water. Work the toothpaste into a lather, then rinse it off and polish with a chamois cloth.

OVENS

Easy Off

❏ If you don't have a self-cleaning oven and don't like the idea of using harsh commercial cleaners, try this solution for stains. Put some vinegar in a spray bottle and spray the inside of your oven well. Sprinkle on some baking soda, then scrub gently with very fine steel wool (available at hardware stores), a plastic scouring pad, or a sponge. Rinse with water.

If Dinner Hits a New Low

❑ To get rid of small stains on the bottom of your oven, sprinkle some salt on the spill before the oven has cooled. (If the oven is already cold, wet the spill, then sprinkle on the salt.) When the oven cools down, scrape away the spill and wash the oven clean.

SINKS AND DRAINS

Wipe Out Those Stains

❑ Eliminate stains on chrome faucets by wiping them down with a little baby oil. Or use full-strength white or apple cider vinegar.

DOLLAR STRETCHER

Free Drain Cleaner

You can stop many drain problems before they start by pouring a kettle of boiling water down your drain every morning after you make tea or coffee. The water will dissolve any grease in the drain, which is the cause of many clogs.

Withdrawing Deposits

❑ Those small deposits that accumulate on chrome fixtures are probably mineral or lime deposits. Here's how to eliminate them. Thoroughly soak several paper towels in white vinegar, then lay the towels around the fixtures, making sure to cover the deposits. Leave the towels in place for at least an hour, preferably overnight. The next morning, remove the towels and wash the fixtures with warm, soapy water.

Plop Plop, Fizz Fizz

❑ To clear a clogged drain, sprinkle ½ cup baking soda down the drain, then add ½ cup white vinegar. Cover the drain with a plate or the lid of a 1-quart yogurt container for about five minutes, then pour 4 to 5 cups boiling water down the drain. (*Don't use this method if you've already tried a commercial drain cleaner. You could accidentally create dangerous fumes.*)

A Hardheaded Showerhead

❏ Those hard spots on your metal showerhead are probably mineral or lime deposits. To get rid of them, remove the showerhead and put it in a large pot with ½ to ¾ cup white vinegar. Boil it for about ten minutes, then rinse well.

(8) Great Cleaning Agents Right in Your Kitchen

You don't need to spend your life's savings on commercial cleaners; you probably have most of what you need right in your kitchen. Start raiding those cupboards now, and you may be surprised at just how many multipurpose cleaning agents you already have on hand.

1. Baking soda. Cleans and deodorizes and can be used as a mild scouring powder for almost anything. Just sprinkle it on a damp sponge.

2. Club soda. Its effervescent action shines ceramic tile and removes some stains from fabric and stainless steel.

3. Cream of tartar. A very mild acid available in the spice section of any grocery store. Put a little in some water to boil stains out of aluminum. Combined with lemon juice, it removes ink stains from carpets.

4. Flour. Mix it with vinegar and salt to make brass polish.

5. Lemon. A mild, all-purpose acid. Mix it with a little cream of tartar to clean brass. Add some borax (available at hardware stores) to clean your toilet bowl. Combine it with a little oil to hide scratches in wooden furniture.

6. Olive oil. An ingredient in homemade furniture polish. It also protects brass from tarnish.

7. Salt. A mild but effective abrasive. Mix it with vinegar to clean your brass. Sprinkle it on warm spills in your oven; when it cools off, spills wipe away.

8. Vinegar. Along with baking soda, probably the most versatile substance in your kitchen. A mild acid that cleans and shines. Mixed with salt, it cleans copper. Mixed with water, it cleans windows and mirrors. Straight up, it dissolves mineral deposits around faucets.

Tidy Bowl

❑ Clean your toilet by sprinkling it with baking soda, then spraying it with white vinegar. Let the mixture sit for a minute, then scrub with a toilet brush.

❑ If your toilet bowl requires a little more elbow grease, mix some borax (available at hardware stores) and lemon juice into a paste that's the consistency of toothpaste. Flush the toilet to wet the sides, put on some rubber gloves, and smear the paste on the inside of the bowl. Let it sit for two hours. Scrub with a toilet brush, then flush.

FLOORS

Clean Enough to Eat Off

❑ To clean linoleum floors, mop with a mixture of ¾ cup white vinegar and 1 gallon hot water. There's no need to rinse.

TIME SAVER

Plug, Unplug, Plug . . .

Having to unplug your vacuum cleaner and move it from room to room wastes a lot of time and energy. Save yourself both by investing in a 25-foot or longer extension cord, which will allow you to move freely around your house.

Remove That Wax Buildup

❑ Over the years, dirt gets trapped under the layers of wax on vinyl flooring, leaving the floor looking grimy. To remove the wax buildup, pour some club soda on a small area and scrub well. Let it sit for a few minutes, then wipe clean. Repeat for the rest of the floor.

❑ To clean wax buildup on a linoleum floor, combine three parts water and one part rubbing alcohol. Use the solution to scrub the floor well with a mop or brush, then rinse thoroughly. Wear rubber gloves, and make sure the room is well ventilated; the alcohol fumes can be hazardous.

Fight Grime

❑ To remove heavy-duty dirt from a vinyl, linoleum, or painted wood floor, dissolve 2 tablespoons TSP or an-

A Clean House Isn't Worth Dying For

Before you try one more experiment to get rid of that stubborn stain, remember that there is such a thing as going too far. Always keep in mind these four basic precautions.

1. Never ever mix household bleach with ammonia, vinegar, or toilet bowl cleaner. Those combinations can cause dangerous, even deadly fumes.

2. Once you've used a commercial drain cleaner, don't try another homemade remedy until you're absolutely sure the commercial cleaner has been totally flushed out of the drainpipe and standing water. Many commercial products contain lye, and the combination of drain cleaner and your home remedy may create dangerous fumes.

3. Always wear rubber gloves when working with chemicals, and be sure to open the windows—good ventilation is a must.

4. If you prepare your own cleaning solutions, store them in clean glass containers and label them well. Never store them in old food containers or keep them in an area where they might be mistaken for food, especially if there are young children around.

other product containing trisodium phosphate in 2 gallons hot water. Scrub the floor with the mixture, then rinse thoroughly. (Trisodium phosphate is a strong multipurpose cleaner, and it's generally one of the main ingredients in dishwasher detergents. You may substitute the latter if you wish.)

Wood You Please Clean Me?

❑ The best way to clean a wood floor with a polyurethane finish is to mop it with warm water once a week or so.

❑ Alternatively, mop a dirty wood floor with ¼ cup white vinegar mixed with 1 gallon warm water.

How the Third Little Pig Cleaned His Floor

❑ Cleaning brick and stone floors can be a challenge, but once again, vinegar comes to the rescue. Mix 1 cup white vinegar with 1 gallon hot water. Scrub the floor with a brush, then rinse.

CARPETING

Take That Sword Fight Outside!

❏ You can remove bloodstains from carpeting by first blotting the spot with some club soda or ice water. Remember to blot, not rub; rubbing will spread the stain. Dry the area with a clean towel, also using a blotting motion.

Mightier Than the Pen?

❏ Ink stains on your carpet don't necessarily spell disaster. Sprinkle the stain with cream of tartar (available in the spice section of any grocery store), then lemon juice. Dab these cleaners into the stain, let the whole thing sit for a minute or so, then remove the powder with a clean brush. Finally, sponge the spot with a little warm water, being careful not to saturate the spot. Repeat if necessary.

❏ Alternatively, blot rubbing alcohol onto the stain with a clean, dry cloth or a damp sponge. Wear gloves for this job and make sure the room is well ventilated.

Until That Puppy's Housebroken . . .

❏ Here's a way to get urine stains out of the carpet. Blot up as much of the urine as possible with dry paper towels. Then combine 1 tablespoon white vinegar with 2 tablespoons dishwashing liquid and dab that onto the stain with a damp sponge. Let it sit for 15 to 20 minutes, then rinse with lukewarm water and a sponge, making sure to blot and not rub. As with any stain removal method, test this in an inconspicuous spot to be sure it doesn't discolor the rug.

❏ Alternatively, pour a little 3 percent hydrogen peroxide solution (or ammonia or rubbing alcohol) right on the urine stain and dab. Rinse by blotting with water on a sponge, then shampoo the rug as usual. Test this method on a hidden spot to be sure it doesn't discolor the rug. And wear rubber gloves, as some of these solutions can be irritating.

WOODEN FURNITURE

Good on Salads, Too

❏ You can eliminate some scratches in finished wooden furniture by combining equal parts lemon juice and vegetable oil, then rubbing the solution into the scratches with a soft, clean cloth. Keep rubbing until the scratches disappear. Try this method on a hidden spot first to be sure it doesn't damage the finish.

Next Time, Use a Coaster

❏ If you have a water ring on a finished wooden table, squeeze a little toothpaste (not the gel type) onto a damp cloth and rub the ring gently. Rinse and dry well.

 TIME SAVER

How to Set Up a Mudroom

One way to spend less time cleaning your home is to prevent the dirt from getting in. Short of living in a plastic bubble, however, what can you do? Set up a mudroom! Here's what you'll need.

• **Boot brush.** A heavy brush on a short stand for brushing mud from the bottoms of shoes and boots. Place it outside the door, so folks can clean their shoes or boots before they step in.

• **Horsehair or sisal floor mat.** Place this inside the door and wipe your feet on it.

• **Bench.** So folks can sit down to remove boots and shoes.

• **Hooks and shelves.** Make sure there are plenty for coats, hats, mittens, and scarves. Shaker pegs are great because you can move them around easily. You can find inexpensive shelves and brackets at many hardware stores and almost any home center. Place an absorbent, washable mat under the hooks and shelves to catch drips.

• **Towels.** Especially during winter, keep a big basket of clean, dry rags or towels in the mudroom for wiping hands. Or purchase a jug of premoistened towelettes and some paper towels for the job.

WALLS

Or Tell Them It's Part of the Pattern

❏ You can remove many stains from fabric wallpaper by dabbing them with club soda on a soft, clean cloth. Remember to dab, not rub, because rubbing may spread the stain. Test a hidden area of the wallpaper (say, behind the sofa and near the floor) before you start on the stain to be sure it will stand up to this treatment.

❏ Wash dirty vinyl wallpaper with 2 tablespoons powdered dishwasher detergent mixed with 1 gallon warm water. Test this solution on a hidden spot first to make sure the dyes are colorfast and the water won't dissolve the glue.

Sponge That Shower Stall

❏ An effective way to clean tile walls is with a solution of ¼ cup white vinegar and 1 gallon hot (as hot as you can stand it) water. Wipe the walls with a sponge or plastic scouring pad. You don't need to rinse.

WINDOWS

A Clear Solution

❏ Clean dirty windows with a solution of ½ cup ammonia and 1 gallon hot water. If the windows are greasy (in the kitchen, for instance) or smoky, add 2 cups rubbing alcohol to the water.

❏ Alternatively, wash your windows with a mixture of equal parts white vinegar and warm water.

Don't Streak Up on Me

❏ If you can't seem to wash a window without producing streaks, save the job for a cloudy day or wait

---

TIME SAVER

The Lazy Way to Clean

It's time-consuming to have to empty out your utensil and junk drawers to dust and vacuum inside. Here's one handy solution. Remove the attachment from the end of your vacuum cleaner hose and cover the hose with a piece of cheesecloth or old pantyhose. Secure the covering with electrical tape or some rubber bands. The fabric will prevent objects from getting sucked into the hose but allow dust to pass through. This method works for vacuuming around your desk and computer, too.

---

until after the sun goes down. Streaking sometimes occurs when the washing fluid dries too quickly. If you wash the windows in the evening, the heat won't be so intense, and streaks won't be as likely to form.

Yesterday's News

❏ If you have both lint and streaks on your windows right after you wash them, stop drying them with regular paper towels. You can use lint-free paper towels, but a less expensive alternative is old newspaper. To keep your hands from turning black, invest in some thin surgical gloves, which you can buy at almost any pharmacy. And don't use today's paper; the ink will be fresher and more likely to come off.

CLOTHING AND FABRIC

Or You Could Use a Pocket Protector

❏ You can eliminate some ink stains from fabric by pretreating them with onion or lemon juice, salt water, or a little milk. Rub the liquid into the stain, rinse, and wash as usual.

A Fruity Solution

❏ Remove fruit or tea stains from clothing by holding the fabric taut over the sink and having a friend pour boiling water on the stain until it disappears. Be careful not to burn your hands.

❏ If no one is available to help with this, stretch the fabric over an embroidery hoop. If the hoop is small, place it over a large bowl to hold it above the sink's surface and avoid burns. Or secure the fabric over the bowl with a large rubber band or by tucking it under the bowl. Then pour the hot water onto the stain.

Raid your crafts supplies for help with fruit stains. Stretch the stained fabric over an embroidery hoop, then pour boiling water on it.

Help for Old Yeller

❏ If your washable silks or woolens have yellowed over time, sponge them with a mixture of 1 tablespoon white vinegar and 2 cups warm water. Rinse, then wash as usual.

No Licking!

❏ You can remove chocolate stains from most clothing by soaking the stains in club soda before you wash the garment.

The Real Thing

❏ To remove a recent cola stain from fabric, dab it with white vinegar, then wash as usual. The stain needs to be fairly fresh—no more than a day or so old—for this method to work.

LEATHER AND SUEDE

Shine On

❏ Have you run out of shoe polish on the night of your big date? Don't worry; you have other options. Olive oil will shine most types of leather, and lemon juice will polish black or tan leather. Follow by buffing with a chamois cloth.

Give It the Brush-Off

❏ Grease stains on suede are ugly but not impossible to remove. Sponge the spot with white vinegar and let it dry. Then brush the suede well to restore the nap.

Or Rub It Out

❏ Remove spots on suede with an art gum eraser (you can buy one at most office supply and all art supply stores), then brush with a stiff suede brush. If the stain remains, buff the spot very lightly with an emery board or a piece of fine-grit sandpaper.

FOOD AND COOKING ODORS

Start That Candlelight Dinner Early

❑ The scent of onions does its worst damage when you first cut the vegetables up. To keep from crying all the way to the dinner table, place a candle next to your cutting board and light it before you begin to slice. The candle will burn the gases that the onions release before they can reach your eyes.

Odor Be Gone

❑ Sometimes when you chop onions or garlic, your hands will smell for hours afterward. Remove that odor by running your hands under cold water while rubbing a piece of stainless steel.

❑ You also can wipe the smell of garlic or onion from your hands by rubbing them with a tablespoon of salt. In just a few seconds, the salt will absorb the oil and the smell that goes with it.

Vinegar Soup

❑ Scorched food has its own pungent smell. Get rid of it by boiling 2 cups water on the stove, then adding ½ cup vinegar and letting the mixture simmer for 10 to 15 minutes. This should overpower the smoky scent.

Don't Let the Scent of Salmon Linger

❑ To keep the smell of cooked salmon at a minimum, squeeze lemon juice on the cut side of the fillet (or on both sides of a steak) about an hour before you cook it. This will help neutralize the odor of the flesh and keep your refrigerator from smelling like fish, too.

St. Patrick Would Be Proud

❏ Ready to cook the cabbage for your annual St. Patrick's Day feast but dreading the odor? Put about a cup of vinegar into a container next to the pot of simmering cabbage, and it will absorb the odor.

☑ PROBLEM PREVENTED

No More Tears

It's no fun to spend hours laboring over a gourmet meal, only to find that your hands reek embarrassingly of onion. You can avoid this if you plan ahead. Just before you slice onions, rub your fingers with vinegar to coat them against the oil. Then pour more vinegar over your fingers after you slice the onions to remove the rest of the scent.

Deodorize Your Dinner

❏ To reduce the strong cooking odors associated with vegetables such as broccoli, cauliflower, and brussels sprouts, add a couple of slices of red pepper to the pot while they cook. This works for both boiling and steaming vegetables and won't affect the flavor.

Something's Fishy Here

❏ The smell of baked fish is great just before dinner but awful the next morning. To get rid of it, boil some water in a saucepan and throw in 2 cinnamon sticks or 2 teaspoons whole cloves, ground cinnamon, or allspice. Remove the water from the heat. As it cools, it will give off a pleasant odor that will mask that fishy smell.

❏ Another way to get rid of the smell of cooked fish is to slice a lemon and spread the slices in a pie plate. Heat the oven to 200°F, then bake the lemon slices for about 20 minutes. They will give off a wonderfully fresh scent.

When Leftovers Leave Leftover Smells

❏ Plastic containers for leftovers seem to collect garlic, onion, and stale food odors. To get rid of such smells, put 2 tablespoons vinegar in each container. Then seal the containers and shake them up so that the vinegar is splashed on every surface. Leave them sealed for up to 2 hours or until you do dishes, then wash them as usual.

REFRIGERATORS

Wipeout!

❏ Some food odors such as fish and rotten eggs tend to linger in the shelves and liner of the fridge. To get rid of them, make a solution of ¼ cup baking soda and 1 quart warm water and use it to wipe down the walls and shelves of the refrigerator. The baking soda is a natural deodorizer and is just abrasive enough to clean the surfaces without scratching them.

Run It on Empty

❏ Some food odors are particularly stubborn. To kill them off, empty the refrigerator and move the temperature dial to its lowest setting (the warmest possible temperature). Spread activated charcoal in shallow pans and put a pan on each shelf of the refrigerator and freezer. Sprinkle a few briquettes in the crisper drawer, too. Then leave the refrigerator running on low for several days. The charcoal will pull the moisture and odors out of the air. Once the odors are gone, you can still use the charcoal for your grill.

We Have News for You

❏ Another way to absorb serious food odors is to pack the refrigerator shelves with crumpled newspaper. Sprinkle the newspaper with water or set a cup of water on the top shelf. Let the refrigerator run for about five days, then remove the newspaper and wipe down the inside of the refrigerator to get rid of the ink.

Try a Little Iced Coffee

❏ Odors from the refrigerator often migrate to the freezer section, where they taint ice cream and ice cubes. You can deodorize your freezer with ground coffee. Scatter about a cup of freshly ground coffee in a shallow bowl and keep it uncovered in the freezer for a couple of days. The coffee will both absorb and mask foul odors.

MICROWAVE OVENS

A Clean Swipe

❑ Microwave ovens are so small and are used so frequently that they can accumulate odors quickly. The best way to make them odor-free is to keep them clean. Working while any spills or spatters are still fresh, dip a sponge in hot water, squeeze it out, and then dip it in baking soda or vinegar. Use it to lightly wipe down the inside of the oven.

Tea for Two

❑ Another way to freshen the microwave is to put 1 tablespoon lemon juice in a mug of water and heat it on High for 1 or 2 minutes. As it heats up, the juice mixture will freshen the inside of the oven, and when the mug comes out, it will be ready for a tea bag.

DRAINS AND GARBAGE DISPOSALS

Sink Stinks

❑ To eliminate unpleasant odors caused by a dirty kitchen drain, sprinkle 2 heaping tablespoons baking soda in the drain, then gently pour in ¼ cup boiling water. Let it sit for five to ten minutes, then flush well with running water.

An Iced Drink with a Twist of Lemon

❑ If your disposal smells bad, it probably means that the blades are dirty. Old food particles tend to cling to the blades and rot. To clean the blades, run a few ice cubes or lemon wedges through the system.

CLOSED SPACES

The Closet Collection

❑ Closets collect odors from clothing and shoes. To freshen the air, put a couple of briquettes of activated charcoal (from your outdoor grill) in the corners of the

The Top 5 Odor-Eaters That You Already Have On Hand

There's no need to run out and buy fancy room deodorizers to cover up that stale fish or spilled perfume. Most likely, you already have everything you need to keep your house smelling fresh.

1. Baking soda freshens everything from diaper pails to bathwater. It's especially effective on acidic smells such as body odor and stale food and in small spaces that collect odors—the freezer, the microwave, or a closed-up suitcase.

2. Fresh air is the cheapest and most effective air freshener. Open windows work magic on everything from stuffy rooms to cars that reek of cigarettes. To treat stale-smelling carpets and closets, get out the window fan, aim it toward the offensive area, and turn it on. The best part is that fresh air doesn't cost a thing.

3. Ground coffee takes the sting out of pungent odors such as fish, soiled leather, and stale food in the freezer. You can deodorize your whole kitchen by making a pot of coffee, then using the grounds to freshen your garbage can.

4. Hydrogen peroxide and water form the basis for many commercial odor eliminators. Use the combination to get rid of organic smells such as perspiration and garbage can odors.

5. Vinegar neutralizes the sulfur smells that baking soda can't. It works especially well on fabric and on bathroom surfaces.

closet. They will absorb odor and moisture and keep the air fresh. Change the briquettes once a season, and your closets will stay fresh smelling.

Look for the Cedar Lining

❑ To get the smell of mothballs out of a cedar chest, rub the inside of the chest with fine-grit sandpaper. The paper will scrape away the chemicals, while the heat from the friction will revive the original cedar scent.

Pack In the Freshness

❑ If your suitcase smells like the attic where it is stored, pour 1 cup baking soda into it the night before

Closed Spaces

you pack. Zip up the suitcase and shake it. Vacuum it the next day, and it should smell fresh and new.

❏ To keep odors from building up between trips, fill your suitcase with crumpled newspaper before putting it away.

Gym Bags: No Sweat!

❏ Get perspiration odors out of a vinyl gym bag by making a solution of equal parts hydrogen peroxide and water. Sponge out the interior of the bag with the solution, then wipe it down with water. The solution may cause the bag's colors to fade, but since you're only wiping down the inside, who's to know?

❏ To protect that gym bag from accumulating new odors, make your own sachets. Pour ¼ cup baking

---

ONE PERSON'S SOLUTION

Quick! Company's Coming!

We don't use our guest bedroom much, and the air gets a little stale. Freshening up the room just before company comes isn't a problem in the summer months, when I can open the windows, but during the Christmas season, I can't do that. Instead, I soak a few cotton balls with some scented oils such as oil of clove, cinnamon, or wintergreen. You can get the oils at health food stores, or in a pinch you can use extracts from the supermarket. I tuck a soaked cotton ball in the heat register. As the room heats up, the oil perfumes the air.

—MILDRED JENSEN
Hastings, Nebraska

soda on a small cotton cloth. (You can cut an old T-shirt into squares for this.) Add a few teaspoons of dried herbs such as rosemary or mint, or use slivers of deodorant soap. (Here's your chance to chop up and use those little bars of soap from hotels or to use up the remains of standard-size bars.) Secure the ends of the cloth with a rubber band. Toss a couple of sachets into the gym bag and leave them there.

UPHOLSTERED FURNITURE

Armchair Urinalysis

❏ Once a young pet has made his first mistake on your favorite couch, the animal is likely to return to the scene of the crime unless you get rid of the smell. To get the odor out of the couch or other upholstered furniture, dampen a sponge with rubbing alcohol or a urine neutralizer (from a pet store). Check the manufacturer's label to see if the upholstery is colorfast, and test an inconspicuous area (such as the back of the couch) to be sure the solution won't discolor the fabric. If the test is successful, blot the mixture onto the stain, then rinse sparingly with water. Don't soak the area, or you may leave water stains on the fabric. Blot out as much of the liquid as you can with a clean, white towel.

❏ If you think that alcohol or neutralizer will damage the fabric, try blotting the stain with a paste made of equal parts white vinegar and baking soda. Blot again with a clean, damp sponge and let it dry.

CLOTHING

Eau de Mothballs

❏ Clothes that have been stored with mothballs carry a pungent chemical smell. The best way to get rid of it

Odors

is to hang the clothes outside, preferably for several days.

❏ If the scent lingers, wash the clothes with heavy-duty laundry detergent. (The label will identify it that way.) In severe cases, add 1 cup white vinegar to your washing machine after it has filled with water but before you add the clothes. *Never add vinegar to wash water that has chlorine bleach in it. The mixture will create toxic fumes. If your detergent contains bleach or if you've added bleach to the load already, skip the vinegar.*

❏ Some fabrics can't be washed. For these you'll need scented fabric softener sheets (the kind normally used in the dryer). Place the clothing in a plastic garment bag with a couple of these sheets and seal the bag shut for two to three days. By then the perfume in the dryer sheets will have chased away the mothball smell.

⏰ **TIME SAVER**

Mint-Hating Moths

One way to avoid dealing with the awful smell of mothballs is to avoid using them altogether. Try storing your clothing with sachets of dried lavender or equal parts dried rosemary and mint. Like most insects, moths are repelled by herbs with strong odors.

When the Gym Clothes Get a Workout

❏ To get perspiration odors out of clothing, dampen the affected area and then rub deodorant soap into it before dropping it into the washing machine. The soap will work on your clothing just as it works on your skin. Wash the clothing at the hottest water temperature recommended for that fabric.

❏ To treat gym clothes or work clothes that are regularly soaked in perspiration, add 1 cup white vinegar to your washing machine after it's filled with water but before the wash cycle begins. The vinegar will cut the sweat. *Do not use this technique if you've already added bleach to the wash water. The combination will create toxic fumes.*

Tobacco Smoke: When the Steam Clears

❏ Steam tobacco smoke from your clothes by adding 1 cup white vinegar to a bathtub of hot water. Hang your clothes over the tub until the bathwater cools, and the smoke will be gone.

Help for Heavy Smokers

❑ To remove smoke from heavy clothes such as wool sweaters and blue jeans, put them in the dryer (on Low or Air-Dry) with a wet towel and a fabric softener sheet for about ten minutes.

OTHER ODORS

Before Those Shoes Go Back in the Box

❑ If you put away some shoes for the winter, push a bit of crumpled newspaper into the toe of each shoe. This will freshen up the footwear while it's in storage.

❑ An alternative is to put a few activated charcoal briquettes (from your outdoor grill) in the box with your shoes before you put them away.

Paint: Beyond the Pail

❑ To help air out a freshly painted room, cut an onion into several large sections and drop the pieces in a pail of water in the middle of the floor. The gases released by the onion will neutralize the fumes.

It Sounds Like the Vacuum, but It Smells Like a Pie

❑ One of the worst parts of vacuuming is the smell of the vacuum bag. Get rid of it by putting a drop or two of cinnamon oil on each new bag. Scented oils are available at most health food stores. The heat from the motor will release the scent, and the more you vacuum, the better the room will smell.

HOME DECORATING
Those Optimal Illusions

PLANNING AND ARRANGING

From the Ground Up

❏ If you're redecorating an entire room and aren't sure where to start, try selecting the floor covering first. Because the floor is the biggest expanse in the room, it's important to decide how you want to treat it before you move on to things such as furniture and curtains. Many people prefer to start with neutral-colored carpets, on the theory that this gives them more flexibility in decorating the rest of the room. That's perfectly fine, but if your tastes run in a different direction, don't be afraid of multicolored rugs with complex designs. You can build on any of those colors with other furnishings.

But Will You Hate It Tomorrow?

❏ Furniture is a major investment, and the higher the price tag, the more mileage you'll want to get out of a piece. So how do you choose furniture you won't get sick of? Unless money is no object, it's wiser to be more conservative with big, expensive pieces (sofas, dining room tables) and get adventurous with things you can change easily—window treatments, paint colors, fabrics and pillows, lamps and other accessories. Antiques are less of a problem because they've already withstood the test of time. But beware of furniture that's expensive *and* trendy—today's hippest looks are tomorrow's flower power sofas.

No-Sweat Layouts

❏ If you're dying to rearrange the furniture but your options seem limited, experimenting on graph paper could help you find a new solution without a lot of heavy lifting. Draw a layout with your room's dimensions, making note of all fixed features such as doorways, windows, radiators, and electrical outlets. Measure each piece of furniture, and using the same scale as the room layout, cut out shapes to represent each piece. (Most people find it easier to work with two-dimensional diagrams. But before you move something, measure it to make sure the third dimension fits, too.) Try placing a piece diagonally in the corner, or move some chairs away from the wall into a freestanding arrangement. You might need to add or remove only one small element—a lamp here, an end table there—to make an arrangement work.

Mix and Match

❏ Are you bored to death with the matching bedroom set you've had since you got married? When you need a change but don't want to replace furniture that's still in good condition, break up the set and redistribute it throughout the house. Exchange a chest of drawers with one from another bedroom; switch a nightstand with an end table from the den. Taking an eclectic approach will add more personality to a cookie-cutter room.

CARPETING

Go for Rugged Rugs

❏ To stretch your redecorating budget, look for carpets that are stain resistant and made of synthetic materials with a tight twist; this gives resiliency. Looser fabrics such as yarn are less resilient and are likely to

$ DOLLAR STRETCHER

Steal That Color!

It's easy to fall in love with one of those fashionable new paint colors, but the price can be enough to break your heart. Don't despair. Ask your paint store or home center to match your favorite hue by mixing less expensive brands. The store should be able to come very close.

show matting over time. If it turns out that your stain-resistant carpet really isn't, you can request and receive a replacement from the manufacturer or your money back.

Carpets for Special Needs

❑ If you have children or pets or are laying the carpet in a high-traffic area, how do you know which materials will hide the soil? Lean toward 100 percent nylon, multicolored carpets.

❑ If you don't want the grain of the carpet to show, revealing multiple footprints or sweeps with the vacuum, look for trackless carpets. A berber carpet, which is made of a "nubby" yarn, is another good choice—unless you have pets. The yarn used in berber carpets is generally "continuous filament," so if a nub gets snagged under tabby's claws, it could pull a whole line of yarn. Avoid a saxonate or velvet finish, which will only highlight the tracks.

PROBLEM ROOMS

The Old Mirror Trick, Revisited

❑ Small, boxy rooms are often both unattractive and claustrophobic. Mirror-covered walls are one solution to this age-old problem, but they can make you dizzy, and besides, they went out with the eighties. For an updated and more subtle effect, hang a series of identical full-length mirrors, evenly spaced, on a section of one wall. The inexpensive closet-door mirrors sold in discount stores will work just fine. Figure out how many you'll need to fill the available space (use at least three). Place them at midwall level two to three inches apart. Later, for a new perspective, move the mirrors to a different spot.

It Doubles As a Bowling Alley

❑ Long, narrow rooms are a big decorating challenge and difficult to arrange. So how do you de-emphasize the bowling alley look? Try installing built-in cabinets at one or both ends of the room, making them just as deep as you need. The cabinets will make the room's dimensions seem less extreme and will give you storage space for out-of-season clothing, extra bedding, toys and games, and any other stuff you want to stow out of sight.

ONE PERSON'S SOLUTION
A Room with No View

I have a good news/bad news kitchen. The good news is that it has a fairly large window—not something one takes for granted in a Manhattan apartment. The bad news? All I get to look at is the brick wall of a building about ten feet away.

I wanted to hide the view but didn't relish the idea of covering up the window with curtains or a shade. The kitchen is pretty small and narrow, and I wanted to keep it as open and airy as possible. To divert attention away from the ugly view, I mounted three pine shelves on the wall and extended them right across the lower part of the window. (For ventilation, I can lower the window from the top.) Though only six inches deep, the shelves give me plenty of much-needed storage space, which I use to display my collection of colored-glass dishes and objects. The effect is dramatic and striking—and when the light comes through the window and hits the colored glass, it sparkles all over the room. All in all, it's a big improvement over the brick wall next door!

—ROSE RAWLINGS
New York, New York

Home Decorating

❏ To soften the appearance of a room that's long and narrow, try painting the end walls a darker color than the side walls. This will make them appear to be closer together and will make the room seem better proportioned.

6 Claustrophobia Fighters

Small, boxy rooms can sometimes make you feel as if the walls are closing in. But the way you decorate a small room can make a big difference. A light touch generally works best for creating a more open feeling—lighter colors, fewer big objects, simpler patterns and window treatments. If a tiny space has you pining for the wide-open prairie, keep the following guidelines in mind.

1. Paint the walls a white, neutral, or pale shade. Use the same color on the ceiling. Avoid dark colors, which absorb light and make rooms feel smaller.

2. Think continuity. Choose either a monochromatic color scheme or closely related hues. Linking together the room's largest areas—walls, floors, dominant furnishings—with variations of the same color will let your eye travel around the room with less interruption, creating an atmosphere of calm and serenity rather than one of claustrophobia. Combine different textures and work in brighter-colored accessories to add interest.

3. Avoid wallpaper with big, loud, or busy designs. This goes for slipcovers and bedcoverings, too. Bold designs will overpower a small space.

4. Think about scale. Choose smaller furniture that reflects the scale of the room. Don't overwhelm a small area with a huge sofa that blocks traffic or takes up most of the available space. You're better off with a greater number of smaller items because you'll have more flexibility to create interesting arrangements. Include a sofa or chairs with legs—they look less bulky than pieces that sit directly on the floor.

5. Keep clutter to a minimum. Instead of displaying photos and knickknacks on tables, mount them on walls or arrange them on narrow shelves.

6. Give your windows some breathing room. Use airy curtains, simple shades, or blinds. Or if possible, leave the windows bare. Stay away from elaborate window treatments and heavy drapes.

Part-Time Walls

❏ If family members need more privacy but you don't have a lot of extra space, create a separate nook by using freestanding shelves as room dividers. This is a good approach for kids who are looking for more privacy when sharing a room or for anyone who wants to set off a work space from public view. It provides extra storage space, too. Place the shelves perpendicular to the wall to define your private zone. Load them up for maximum privacy or keep them relatively open and airy. The unit should be wide enough to stand solidly on the floor. Depending on your needs, you can use industrial metal shelving from the hardware store or a wooden étagère purchased at a furniture store or home center. Don't use tall bookcases for this purpose—they'll tip over too easily.

Know When to Fold Up

❏ Another way to increase privacy is with folding screens. The freestanding variety, usually with fabric panels, can be found at most home centers. Since they need not reach all the way to the ceiling, air can circulate through the space at the top—especially important if your part-time room has no window. You can also make your own screens or have them custom-made and installed on a sliding track. Those with translucent panels, such as Japanese shoji screens, offer privacy while letting in light.

FURNITURE

The Low-Budget Work Space

❏ Good office desks are expensive, heavy, and bulky. If you need a desk only for occasional use, or if you need a second work space in a home office or sewing room, you can save both money and space by buying a sheet of half-inch plywood or three-quarter-inch pressboard (building supply stores often sell them precut to the appropriate size). Place it on top of a pair of two-drawer file cabinets and use laminated edging to protect against splinters. Voilà! A desk or craft table with drawers.

No Sunbathing Allowed

❏ It's pretty common for good wooden furniture to bleach out over time when exposed to direct sunlight. If you notice that a favorite piece is starting to fade, act quickly before it loses both the beauty and the protection offered by its original finish. Move that special piece out of the direct sun—beside the window rather than in front of it, for instance. The piece will maintain its original color a lot longer.

❏ The same principle applies to upholstered furniture. Move sofas, armchairs, and other upholstered items as far as possible from direct sunlight, and you'll keep the fabric looking bright and crisp longer.

Damage Control

❏ Is your wooden furniture cracking or warping? It may be too close to a heat source such as a radiator or hot-air vent. Move it away or, if necessary, fasten blocks of wood or molding to the floor so the furniture can't slide too close to the heat.

❏ If your wooden furniture suddenly starts to darken, it may be a victim of mildew. The way to stop mildew from spreading is to dry things out. Make sure any humidifiers or vaporizers are aimed away from wooden furniture and take any other steps you can to decrease the humidity in the room (run a fan occasionally, for instance, to keep the air circulating). If all else fails, consider moving the affected furniture to another, drier room.

Un-Scratch the Surface

❏ To camouflage scratches on wooden furniture, apply a few drops of salad oil or other light oil to the scratch. Add a little pumice (available at paint and hardware stores). Wrap a wooden block with a piece of felt and use it to rub in the oil and pumice until the scratch disappears.

WINDOWS AND WALLS

Dramatize Those Dinky Windows

❏ Small, boxy windows can be a decorating challenge, but you can make them look more impressive by cheating a bit when you hang curtains or drapes. To make a window look longer, mount the drapes higher than you ordinarily would, adding a valance to prevent the wall from showing. Use an extra-wide curtain and rod. To make a window look wider, let the fabric folds hang just inside the bottom edge and over part of the sidewalls.

Make a short window look longer by mounting the drapes above the window and adding a valance (A). A narrow window will look wider if you extend the edges of the drapes over adjoining walls (B).

A   VALANCE

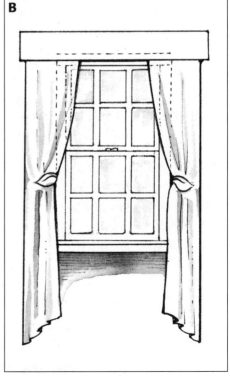

B

Scene of the Hanging

❏ You may have found a great painting or print, but that's only the first step in decorating your walls. Now you need to figure out just where to hang it. You can center the art on the wall, on a segment of the wall, or over a piece of furniture—depending in part on whether you plan to rearrange the furniture frequently. Centering a painting over the sofa is fine if you expect to leave the sofa in the same spot for a while, but if you want the option of moving it around without rehanging all your wall decorations, it's better to center the artwork on the wall instead.

❏ Hang a picture slightly lower if it will be seen most often from a sitting position. Hang it higher in a standing-up spot such as a hallway or foyer. If the artwork is very large, hang it in an open area where you'll be able to get far enough away to take it all in. Arrange smaller pictures together in a group for greater impact; a little picture will get lost on a big wall.

The Floor Plan

❏ When you're hanging a group of nonsymmetrical pictures on one wall, it can be difficult to figure out exactly how you want to display them. One approach is to lay the pieces out on the floor to plan your arrangement. When you've decided on a layout, hang the pictures on the wall, starting from the center and working out.

Cover-Up!

❏ To deal with walls that have small cracks and bumps, cover them with solid vinyl wallpaper that has

---

TIME SAVER

Quickie Curtains

Can't find the right curtains? Before you sew your own from fabric or bedsheets, try looking for a 100 percent cotton or cotton-polyester blend shower curtain in a style and color you like. Department stores, home centers, and mail-order catalogs carry a wide range of attractive designs that can easily be adjusted to fit a window. And with these curtains, unlike those made from sheets or fabric, you won't need to add a lining for them to hang well. Those with tab tops or tie-ons are a snap to hang; you can also use café clips or run a decorative ribbon through the grommets. Save sewing time by using iron-on hem tape wherever you need to make adjustments.

a fabric or vinyl backing. Textured wallpaper is especially good for this purpose.

COLLECTIONS

Try a Little Group Mentality

❑ You may call it junk, treasures, or objets d'art, but when there's too much of it in the wrong places, it detracts from the look and comfort of your home. Get control over clutter by dividing it into three groups: the Good (collections and treasures), the Bad (useless, broken, or outdated items), and the Ugly (things you need but don't want to look at). Throw out the Bad right away so you can focus on displaying the Good and storing the Ugly.

The Display's the Thing

❑ A collection of similar items can be an impressive decorating touch, or it can look like nothing more than a jumble of odds and ends. To reduce the impression of clutter, try displaying your collection on a wall. This keeps tabletops and other surfaces clear and creates a new focal point that draws the eye upward.

> ✔ **PROBLEM PREVENTED**
>
> ## Nail with Finesse
>
> To avoiding damaging the wall when hanging pictures, nail with short, steady taps. Old plaster may crack, so go gently. If you're very careful putting the nail in, you'll make only a small hole. And don't apply tape to the wall before you nail—the glue will be hard to remove later on.

❑ Another way to decrease clutter and increase the impact of your collections is to group items of similar scale and place them in a setting that's appropriate to their size. Smaller items (a collection of matchbooks or Pez dispensers) will look best mounted in a box or display case with just-big-enough compartments. Larger items such as cookie jars can be grouped on a shelf.

Sometimes More Is More

❑ Want your stuff to make more of a statement? Sometimes the problem is too *few* items in one place. For example, if you have unused vases scattered all over the house, gather them up and display them together. If this results in a hodgepodge, try separating them by style or color: Group colorful ceramics in one spot, elegant glass in another. Displaying similar items together can create a dramatic impact.

"Found Art" for Your Walls

Who says walls are only for pictures and mirrors? Look for "art" in unexpected places and solve several decorating problems at once: Cover blank walls, express your personality, and maybe even clear out the closets. Items that represent your family's interests and activities are a natural choice—especially if you already have them lying around the house. Following are some ideas to get you started.

Antique tools
Barbie dolls or paper dolls
Birdcages
Fishing lures
45 rpm records
Frisbees
Hats (straw hats, bowlers, fedoras, or caps)
Jersey numbers from footraces
Kites
Maps
Masks
Musical instruments
Sheet music covers
Tennis rackets
Theater programs
Travel souvenirs

Contain Yourself

❏ Does your home suffer from chronic disorganization? You can turn clutter into a decorating opportunity if you start by finding the right containers. Be on the lookout for jars, boxes, bowls, baskets, and other receptacles you can use to store and display your treasures. Search your home for little-used items you can adapt. Then check out the possibilities at flea markets and garage sales. Keep an eye out for an old wooden or plastic milk crate, for instance, and cut it down to make a display case for a ceramic cow collection. Or pick up an old soda crate or two. They're just a few inches deep, and the compartments make great display nooks for kids' small action figures or tiny toys.

❏ When trying to put your house in order, think about what you need to contain and be imaginative in choosing the right containers. Use goldfish bowls or glass jars to hold marbles, buttons, or pins. An old medicine cabinet, spice rack, or dresser drawer can be turned into a display case for a wall-mounted collection. If you sew a lot, store spools of thread in flat file drawers. The rule of thumb is, if it's meant to hold stuff, put something in it.

Outside the House

I once knew a woman whose property had been bought by the state to make room for a new highway. The woman didn't want to lose her house, so she bought another piece of land just up the road and hired me and my crew to move the house there.

When I came by with my men to do the job, the woman took me aside, showed me a raised stone flower bed that she loved, and asked if we could move that, too. The flower bed was about 3 or 4 feet wide and 30 inches high, so the woman could stand up while she worked in it. I told her I didn't think we could move it in one piece, but we might be able to take

it apart and bring it along that way. Since she couldn't afford that much work, we moved the house without it, but I didn't forget that flower bed. While the other men were working at the new location, I asked my loader operator to go down to the old site and see if he could get his bucket under the bed. I told him that if it fell apart, he should just leave it, but if it didn't, he should bring it on up the hill and set it next to the house. Whoever did the masonry on that flower bed did good work, because we were able to get it to the new location in one piece—and the woman was tickled when she saw it.

I learned a long time ago that it pays to consider both simple and unconventional ways to solve problems. In "Yard and Garden," you'll find all sorts of ideas for coping with crabgrass, protecting plants from frost damage, getting rid of all those zucchini, and making floral bouquets last longer. And if your biggest outdoor dilemmas are animal rather than vegetable, look to "Animal Pests" for ingenious ways to discourage mosquitoes, skunks, and everything in between. Whether you're trying to keep the raccoons out of the garbage or the mint plants out of the front yard, you'll find the perfect solutions here.

ANIMAL PESTS
The Skunk in the Woodshed and Other Dilemmas

BATS

Don't Give Them an Opening

❑ When you see a bat in your house and you don't think it came through the attic, how can you make sure no more bats will get in? Most bats that come into the main part of a house get in accidentally, not because they're looking for a new home, so the problem may be with your door and window screens. Make an inspection of your house, checking each screen for a very large opening. Repairing the gap should prevent a return appearance.

BEES

Excuse Me, Madam, I Thought You Were a Gardenia

❑ While you're outside, you'll attract fewer bees if you eschew flowery perfumes and clothing with big floral prints.

Oh, That Stings!

❑ To deaden the pain of a bee sting, apply ice to the affected area after washing it with warm, soapy water. This will soothe the pain and reduce the swelling.

❑ You can also soothe a bee sting witha simple treatment straight from your kitchen cupboard. Just make a thin paste of baking soda and cold water and dab it on the sting.

Bees

BIRDS

Woody Shouldn't Live Here Anymore

❏ Bird enthusiasts enjoy spotting the occasional woodpecker, but one that sticks around can turn into a real pest. A good way to get rid of a persistent woodpecker is to hang pie plates over the area where it likes to peck. The plates will turn in the wind and catch the sunlight, and the flashing light will frighten the bird away.

❏ If an annoying woodpecker often visits one small area, you might try something called a bitter agent. Available at most hardware stores, this is a strong-tasting chemical that you can apply to the wood to repel the bird. It won't harm the woodpecker, but it will send the bird down the street.

Say Bye-Bye to the Birdies

SCREEN

Screen all avian callers by sealing off any area where the original building overlaps a new addition to your home.

❏ The best way to keep pigeons from roosting on your house is to eliminate the places where they like to live. They are especially fond of eaves, as well as any addition to a house where the old building overlaps the new construction. (This creates a cozy shelter for them.) Shoo away unwanted guests, then seal off those areas with galvanized steel screening from the hardware store. That will prevent them from coming back.

BLACKFLIES

Why Brides Don't Worry about Blackflies

❏ When it's springtime in the North, the blackflies can be vicious. Wearing long pants and long sleeves is a start, but it isn't enough to keep them away; they often bite even more ferociously once they're under a cuff or sleeve. What can you do to minimize their mischief? Be sure to tuck your pants into your socks and your sleeves into your gloves before working in the garden.

❑ What about your face and neck, the favorite targets of blackflies? To protect these areas, get a few yards of fine netting (the same material used to make bridal veils) from a fabric store. The netting has to be fine enough to keep the flies out and yet not so dense that you can't see through it. Wrap this over your wide-brimmed gardening hat and tuck it into your shirt collar so that it covers your face and neck. That should keep the flies out of your face.

CUTWORMS

Keep Plants Surrounded

❑ Keeping cutworms away from your favorite plants is easy if you have a supply of plastic milk or soda bottles. Use your garden shears to cut off the bottom and top of each bottle. Then cut each tube into rings three inches wide. Work each ring into the soil around the plant to a depth of two inches. Leave one inch of plastic visible above the soil to keep out worms that are crawling along the surface.

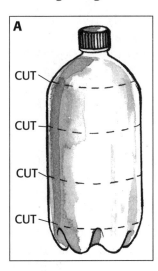

The worms crawl in; the worms crawl out—but they can't get through plastic. To protect seedlings against cutworm damage, cut three-inch-wide rings from plastic soda or milk bottles (A). Insert a ring in the dirt around each seedling (B), leaving one inch extending above the ground.

DEER

Foiled Again!

❑ To keep deer from snacking on the tender bark of a young tree, wrap the base of the tree in aluminum foil

Animal Pests

up to about your waist level. This is also a deterrent for gypsy moths.

❏ Sometimes you can repel deer by making them think you are lurking just around the corner. Ask your local beauty parlor for hair clippings, then scatter the hair in and around the plants so the scent of humans lingers through the night.

Don't Let Bambi Harvest Your Garden

❏ Rabbit fencing—the wire kind with two-inch rectangular openings—will deter deer if you form it into semicircles and place it right over vegetables, sealing the ends, of course.

The One-Scent Solution

❏ If deer are a problem in your flower garden, try scattering mothballs on the ground or tying them up in old panty hose and hanging them from the garden fence. *Do not use this approach if there's any chance that children or pets will find and eat the mothballs, and never scatter mothballs in a vegetable garden. The chemicals in the mothballs are toxic.*

MOLES

Go Underground

❏ Moles will destroy ornamental plants while they burrow underground in search of grubs. One way to control the moles is to treat your lawn with a biological grub-control agent (available at garden centers). If you take away the mole's food supply, it will move on.

❏ An old-time technique that still gets rid of moles is to bury a large coffee can below a mole tunnel and

DOLLAR STRETCHER

Spice It Up

You can get more use out of your deer and insect repellents if you dilute them with a spicy pepper spray. Fill a bucket with water and add a few handfuls of chopped jalapeño peppers. (Or use quartered onions, garlic, marigolds, or rhubarb leaves instead.) Let the mixture "cook" in the sun for a week. When it is really spicy, strain the liquid and discard the peppers. Then mix up a solution of four parts pepper solution and one part commercial repellent. Put the mixture in a spray bottle and use it to spray everything from your roses to your cornstalks. It will make them less tasty to deer and raccoons looking for a midnight snack. Remember to wash your vegetables carefully before you eat them.

cover the tunnel with a board to keep out daylight. If the can is large enough, a mole traveling the tunnel will fall in and won't be able to climb out. Unless it's released elsewhere shortly after capture, the mole will die after a few hours without food.

MOSQUITOES

Watch Out for Still Waters

❏ If the mosquitoes seem particularly bad this year, check your yard to see if you might be breeding them unintentionally. Mosquitoes need still, stagnant water to reproduce. Even the smallest amount of water can incubate hundreds of thousands of larvae. Empty any wading pools that aren't being used and clean all birdbaths. Change the water in those birdbaths once a week for the rest of the summer.

❏ To stop any mosquito breeding that's taking place on your property, take a tour of the yard and look for any spot likely to collect water in a rainstorm. Throw away old tires. Turn your wheelbarrows upside down or store them in the garage or toolshed. Clean the gutters on your house. And check all plastic tarps, such as swimming pool covers. Half an inch of standing water on top of a plastic sheet will keep the neighborhood scratching all summer.

> ☑ **PROBLEM PREVENTED**
>
> ## Leave the Blue Jeans in the Closet
>
> To discourage mosquitoes, watch what you wear. Light colors are good, but don't dress in dark blue in mosquito country. For some reason, mosquitoes seem to be attracted to dark colors.

Try Biological Warfare

❏ If it's not practical to remove stagnant water from a large area such as a pond, you'll need another approach. You can actually see the mosquito larvae on still water. They look like small, moving worms—that's why they're called wigglers. If you spot these larvae in your wading pool or pond, ask at your local hardware store or garden center for a form of bacteria called DTI. The bacteria come in a briquette that will dissolve in the water and kill the pests in their infancy.

This approach is environmentally friendly—except, of course, to the larvae.

They Like a Noontime Siesta

❑ Even if you're not breeding mosquitoes, you run the risk of being bitten every time you go outdoors. You can't stay inside all summer, but you'll get fewer mosquito bites if you plan your outdoor activities for midday. Mosquitoes don't like the hot sun, so they do most of their hunting in the evening and early morning.

✔ PROBLEM PREVENTED

Maggots: The Root of the Problem

When root maggots get into your vegetable garden, they feed on your crops below the ground, destroying their roots and eventually killing the plants. You can ban them from your garden without resorting to chemical warfare. Just try any of these low-tech approaches.

1. Give pests a heap of trouble. Keep them out of your beets, turnips, cabbage, and onions by heaping wood ashes around the base of these seedlings as soon as they come up. This will deter the flies from laying their eggs at the base of these young plants.

2. Dip in. When planting seedlings for any of these varieties, discourage root maggots by dipping the plants' roots in a mixture of equal parts lime and wood ashes before placing them in the ground.

3. Collar those plants. As soon as seedlings are in the ground, fashion a little collar for each plant out of tar paper. Cut a circle out of the paper and make a cut from one edge to the center. Fasten the collar snugly around the base of the plant. The paper will block pests from laying their eggs on the plant, and its smell will keep them away for good.

Tar-paper those transplants.

Are You Itching to Try This?

❏ To relieve the itch from insect bites, make a paste of baking soda and cold water and apply it to the affected spot.

❏ Another good treatment for mosquito bites is ammonia. Apply it directly to the bite with a cotton swab. Ammonia will numb the area and keep you from scratching it. In fact, it is the main ingredient in those itch-relief products you find in the drugstore.

RACCOONS

Garbage In, Raccoon Out

❏ Raccoons in the garbage can be a terrific nuisance, and in most urban areas you won't solve the problem by putting a lid—even an interlocking lid—on the garbage can. The raccoon has the dual advantages of determination and an opposable thumb; these critters have even been known to unscrew bottle caps! If you're plagued by a smart raccoon going after your garbage, *do* put a lid on the can. Then secure it with a bungee cord hitched to the can's handles.

Keep masked scavengers out of the garbage. Put a lid on it—and then secure that lid with a bungee cord.

The Electrified Garden

❏ To keep raccoons out of a garden that's relatively near the house, try stringing Christmas lights (particularly the kind that blink) around your cornstalks and leaving them on all night.

SKUNKS

They Prefer Their Own Perfume

❏ If a skunk has made a summer home of your woodshed or garage, you can gently encourage it to leave. Oddly enough, skunks are generally turned off by perfumes. Try hanging one or even two room deodorizers in the small area the skunk has invaded. The animal will likely move on, and then you can seal up its entrance hole so it won't come back.

SLUGS

There Are Some Lines They Won't Cross

❑ If slugs are a problem in sunny areas of your garden, surround your seedlings with cocoa bean mulch (available at most garden centers). Slugs don't like to crawl over it, so they'll stay away from your plants. Be sure to use the mulch only on plants that get a lot of sun. If used in the shade, cocoa bean mulch tends to mildew.

❑ In shady areas, try mulching with crushed seashells. Slugs don't like the sharp edges.

Drinking and Diving

❑ You can trap slugs with a little beer, cola, or sugar water. Place your beverage of choice in shallow pans near infested plants and leave it overnight. The beer or other beverage will attract the slugs, which will drown when they try to drink.

SPIDERS

Neatness Counts

❑ If spiders make a home near your house, they are just a few steps away from becoming your roommates. How can you keep them out? The best way is to keep the leaf litter out of your gutters and away from the base of the house. Clear the gutters each fall and rake up any leaves that have drifted in around shrubs near

---

☑ PROBLEM PREVENTED

Natural Allies for the Gardener

If you don't want to spray your garden with an insecticide, try planting things that will keep bugs away naturally. Marigolds planted around the border of a garden, for example, will deter many insects, and they are especially good at luring Japanese beetles away from your herbs and vegetables. In the morning, you will find hundreds of groggy bugs clinging to the marigold blossoms; simply pluck them off and kill them by dropping them into a bucket of turpentine. Other battles call for other allies. Try these.

PLANT	TO DISCOURAGE
Basil and rosemary	Mosquitoes and flies
Garlic	Slugs
Mint	Cabbageworms
Nasturtiums	Aphids

---

the house. Keep garden areas around the house clear of leaves, too.

❏ If you are seriously concerned about keeping crawling insects away from your house, mulch around the foundation with crushed stone. The stone should cover the ground for a good 12 inches around the house. Unlike bark mulch, which makes a dark, moist bed for insects, the stone will stay dry and hot, forming a natural spider and insect repellent.

SQUASH BUGS

Horton Hatches a What?

❏ Your chances for beating squash bugs are best if you seek and destroy them early in the season, before they hatch. At that time, the yellow egg clusters are easily visible on the undersides of leaves. In fact, you can even spot them from the tops of the leaves; just look for spots that seem to pucker under the weight of the eggs. Then pick them off and kill them immediately.

Late Sleepers Get Squished

❏ To get rid of the bugs that will eat your cucumbers and squash all season long, take a tour of the garden early each morning. Because the bugs will be sitting on the leaves and will still be sluggish, it will be easy to pluck them off and squish them before they do any more damage.

SQUIRRELS

Baffle That Critter

❏ If your bird feeder sits on a pole and you're pestered by squirrels stealing the seed you put out for the birds, go to the pet store and buy a squirrel baffle. This is a

---

⏰ TIME SAVER

A Sweet Solution

If you don't want to go plant by plant to pick off worms, snails, and beetles, you can make a simple trap for them instead. Place a small board or old shingle near the infested plants. Make sure one corner is propped up enough so that the bugs can crawl underneath. To sweeten the deal, spread honey or molasses on the underside of your trap. Early the next morning, check for results. The trap should be crawling with invaders that have been lured away from your garden. You can then dispose of them without having to spray your plants with insecticide.

Animal Pests

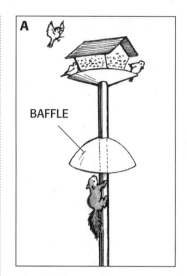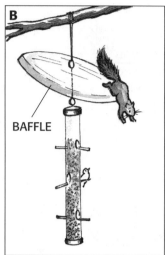

Baffle those squirrels and keep them away from bird feeders. One type of baffle works for a feeder on a pole (A). Another protects hanging types (B).

plastic dome that you attach under the feeder. It curves downward and away from the feeder, providing a barrier against upwardly mobile squirrels. Make sure the baffle is high enough so that squirrels can't jump past it. (An alternative version, designed for hanging feeders, is mounted *above* the feeder.)

❏ Another approach is to make a squirrel baffle yourself by cutting a rigid, collarlike disk from aluminum flashing.

Bird Food That Squirrels Don't Like

❏ If even a baffle doesn't keep the squirrels away from your bird feeder, you may want to back up your baffle with a commercial repellent. Ask at your local hardware store for a repellent containing capsicum pepper powder (Squirrel Away is one such product) and mix it right in with the birdseed. Squirrels will find the powder irritating to touch and taste, but it won't actually harm them. Birds, which have no receptors in their brains for the pepper sensation, won't even notice it. But you will, so be sure to wash your hands thoroughly after touching it!

On Shaky Ground

❏ To keep squirrels from invading a hanging bird feeder, try moving the feeder to a branch that will just support its weight. When the squirrel makes its entrance, it will feel the branch begin to give and back off.

❏ You can reinforce the wire your bird feeder hangs from by wrapping it with a little barbed wire. Wrap a little more around the branch that supports it. Once you do this, squirrels are likely to find the neighbor's feeder much more attractive.

TERMITES

Know Where to Look

❏ You suspect your house may be infested with termites, and you're anxious to find out for sure. You can tell you have termites if you see their mud tubes running up your basement walls. Subterranean termites— the most common kind—have to build protective tubes across dry areas such as masonry foundation walls or concrete slabs to reach the wooden parts of the house. But even if you don't see those shelter tubes in the basement or around your home's foundation, you may not be free and clear of termites. A termite's favorite place to eat is under the front porch in that gap between your front stairs and the house. This is a great spot for termites because it provides both darkness and shelter. If you want to be sure that termites haven't moved in, check under the porch for those infamous mud tubes.

Your new tenants could be termites. Watch out for their signature mud tubes on basement walls.

An Early-Warning System

❏ The signature mud tubes of termites aren't always visible, so if you're still concerned about a possible termite takeover even though you don't see any mud tubes, check the way exterminators do. At the hardware store or lumberyard, buy a few pieces of soft pine. Narrow strips, about 12 inches in length, will do just fine. (You can also use scrap pieces as long as they're made of softwood.) Position the strips about 3 to 4 inches from your house's foundation, then use a hammer to drive them 8 inches into the ground. Check

Termites

Bug Busters

When it comes to deterring insect pests, Mother Nature can be your best friend—if you work with her and not against her. For example:

• **Encourage your kids to bring home toads they find** and release them in your garden. A single healthy toad will eat thousands of bugs each month and do no damage to your lawn and garden.

• **Install a bat house** (available in kit form from garden centers and mail-order suppliers such as L.L. Bean) on your property. A bat will kill and consume thousands of bugs each night—mostly mosquitoes, not the beneficial insects that help pollinate flowers and provide food for songbirds, frogs, and other wildlife.

• **Get to know what a praying mantis looks like** so that you'll never, ever kill one. A single one of these insects will feed on thousands of the bugs that want to destroy your garden. You can even buy praying mantis eggs from some mail-order companies, then breed the insects in your garden.

The praying mantis: a gardener's friend.

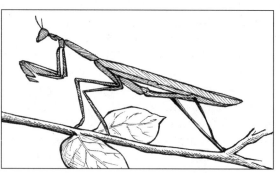

these stakes every couple of months. If termites have eaten away at the wood, chances are they have invaded your home as well. It's time to call the exterminator.

TICKS

They're Just Waiting for a Lift

❑ One easy way to ward off ticks is to wear long pants and tuck them into your socks. The farther a tick has to crawl, the more likely you are to spot it or knock it off accidentally. Ticks don't actually drop out of the trees. Instead, they cling to blades of grass and the leaves of low bushes, waiting for you to brush by and pick them up. Then they crawl upward, looking for a place to bite.

Read Those Labels

❏ You can also deter ticks by treating your clothing with a chemical called permethrin. When you shop for a tick repellent, check for this as a main ingredient.

Pluck It Out

❏ If a tick latches onto you, it's important to remove it as quickly as possible—but exactly how do you do that? Use sharp tweezers to pull the tick out, then wash the area with warm water. If the insect's head breaks off under your skin, apply antiseptic, then remove the head as you would a splinter.

ONE PERSON'S SOLUTION

The Heat Is On

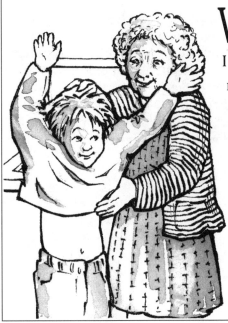

When my grandchildren have been playing outside all day, I want to check their clothes to make sure they haven't gathered up any ticks, but they don't like to sit still for that. Now I just toss their play clothes into the dryer for a few minutes. That dries up any ticks and kills them. Then I shake the dead ticks out over the trash can.

—BEV MIDDLETON
Gothenburg, Nebraska

Does It Measure Up?

❏ Concerned about whether a tick bite will lead to Lyme disease? Soon after being bitten, place a small plastic bag over the affected area and use a laundry marking pen to draw a circle on the bag around the bite. The circle should form a loose outline of the red, infected skin. Each day after you shower, hold the marked bag over the bite. The warm water from the shower will accentuate any rash—the warning sign of Lyme disease—and the circle on the bag will help you to determine whether the rash is expanding. If the rash crosses the line, see a doctor.

❏ What do you need to tell the doctor when you see her about that tick bite? If you do have Lyme disease, she'll want to know the date the infection began. So anytime you're bitten by a tick, write down on the calendar the date of the bite. Then you'll be prepared if it turns out you're infected.

WOODCHUCKS

In the Trenches

❏ If you have a real problem with woodchucks, you may have to do what they do: Burrow. Dig a narrow trench, at least a foot deep, around the perimeter of your garden. Line the trench with cinder blocks or bricks, or use sheets of metal or wire mesh. Then fill in the trench with dirt. Since woodchucks spend most of their time underground, you need to place the barrier where they are most likely to find it.

Give Them a Shock

❏ If the trench doesn't deter your woodchucks, try stringing electric fencing around the garden. (Be sure to follow the manufacturer's directions for maintaining the fence and the area immediately around it.) That may stop those animals bold enough to approach the garden aboveground.

YARD AND GARDEN
The Not-So-Green-Thumb Blues

LAWNS

Inch by Inch

❏ Everyone knows that healthy lawns need watering. The problem comes in determining how *much* water yours needs. A lawn that doesn't receive enough water will start to look dull, and one that gets too much will require excessive mowing and be less resistant to disease. What's just right? The rule of thumb in the heat of summer is that sunny areas should receive an inch of water a week, either from rainfall or from your sprinkler. Shady areas require less water because they don't dry out as quickly.

Measure for Measure

❏ Every sprinkler is different, so how do you know how long to leave yours on to deliver the equivalent of an inch of rainfall? Measure its output. Put a small cup ten feet from the head of your sprinkler. Come back in 20 minutes and measure the amount of water that has accumulated in the cup. This approach requires some trial and error, but if you test a few times, you'll be able to figure out roughly how long it takes to deposit an inch of water in the cup—and on the lawn.

⏰ TIME SAVER

Make the First Cut the Last

When the mowing is heavy, as in an overgrown field, you make the job harder if you have to fight previously cut grass. To save some sweat, plan your cuts so that you always discharge or lay down cut grass on top of cut grass—not on uncut areas where you are going to work next.

Yard and Garden

It Needs to Sink In

❑ During the hottest, driest days of summer, it sometimes seems that the water from the sprinkler evaporates as soon as it hits the lawn—and that doesn't help the grass much. To beat the heat, plan your watering for first thing in the morning or early in the evening, when the surface of the lawn isn't quite so hot.

Everything's Coming Up Mushrooms

❑ It can be disconcerting to wake up one morning in the middle of summer and find that you've accidentally started a mushroom farm in the backyard. Mushrooms flourish in areas that are wet and dark, so to get rid of them, you need to change your lawn-watering habits. Turn on the sprinkler less often or, if you've been watering in the evening, adjust your schedule and do it in the morning instead. This will give the roots plenty of time to absorb the moisture before darkness sets in again.

Make Weeds Feel Unwelcome

❑ Trying to keep weeds out of your lawn? Get back to basics. Mow the lawn consistently, water it deeply (thoroughly soaking the yard instead of providing just a brief sprinkling), and feed it frequently. If you do all these things, the grass will develop a strong and deep root system that will be impenetrable to outsiders such as crabgrass.

Curb That Crabgrass

❑ Sometimes it seems that crabgrass, like the proverbial cat, has at least nine lives. You may kill it, but as soon as you reseed the lawn in hot weather, the crabgrass reappears and overpowers the new seedlings. The solution is to attack

---

✔ PROBLEM PREVENTED

Mower Protection

When you're cutting back an overgrown field, it's not uncommon for even a heavy-duty mower to overheat, potentially warping the parts or otherwise leading to an early demise. You can reduce the chances of that happening if you inspect and clean the cooling fins around the engine regularly. Pay particular attention to the fins surrounding the spark plug (the cylinder head) and under the starter flywheel. Also check the crankcase oil and the air cleaner after every five hours of use; they'll both get dirty faster under heavy work conditions.

the crabgrass in two stages. First, apply corn gluten meal, an organic preemergent. Do this in the spring—when the soil is still cold and the crabgrass is weakest. (Crabgrass is an annual weed, so it starts from seed every year. The preemergent prevents the seed from germinating—and if the seed can't sprout, it can't grow.) For the next few months, bear with the bare spots where the crabgrass used to be. Finally, reseed your lawn in the fall. This will allow the new grass time to grow strong before the next summer's attack. Corn gluten meal is available by mail from Gardens Alive! at 5100 Schenley Place, Lawrenceburg, Indiana 47025.

Sometimes It Takes a Little Extra Effort

❏ Just when you think you've gotten all the crabgrass, it starts showing up again along the edges of driveways, sidewalks, and other paved areas. This isn't surprising. The tenacious weed loves sunny locations and soil temperatures above 50°F—just the conditions that exist in sections where hot sidewalks warm the adjacent soil. To be sure you're getting all the crabgrass, apply extra doses of corn gluten meal along these potential entry points when you treat the rest of the lawn. Be careful not to overdo it, or you'll burn the lawn.

To Everything, There Is an Order

❏ If you plan to use corn gluten meal, do your raking beforehand. Raking a preemergent-treated lawn breaks down the crabgrass barrier you just created.

Deadline for Dandelions

❏ Sometimes it seems impossible to clear the dandelions from your lawn without clearing the grass, too.

TIME SAVER

Moss: The Ultimate Seed Starter

Sometimes a lawn can look wonderfully lush and green from a distance, but when you get up close, it turns out that the entire yard is covered with moss. If you're anxious to replace moss with grass, relax. You don't need to rip out the moss. (If you did, it would just grow back anyway.) Instead, throw your grass seed right on top of it. Because moss holds moisture, it will help the seed germinate. Eventually, the grass will naturally displace the moss.

But Mom, I'm Not Just Being Lazy . . .

If your grass clippings aren't too heavy, leave them on the lawn once in a while instead of raking them up. They won't build up thatch; that's an old wives' tale. They *will* add nutrients to the soil.

Using corn gluten meal *will* get rid of dandelions as well as crabgrass, but if you apply it at the same time you reseed your lawn—as some folks suggest—it also will keep the grass from taking root. Follow this rule instead: Zap the dandelions when the forsythia blossoms are about to fall. (In the Northeast, that's the first or second week of May.) Then seed your lawn later in the season. That way, the grass will grow and the dandelions won't.

Watch Out for Brownouts

❏ If the lawn browns suddenly in the days following a mowing, you may have cut it too short. Closely cropped lawns lose a lot of moisture in summer heat, and a sudden, close shave may cause the lawn to go dormant. To rescue it, give it half an inch of water for each of the next couple of days—and raise the height of the mower blade next time you mow.

❏ If your lawn suddenly turns brown and you're sure you haven't overcut it, check the sharpness of your mower blades. A sudden browning can mean that the dull blades are tearing up the grass instead of cutting it.

FRUITS AND VEGETABLES

Strawberry Jars: Pipe It In

❏ The trouble with strawberry jars is that it's tough to get water down to the strawberries on the bottom without flooding the ones up top. You can avoid this by purchasing a length of polyvinyl chloride (PVC) piping from the hardware store when you buy your strawberry jar. Make sure the piping is as tall as the jar, with a diameter of 1½ to 2 inches and small holes along its entire

It's a sprinkler system that works from the inside out. Start with a length of PVC piping that has holes drilled in it (A). Insert the piping in the middle of the strawberry jar (B), then surround it with dirt and plants.

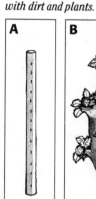
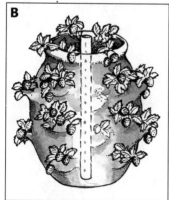

A   **B**

length. (You can buy the piping with holes already in it, or you can easily drill your own.) Stand this instant irrigator upright in the center of the jar, then fill in the dirt and plants around it. When the plants need a drink, just pour the water into the pipe to refresh the whole jar at once.

Where Does Your Garden Go?

❏ When you start a new vegetable garden, the first problem you face is deciding where to put it. Before settling on a location, watch your yard for a day or so to find a spot that gets good sunlight all day long. That's where your vegetable garden should go, because your plants will need sunlight more than anything else.

You Didn't Want to Mow There Anyway

❏ If you're having a hard time finding a location that you're sure will get sufficient sun for gardening, try a south or southwestern slope. The more perpendicular the soil is to the sun, the more exposure it will receive. (The ground also heats up more quickly in such a spot, reducing the danger of frost.)

ONE PERSON'S SOLUTION

A Gardener's Six-Pack

I'm forever sending potted seedlings home with friends, but they've always had trouble getting the plants home without leaving dirt all over the backseat. One day my husband had an  idea. He cropped the top off a grocery bag to make a kind of tray. It fits six plants nicely, and now they never fall over.

—MARTHA PAUL
Putnam, Connecticut

Fruits and Vegetables

*It's Always Darkest
Where You Want to Grow Something*

❏ If you're concerned that your garden won't receive enough sun, orient your rows east to west. That will allow you to take full advantage of the available sunlight. Locate tall plants, such as corn, beans, and tomatoes, to the north so they won't shade the shorter plants.

It's an Ill Wind . . .

❏ Strong or constant wind bruises and breaks stems, which diverts plant resources from growth to healing. It also carries disease-bearing spores and bacteria, erodes topsoil, and carries away moisture and warmth that your plants need to survive. To protect against potential wind damage, site your garden behind a wind barrier such as a hedge, trees, fence, or building.

❏ In the case of particularly vulnerable young vegetables such as tomatoes, protect individual plants from wind damage by encircling them with wire cages and wrapping the cages with clear plastic.

Help for Forgetful Gardeners

❏ Do you find that after you've planted your vegetable seeds but before they've germinated, you sometimes lose track of what's planted where? Here's an easy solution for one pair of crops: Plant carrots and radishes together by mixing the seeds at planting time. The radishes will come up almost immediately and will mark your carrot row so that you won't forget about it and plant over it. Carrots take a while to germinate, so the radishes will be ready to harvest well before the carrots will need the room.

PROBLEM PREVENTED

Don't Let Veggies Wither While You Wander

It's tough to leave for vacation knowing that while you're gone, your best vegetables will wither on the vine. To avoid this problem, invite nongardening neighbors to help themselves to the vegetables in your garden while you're away. They can repay you with a little bit of weeding and watering—or maybe a fresh carrot cake when you return!

Frost Protection from the Dairy Section

❏ Every year, it seems that as soon as the seedlings are out, one more frost strikes, killing all the tender young plants. To combat this perennial weather problem, make frost covers for your plants from plastic milk jugs. Cut out the bottoms but keep the caps on. When a frost is predicted, take these modified jugs out to the garden and set one over each seedling to provide overnight protection.

Bottoms off! Then place empty milk jugs over those precious seedlings for instant frost protection.

Get Tired!

❏ If cold weather is a particular concern in your area, you need to help the soil retain as much warmth as possible. One way to do this is to turn old automobile tires into raised beds for melons, cucumbers, and squash. Each raised bed provides a small, neat patch of warm soil, and the dark color tends to hold the heat, making the tires especially good for growing watermelons.

Raised Beds: An Easy Reach

❏ Raised beds are a great idea, but sometimes it's a strain—literally—to reach the plants in them. In that case, rethink the dimensions of the beds. Each can be as long as you like but no more than four feet wide. That way, you have to reach no more than two feet on either side to weed the bed.

The Birthplace of the Great Pumpkin

❏ If you want to grow huge pumpkins for Halloween, toss some seeds

---

✔ PROBLEM PREVENTED

Raised Beds: The Ties That Bind

If you decide to border your raised beds with railroad ties, don't use the kind that have been treated with creosote or other chemicals. The chemicals will seep into the soil and damage your vegetables. Use untreated ties, even though they won't last as long.

Fruits and Vegetables

onto the compost pile. The resulting crop will be absolutely enormous.

Don't Encourage Shallow Characters

❏ How can you keep drought and disease from destroying your garden? Build up your plants' roots before they're threatened by paying careful attention to watering. The temptation when watering any garden is to run the sprinkler just until the ground is damp. But plants that find water only on the surface will have shallow roots and be very susceptible to drought and disease. To encourage a strong, deep root system, give your plants real showers of 20 minutes or more. With a good start, they will be better able to withstand the heat later in the season.

Tomatoes: You Can Channel Their Energy

❏ Tired of tomatoes that don't quite develop before the first frost wipes them out? Try a little triage. When you're getting close to the end of the growing season—about six weeks before the predicted first frost—tour your garden and pinch off any new blooms on the tomato plants. The fruits that would otherwise form from them will never mature before the frost anyway, and this way they won't take energy away from tomatoes that are already starting to ripen.

Too Much of a Good Thing

❏ If your vegetable garden produces more bounty than your family and friends can possibly consume in the summer, save some of it. You can keep carrots and other root vegetables throughout the winter if you have a basement or root cellar that stays cool. All you need is a packing crate and some clean sand, which is available in 50-pound bags at large hardware stores. (Ask for play sand, which is a finer, cleaner grade.) Fill your crate with alternating layers of vegetables and sand—being sure to use enough sand so that the roots don't touch. The sand will keep mold at bay and also keep the vegetables from drying out before you need them for winter soups and salads.

Freezer Corn: Lend Me an Ear

❏ If you have an overabundance of corn, husk the extra ears and wrap each one individually in waxed paper, then store them in plastic freezer bags. They will keep well in the freezer until your next corn craving strikes. Be sure to let the ears defrost in the fridge before cooking, then boil them as usual.

Win Friends and Influence Neighbors

❏ If your harvest is too good, consider giving the excess to your local food pantry. These organizations always need donations during the summer, when many donors are vacationing.

❏ Another way to deal with an overproductive garden is to organize a vegetable swap. In addition to adding a change of pace to your vegetable platter, this is a great way to taste new varieties that your neighbors have discovered grow well in your area.

HERB GARDENS

Avoid Junior Mints

❏ Mint will take over your entire garden if you let it. To keep it from doing just that, plant it in the corner of your yard, well away from the garden patch. Don't worry about the shade; mint does well without much sunlight.

❏ Another way to keep mint from covering your entire yard is to pot

✔ PROBLEM PREVENTED

Do Your Mints Meet?

If you have more than one kind of mint (peppermint, spearmint, chocolate mint), they're likely to cross-pollinate and lose their flavor. To prevent this, plant them at opposite ends of the yard.

it first and then plant the pot wherever you want it to grow. Follow up by turning the pot once a month to keep runners from heading out into your garden. (This works with rosemary, too.)

Most Herbs Should Not Be Blonds

❏ If you notice a sudden yellowing in your herb garden, or if your herbs drop their leaves, you may be overwatering them. Most herbs are Mediterranean—which means that they like sunshine and don't like to sit in soupy soil. If you pinch off the dead leaves and give them a week or so to dry out, they will probably perk up.

Slow-Sow Cilantro

❏ The problem with herbs such as cilantro is that they mature and go to seed so quickly. But you can have cilantro all season long if you plant it by the half row. Cilantro matures in about four weeks, so here's what you should do: Plant half of the row, then wait two weeks before planting the other half. In two more weeks, the first half will be ready to harvest. Then you can clear it and plant some more. (This works for dill, too.)

FLOWER GARDENS

DOLLAR STRETCHER

I'll Trade My Violets for Your Verbena

If you're looking to add variety to your garden but don't want to invest a fortune in new plants, organize a seedling swap next spring. It's a great way to get rid of extra seedlings and to fill in your garden for free.

By Prearrangement Only

❏ Do you find it hard to visualize how a new garden arrangement will look? Before planting your flowers, always place them on top of the ground first and make sure you're pleased with the effect. Then go ahead and plant them in their new homes.

Don't Tear Us Apart

❏ If you need to divide an overgrown plant but aren't quite sure

Where Have All the Flowers Gone?

Fresh flowers are one of the greatest joys of summer—but not if they wilt as soon as you put them in the vase. Here are five ways to make your bouquets last longer.

1. Start early. Flowers cut first thing in the morning have a higher moisture content than those plucked in the afternoon, so they'll hold up longer.

2. Cut again. If you're working with flowers from the florist, give them a fresh cut on an angle before putting them into a vase of tap water. The stems will probably have dried out, and the fresh cut will help them take up the water in the vase.

3. Mix things up. Cut flowers will stay fresh longer if you spike the water in their vase with a little sugar and bleach. Try a solution of 2 drops bleach, 1 teaspoon sugar, and 1 quart water. Or give them a little lemon-flavored soft drink. A mixture of 1/4 cup soft drink and 1 quart warm water should do the trick. The sugar in the soda will help to replenish the flowers' lost glucose, the lemon will lower the pH, and the carbonation will inhibit the growth of bacteria.

4. Keep it cool. Heat and sunlight will quickly wilt cut flowers. To hold on to your bouquets longer, keep vases of flowers away from TV sets, CD players, computers, and windowsills.

5. Allow for change. Keep vases of flowers filled with water and change the water every two days. Give the flower stems a fresh cut every time you change the water. This helps them drink in the water they need to stay fresh.

how to go about it, try digging up the whole thing. Then use a strong, sharp knife to cut it into sections. This actually does less damage to the roots than ripping the plant apart.

Sunflowers Make Good Wallflowers

❑ Some people find the stalks and leaves of sunflowers unattractive. If you're one of those folks, you can camouflage the foliage by planting something else in front of it. A row of marigolds or a low fence will serve the purpose well.

Keep Cut Flowers Smelling Like Roses

Cut flowers should smell as good as they look. To prevent a nasty odor from developing in a vase of flowers, trim off all the leaves that would otherwise end up underwater, *then* place the flowers in the container. Leaves left underwater tend to rot quickly, and you won't like the resulting smell.

Strange Bedfellows

❏ Are your sunflower blossoms smaller than you expected? Take another look at their neighbors. Sunflowers planted near pole beans, tomatoes, and other crops that have large root systems tend to compete with the vegetables for nutrients in the soil. Similarly, sunflowers planted near potatoes and other root vegetables will battle for space—resulting in either small sunflowers or withered vegetables. Plant sunflowers outside the vegetable garden, or at least allow a few feet of space between them and the other plants.

GARDEN TOOLS

Take a Stab at Cleanliness

❏ Spades, hoes, and other garden implements are more effective and last longer if you keep them clean, but that can be a pretty dull task. Here's an easy way to keep garden tools in top condition: Fill a bucket with sand and add enough motor oil to make the sand wet but not soupy. (About 1 quart oil for each gallon of sand will do the trick.) Before you put away your tools, stab the sand with the blade of each one. This will clean off the dirt and clippings from the blade and simultaneously oil the tools to help keep rust at bay. If you keep the bucket in the garage near the spot where you store your tools, you won't forget to use it.

Too Bright to Get Lost

❏ If your garden tools are forever getting lost among the weeds, paint the ends of the handles with fluorescent paint (available at any crafts store). Once you've marked your trowel handle with a bright splash of orange, you'll never lose it in the weeds again.

TREES AND SHRUBS

Placement Tests

❏ Often you can often improve the appearance of a yard by planting a few trees and shrubs in strategic locations. But how do you decide exactly where to put them? One rule of thumb is to remember your lawn mower when planning the arrangement. A few young maples scattered haphazardly across a lawn can turn the ordinary mowing routine into a nightmare. Plant your trees in spots that your lawn mower can easily get around.

❏ When it comes to placing trees in your yard, it's also important to imagine what they'll look like in five or ten years. Are they far enough away from the house, from fencing, and from each other to allow them to grow well? Are they close enough to the house to provide shade? Are they directly under power lines? A few minutes of consideration now will save a bundle of worry and hours of pruning later.

Young Trees: Beat the Wrap

❏ If your new tree comes home wrapped in burlap, it may not be clear just how you're supposed to handle that wrapping. All you need to do is untie the burlap, loosen it from the root ball, and fold it back. Then plant the tree with the burlap intact; the fabric will eventually break down in the soil. When you fold back the burlap, make sure none of it will be visible once you've planted the tree. If the fabric shows aboveground, it will act like a sponge and suck the moisture away from the roots.

That Sinking Feeling

❏ If your newly transplanted tree sinks and lists in its bed as soon as you water it, you may have used the

PROBLEM PREVENTED

A Short Rule for Garden Tools

To avoid back strain, check the length of garden tools before you buy them. Choose hoes, rakes, and shovels that are at least as tall as your shoulder. Longer tools ease the stress on your back and provide better leverage for yard work.

BOARD FOR
ALIGNMENT

SOLID EARTH

When transplanting a young tree, dig a hole no deeper than the root ball but about twice as wide. Place the root ball in the hole, then check the depth by placing a board across the top of the hole. It should be flush with the surface of the root ball.

wrong technique when placing it in its new home. When planting a new tree, the temptation is to dig a very deep hole, then partially refill it with loose soil before putting in the tree. As soon as you water it, the loose soil will deflate, and the tree will move in its soft bed. To correct this, dig a *shallow* hole for your transplant in a new spot. The hole should be approximately twice as wide as the root ball. Set the tree in place, making sure the root ball sits on hard ground and the top is flush with the rest of your yard. (You can check this by laying a board across the top of the root ball. The board should rest evenly on the ground around the hole.) Then fill in the remaining area around the root ball with loose soil. This will give the young tree a firm foundation for growth.

New Trees Like Chinese Water Torture

❏ New trees and shrubs need almost constant watering for the first couple of seasons. So how do you see that they get it? Buy what's called a soaker hose from your garden center. This is a flat hose with little holes all along its length to provide a constant, slow-drip form of watering. Wind the hose around the base of the new tree or thread it through the branches of young shrubbery and leave it there all summer long. Turn the hose on for several hours every other day, just enough to generate a slow but steady drip.

Shrubbery: The Root of the Problem

❏ When you buy shrubbery from a garden center, you may find that it's become pot-bound. That means that its roots grow in a circular pattern as they follow the wall of the pot—the result of growing up in a container. The natural tendency of such plants is for the roots to continue to swirl in the ground after you plant the shrub, stunting the plant's growth. You can correct this problem before planting. Take a sharp knife and score several of the roots top to bottom. Rather than hurting the shrub, this will actually free the roots and allow them to grow outward.

 Uses for an Old Garden Hose

When your hose is ready to be retired from the garden, it may still have plenty of life left in it. You just need to refocus its energies. For instance:

1. Turn it into a soaker hose for your shrubs and seedlings. With an ice pick, poke holes about three inches apart along the length of the hose. Then wrap the greenery in the hose.

2. Make an extension nozzle. Attach the old hose to the faucet outside your home, then cut off the hose about 12 to 18 inches from the faucet. The extra length will form a kind of extended nozzle, making it much easier to fill buckets or take a drink.

3. Stake up trees. Cut the hose into 6- to 12-inch lengths. String wire through the hose, then tie the wired contraption around young trees to secure them to stakes. The hose will form an effective padding for the tree as it grows so that the wire won't scratch it. (Remember to adjust this contraption periodically as the tree increases in size.) In fact,

the tree-staking kits you can buy at garden centers are essentially wire, stakes, and a couple of lengths of old garden hose.

4. Store your saw. Cut a length of old hose that matches the length of your small saw, then slice the garden hose open lengthwise. Wrap it around the teeth of your saw before storing the saw. The hose will protect the blade

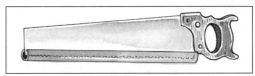

Guard that saw with garden hose.

and anything that might come in contact with it.

5. Make supportive coils to protect boxes stored in the basement. Cut the hose into two- to four-foot lengths and form coils by taping the ends together with electrical tape or duct tape. Put the coils on the damp floor of your garage or unfinished basement. Stack on top of them any cardboard boxes or other items that would otherwise rot from sitting on damp cement.

❏ If you don't like the idea of cutting the roots of your shrubs or you are planting a shrub that's particularly delicate, you can deal with pot-bound roots by untangling them and straightening them out manually. Pay special attention to the roots near the top of the root ball. If these continue to grow in circles, they can stunt the plant's growth.

It's Dying of Thirst

❏ If a tree drops an unusual number of leaves over several weeks' time in the middle of the summer, or if its leaves seem to fade in color, it probably needs more water. To solve this problem, get a soaker hose (a flat garden hose with small holes along its length) at any hardware store or garden center. Wrap the hose loosely around the base of the tree so that it forms a circle four to six feet in diameter. Turn the hose on low for several hours every day for three or four days. The key is to water the ground very slowly over a long period of time so that the moisture will seep deeply into the ground and not run off into the street.

❏ An alternative method for reviving a thirsty tree calls for an old five-gallon bucket that has a hole in it. Fill the bucket with water and place it a few feet from the base of the tree. Let it drain slowly, then move the bucket and refill it. Repeat the process two or three times. Water your ailing tree once a week in this manner until it perks up.

⏰ TIME SAVER

The Portable Trellis

Trellises against the porch or the side of the house are beautiful foundations for roses and climbing ornamentals, but they get in the way of building maintenance. To keep them from being obstacles, make them movable. Mount spacers, such as dowels or hollow tubes, to the back of each trellis so that it stands four to six inches from the wall. Then attach the trellis with long screws or hook-and-eye hardware so that it can be easily disengaged. That way, when it comes time to paint, you can simply unhook the trellis and lay it forward on the ground, plants and all.

Shear Mistakes

❏ Not sure what tool is best for what size pruning job? Small hand shears work best to prune branches that are less than ½ inch in diameter, but don't try to use them on anything larger. You will smash the bark and leave a gash open to disease and insects. (You're also likely to damage the shears.) Use larger lopping shears on branches less than 1½ inches in diameter. For anything larger, use a pruning saw, available from many garden centers.

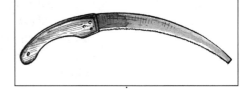

For branches more than 1½ inches in diameter, the prudent choice is a pruning saw.

Branch Surgery: Keep It Sterile

❏ If you are removing a branch that is diseased, you'll want to avoid spreading the infection to the rest of the branches or to other trees. That's easy. Just dip your cutting tool in alcohol or rub alcohol liberally on the blade after each cut. This will sterilize the tool, thus preventing the spread of disease.

Lilac Blues

❏ If your lilac bush has become leggy or overgrown, you can revive it by cutting it back. That means selecting one-third to one-half of the old stalks for pruning right after the spring flowers fade. Cut these stalks down to within three inches of the base. By next spring, the bush will have new, more vigorous stalks to replace the old ones. Over the coming years, you can cut out the rest of the old stalks a few at a time.

FENCES

A Clean Rust Stop

❏ It's no secret that iron and steel fences will rust to pieces if they are not protected with paint, but how do you get paint to stay put where it's already blistering and peeling off? The answer is good preparation. Wait for a clear day without a lot of fog or mist. Then chip, wire-brush, and sand away all paint and scale down to clean, bright metal. Use a rag dipped in mineral spirits to wipe the surface clean of all dust and oils. Then brush on two or more coats of rust-inhibiting primer, either alkyd or acrylic based. (Never use water-based primers on ferrous metals; the water in the paint will promote rust.) Once bare of protection, iron and steel will start to rust almost immediately, so prime as soon as the surface is clean and dry. When the primer has had at least a day to dry, finish up with an acrylic topcoat.

❏ If it's a foggy or misty day when you're ready to clean up your metal fence, hold off. Otherwise, once you have the metal clean, fog or mist will put a fine layer of rust on it before you get a chance to prime. And don't prime when the sun is beating down on your work; the heat will dry the primer prematurely.

Gates: Get a Grip

❏ Wooden gates in fences often get out of square as they age, making them hard to close and difficult to latch. You can true up a sagging gate by adding diagonal support. Try installing a steel turnbuckle and brace (available at hardware stores). Mount the brace to the gate frame with the top end on the hinged side and the bottom end in the corner on the opposite side. Then adjust the turnbuckle until the gate is square.

❏ Another way to bring a wooden fence gate back into square is to support it with a piece of light finish lumber that is one inch thick and anywhere from three to six inches wide. Scrap wood will do just fine. Shim or jack the gate into its proper position, then attach the wood brace with screws.

Shore up a sagging gate with a steel turnbuckle and brace (A), then tighten the turnbuckle (B). Or screw the gate back into position with a piece of scrap wood mounted diagonally (C).

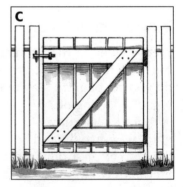

Everyday Living

I t takes a little extra creativity to solve some problems.

The owner of a company I had done some work for had a 30-foot-high TV antenna on his house. He decided he wanted it raised, hoping to get better reception. I agreed to help and met him on a day a crane was available to get me up to the top of the antenna. I went up in a basket and added a 10-foot section to the antenna, but it didn't have the effect he wanted—the next day he had no reception at all. I went back to take the piece off, but when I got there, I found the crane gone. I asked this fellow how he thought I could do the job without a crane, and he said he was sure I would think of something.

I couldn't resist a challenge like that, so when the owner left for the day, I went up on the roof to see where the antenna was attached. Beneath the point where it was bolted to the house was about two extra feet of pole. I sawed that piece off, then lowered the antenna two feet. Then I repeated the process. After making five cuts, I had removed the extra ten feet—and the owner never did figure out how I did it!

Half the fun of problem solving is figuring out a way not just to beat the problem but to beat it with a little ingenuity. That's why this section tells you how to use a slice of bread to salvage a pan of burned rice, why the government is the place to go for great deals on household goods, how you can use old film canisters to organize washers and nuts, one way a nail can become a quick and inexpensive lock for a sliding glass door, and how you can use a raft repair kit to fix a damaged convertible roof.

And that's just the beginning. These are everyday problems, but they're definitely not everyday solutions. In "Cooking," you'll learn how ice cubes can help you to get the perfect crust on home-baked bread and why you should use dental floss to slice cake layers. "Buying Wisely" tells how to save time as well as money when shopping for everything from groceries to clothing to prescription medicines, and it suggests several out-of-the-ordinary places to find bargains. In "The Home Workshop," you'll learn how you can double your shop storage space and strengthen sagging shelves. In "Household Repairs," you'll find fresh ideas for fixing everything from windows that won't open to radiators that won't heat. And if you're stumped by all those mysterious noises under the hood of your pickup, turn to "Cars and Other Vehicles," where you'll also find out which switch you should hit to keep your car from overheating in a summer traffic jam.

FRUITS AND VEGETABLES

Good Humor Bananas

❏ What to do on hot summer days when the kids (or the parents) are clamoring for ice cream and you're worried about all that fat? Try this healthful alternative. Peel some bananas and cut them in half. Insert a Popsicle stick in the end of each half (you can buy these sticks at most kitchen supply stores), wrap the bananas in waxed paper and aluminum foil, and then pop them in the freezer. In a couple of hours, you'll have tasty banana-sicles!

A Quick Fix for Dried Fruit

❏ Dried fruit can be delicious as well as nutritious—but not if it's *too* dry. To plump and soften dried fruit, rinse it in cold water, then place it in a bowl and pour boiling water over it. Let the fruit sit in the water for five to ten minutes, then drain.

Olives Are the Pits

❏ Pitting olives isn't difficult, if you know how to do it. Lay each olive on a cutting board and, with the heel of your hand, push straight down on it. The pit should slip out very easily.

Slip Sliding Away

❏ You can keep your cutting board from sliding all over your kitchen counter while you're chopping onions and peppers. Just dampen a kitchen towel and place it between the counter and the cutting board.

How Green Was My Tomato

❏ You picked your last tomatoes just before the frost, and now your counter is loaded with tomatoes that are still green. What to do? Ripen green tomatoes by placing them in a brown paper bag with an apple or a banana. Place the bag in a warm spot, and in a day or so the tomatoes will be ripe. Apples and bananas give off ethylene gas, a chemical that encourages ripening. Don't set tomatoes on a windowsill because bright, direct sunlight can damage them or cause them to ripen unevenly.

ONE PERSON'S SOLUTION

Can It!

When I have a recipe that calls for canned whole tomatoes to be cut into chunks, I cut the tomatoes while they're still in the can. I remove the lid, insert a knife, and slice right through the tomatoes. It's a lot easier than trying to do it while they're in the pan, it saves me from scraping up the bottoms of my pans, and, best of all, it saves dirtying another bowl.

—NANCY SEATON
Hastings, Nebraska

No Guacamole Tonight

❏ It's difficult to find a perfectly ripe avocado at the grocery store because avocados don't start to ripen until they've been picked from the tree. That means you have to find a way to ripen them yourself. When you get home from the store, put fresh avocados in a brown paper bag. Leave the bag in a warm spot for a few days, and the fruit should be ready to eat.

For Silky Smooth Cobs

❏ Tired of getting corn silk stuck in your teeth when you eat corn on the cob? After you husk the corn, brush straight down the cob with a paper towel. All the silk will come right off.

Spinach: The Nitty-Gritty

❏ No matter where you buy your spinach, you can expect it to be at least a little sandy. How do you get rid of the grit? Here's the best way: Wash your sink well, then fill it with cold water. Trim and discard the spinach stems, then submerge the leaves in the water. Swirl it around to loosen the sand, then pull the spinach out of the water. (Cleaning it the usual way—putting the spinach in a bowl and then pouring the water off— leaves the sand, which is heavier than the water, in the bowl on the spinach.) Rinse the spinach once or twice this way and you'll never serve sandy spinach again (unless you serve spinach at the beach).

Darn Clever, Those Chinese

❏ Tired of the same old same old? Water chestnuts (available canned in the Asian food section of most grocery stores) add real crunch and taste to almost anything, from chicken pot pie to sautéed vegetables to meat loaf. If you buy the sliced ones, all you need to do is drain them and dump the contents of the can into your dish—no cooking or other preparation is necessary.

Go Soak Your . . . Onion!

❏ If chopping onions brings tears to your eyes, try this trick: Slice off the stem and root ends of the onion and

Cooking

soak it in cold water for a couple of minutes before you chop it. This should greatly reduce the tearing.

DAIRY PRODUCTS

Spare the Air

❏ If you're looking for ways to make your liquid dairy products (milk, cream, half-and-half) last longer, repackage them in airtight containers. The cardboard cartons that those products come in let in air, especially once they've been opened. Repackaging the foods will keep them fresh longer.

TIME SAVER

Butter, Cubed

Recipes for pie and other pastry crusts often call for the butter to be cut into small pieces—generally a time-consuming and tedious process. Here's an easy and quick alternative. Start with a chilled stick of butter (put it in the freezer for about five minutes), unwrap it, and cut it in half lengthwise (do not separate the halves). Turn the whole thing over on its side and cut it in half lengthwise again, so that the stick is now divided into four long sticks (don't separate them yet). Finally, make about ten cuts in the butter crosswise. Separate the cubes. Since the butter for pie crusts has to be very cold, you may want to put the cubes back in the freezer for a few minutes before you use them.

Scorch No More

❏ Many baking recipes call for scalded milk, which isn't a problem, except that this sometimes leaves a layer of scorched milk in the bottom of the pan—and that's not easy to clean. Here's a solution. After you pour the milk into the pan and before turning on the heat, add 1 teaspoon sugar, but don't stir it. After you've scalded the milk and poured it out, the bottom of the pan should be scorch-free. Use this solution with sweet dishes only because the sugar will impart a slightly sweet taste.

Egg-stra Fresh

❏ If you like to keep eggs on hand but don't use them up very quickly, you'll need a way to keep them fresh longer. Try storing them in their original carton in your refrigerator rather than on the egg rack. Eggshells are porous, and the carton not only protects them from breaking but also keeps them from drying out and from absorbing odors.

MEAT, FISH, AND POULTRY

Marinade in the Shade

❏ You probably have at least one recipe that calls for a piece of meat, fish, or poultry to be marinated overnight, turning once. If the thought of getting up at 3:00 A.M. to flip a chicken breast doesn't appeal to you, try this solution. Place the marinade and the meat in a sealable plastic bag—one that's just slightly larger than the cut of meat or chicken—and squeeze out all the air. Put that on a plate and set it in the refrigerator. You won't have to flip the meat because the cut will be completely covered by the marinade.

Hold On There

❏ You bought the chicken breasts (or thighs or any other portion) with the skin on because they were so much less expensive than the skinless pieces. But now you have to remove the slippery, slimy skin. To get a better grip on it, grab it with a piece of paper towel.

RICE AND POTATOES

Increase the Flavor, Not the Fat

❏ Plain old white rice is bland, and if you add flavor in the conventional way—by adding butter—you add a lot of fat, too. Want a better way? Next time you prepare rice, liven up the taste by cooking it in broth instead of water. (The amounts stay the same, so if you would have used 1 cup water, substitute exactly 1 cup broth.) Or use some of the water left over from cooked potatoes.

Discourage Stick-to-itiveness

❏ Love rice but hate the cleanup? To simplify the after-dinner chores, spray the bottom of the pan with some

TIME SAVER

Devein Divinely

Deveining shrimp is time-consuming, and if you're trying to do it with a knife, it's easy to cut yourself. A better solution is to use a small pair of clean manicure scissors, which you can find at any drugstore.

nonstick cooking spray before you add the rice and water. That should keep the rice from sticking to the pan.

Too-Sweet Potatoes

❏ If you notice your potatoes have developed an unpleasant sweet taste, you have probably stored them at a temperature lower than 40°F. At lower temperatures, the potatoes will start to convert their starch into sugar. You can reverse that process by moving the potatoes to a warmer (room temperature) spot for a few days.

OTHER FOODS

Just Like Mom . . . But with Less Nagging

❏ There's nothing like a hot, hearty breakfast on a cold winter morning. But who wants to get up at 6:00 A.M. to make it? Here's a deliciously cozy solution. First, if you don't already have one, buy a slow cooker. The largest models cost less than $35, which is a small investment to make for all the use you'll get from it. In the evening, before you go to bed, put all the oatmeal ingredients—old-fashioned (don't use instant or quick-cooking) oats, water, and a pinch of salt—into the pot and put the lid on. Set the cooker on low and let it run all night. Next morning, breakfast will be ready. (You may have to add a little milk to moisten it.)

Cracker Crumb Crush

❏ No true Yankee would buy store-bought cracker crumbs when he could save money by crushing his own, but getting the crackers to a fine, even consistency can be challenging. Try this trick: Place the crackers in a sealable plastic bag and squeeze out the air. Crush the crackers by rolling over the bag with a rolling pin. This trick is most commonly used with saltines, but it also works for graham crackers and even cornflakes.

Hello, Mr. Chips

❏ Don't throw away those stale potato chips—revive them! Place them in a single layer on a baking sheet and set them under the broiler for about five minutes. Keep an eye on them to prevent burning.

BAKING TRICKS

Better Than 4 and 20 Blackbirds

❑ How can you can make your pie crusts special? Try cutting the pastry dough with pinking shears. It adds an especially nice touch to lattice-topped pies.

Flour Freezer

❑ You wanted to save money by purchasing the largest available bag of flour for your holiday baking, but now it's New Year's, and you have more left than you ex-

---

ONE PERSON'S SOLUTION

Sssteam Heat

When I first started making bread, I had trouble getting good, crusty loaves. Then a friend told me that if you toss about a quarter cup of water in the oven right after you put in a loaf of bread, the outside of the loaf will be nice and crusty, like French

bread. It works, but instead of throwing in water, I use three or four ice cubes. I just put them on the bottom of the oven, right after I put in the bread, and close the door. It's a little less intimidating than throwing water in the oven (which makes a huge burst of steam), and it works just as well.

—SUSAN CHOP
Mount Vernon, New York

---

pected. Not to worry. Simply transfer the leftover flour to one or more airtight containers and store it in the freezer. Be sure to let the flour return to room temperature before you use it.

It's a Piece of Cake

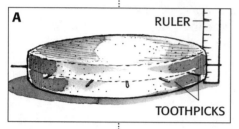

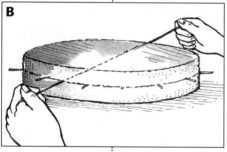

Cutting layers is a piece of cake if you do it by measuring up from the counter, marking the midpoint with toothpicks (A), and slicing the layer with dental floss (B).

❑ Some cake recipes call for you to cut the cake layers in half so that you have two rounds of equal thickness. Anyone who has ever tried doing this knows how dicey it can be. Here's a solution. Insert toothpicks horizontally into the side of the cake at an equal distance from the counter. Measure up from the surface of the counter because that's (fairly) level; the top of the cake probably isn't. When you've gone all around the cake, use the toothpicks as guides while you slice through the layers with a piece of clean, unused fishing line or dental floss.

Pack It Frost(ing)-Free

❑ Wondering how to get your cake to the potluck in one neat piece? Don't frost it until you get there. Pack the layers separately, wrapped in waxed paper or foil, and take the frosting along with you in a separate container. Be sure to bring along any utensils you'll need, and put the whole thing together at your destination.

Better Late Than Never

❑ If you're not reading this until *after* you frosted the cake that you need to transport, set the cake in a box and insert several toothpicks in the top. Cover the cake loosely with plastic wrap or aluminum foil (or put the cover on the box). The toothpicks will keep the wrap or foil from touching the frosting. Take a little extra frosting with you to repair the holes. And don't forget to remove the toothpicks after transport!

EMERGENCY RESCUES

This Is a Stickup!

❏ Many soups and stews need to be stirred frequently to keep them from sticking to the bottom of the pot. If you forget to stir and later find that the soup or stew is obviously sticking, turn off the heat and let the soup sit for a couple of minutes. Don't stir it, or you'll stir up the burned bits on the bottom of the pan. Pour the soup into a new pot. If there's a thick layer of soup on the bottom of the pan and you think you can scrape up the good stuff without hitting the bottom, go ahead, but be careful. Reheat the soup in the new pot—and keep an eye on it this time!

Rice and Easy

❏ If you accidentally burn a pan of rice, just lift the lid and add a slice of bread to the pot while the rice is still in it. Rye bread seems to do the best job of soaking up the burned odor and flavor, but if you don't have rye, use the heel of any other loaf. Leave it for about ten minutes, then remove the bread before serving the rice.

Salt Soup

❏ You may be able to remove some of the excess salt in an overly salty soup or stew by slicing a potato into quarter-inch slices and putting the slices in the pot. Let the mixture cook, covered, until the potato is soft. Then remove the potato from the pot.

> ✔ **PROBLEM PREVENTED**
>
> # Help for the Absentminded Cook
>
> How can you make absolutely sure your double boiler doesn't boil dry if you're distracted for a few minutes? Invest in a few small ball bearings, which you can find at a hardware store. Next time you use your double boiler, place three or four ball bearings in the bottom pot. If the pot boils dry, the bearings will rattle, alerting you to add more water.

MEAL STRETCHERS

Loaves and Dishes

❏ If you're looking for ways to make meat loaf go a little further or even to make it more interesting, try adding some canned, drained chickpeas or boiled potatoes. Mash the chickpeas or potatoes or blend them in a food processor, then add them to the meat mixture. Form it into a loaf, then bake as usual. As a general guideline, you can add about 1 cup mashed chickpeas or potatoes for each pound of meat.

❏ Alternatively, add about 1 cup cooked white or brown rice or uncooked, quick-cooking oatmeal to the mix, then bake as usual.

❏ To add texture and color (in addition to bulk) to your meat loaf, add a handful of whole cooked peas or sliced, raw red bell or hot pepper to the mixture before cooking.

Spuds and Fishes

❏ Eight hungry people are coming for dinner, and at the last minute you discover that you have only four potatoes in the house. Here's how to make four baked potatoes feed eight people. Cut each cooked potato in half lengthwise and scoop out the flesh, being careful not to damage the skin. Place the flesh of the four potatoes in a bowl and whip it with ¼ cup milk or cream and 1 tablespoon butter or margarine. If you like, add about ¼ cup cooked corn or 2 tablespoons bacon bits or Parmesan cheese. Scoop the whipped potatoes back into the skins and heat the stuffed potatoes in the oven until they're warm.

A Triumph of Style Over Substance

❏ If you're preparing a roast beef and you're afraid it won't be enough for the crowd, julienne the meat into strips and fan them out on a plate rather than cutting big slabs for each person. That way, everyone can have some meat, but you can keep the emphasis on the other parts of the meal.

DOLLAR STRETCHER

Focus on Flavor

When you're running low on cash, save money by making meat or chicken just one element—rather than the main attraction—of your meals. Meat or chicken will go further if used as one ingredient in casseroles, stir-fries, soups, and stews.

A Piece of the Pie

❑ Serving dessert to six can be tricky if you have pie for only four. You can make a pie go further if you don't slice it. Instead, try scooping it—crust and all—out of the pan and into bowls. Top it with whipped cream, ice cream, or frozen yogurt.

LEFTOVERS

Sì, Sì, *What You Can Do!*

❑ Stuck with leftovers but tired of chicken salad and cold roast beef sandwiches? With some flour tortillas (available in the refrigerator section of most grocery stores), an onion, a little lemon juice, and some cumin (available in the spice section of any grocery store), you can delight your family with homemade fajitas. To make the filling, cut the beef or chicken into strips. In a frying pan, heat a little vegetable oil, then add some chopped onion. Cook the onion until it is the consistency you like. Add the chicken or beef, a squeeze of lemon juice, and a sprinkling of cumin. Cook until the chicken or beef is heated through. Remove the filling from the pan and keep it warm in the oven. Wipe the pan clean, then heat the tortillas, one at a time, in the pan (they won't stick) until they're very warm. Set them out on the table with the filling, shredded lettuce, and diced tomatoes, and you have a Mexican treat.

Orient Express

❑ Another way to spice up leftover chicken or beef is to sprinkle it with a little soy sauce or hoisin sauce (available in the Asian food section of most grocery stores). Wrap the filling in some warmed tortillas, and you have mu shu chicken, an Asian-style dish. To warm the tortillas, simply place them in a heated frying pan (they won't stick).

TIME SAVER
Take It Off!

If you have more than three or four garlic cloves to peel at once, you can save yourself some aggravation and time by dropping them into a pot of boiling water for about five seconds. Fish out the cloves and put them in a bowl of ice water for about five seconds. You should be able to slip the skins off easily.

❏ If you can't find hoisin sauce at your grocery store, mix together one part soy sauce and one part honey, then adjust to your taste.

A Turkey in Every Pot

❏ Running out of ideas for using up that leftover holiday turkey? Prepare a quick turkey soup or stew. Sauté some chopped onion in a pan until it's translucent, then set aside. Pour canned chicken broth into a pot, then add canned or frozen corn, the sautéed onion, and the leftover turkey, cut into chunks. Heat thoroughly. Just before you are ready to serve the soup, season it with black pepper, poultry seasoning, and perhaps a pinch of cayenne pepper. If you like, add some cooked rice or cooked, cubed potatoes. This works equally well with leftover chicken.

Well Bread

❏ If you have a loaf of bread that you'd like to keep from getting stale, put it in a plastic bag with a stalk of celery.

Grate Idea

❏ If you have a partial loaf of unsliced bread left over, don't toss it out. Instead, put it in a paper bag for a few days until it's good and stale (if you put it in a plastic bag, it'll get moldy). Grate the bread with a box grater, then use the crumbs to bread meat or fish or to thicken soups. It's best to season the crumbs just before you use them.

Cakewalk

❏ There's no need to throw out a cake just because it's gone stale. Remove any icing, then cut the cake into one-inch cubes. Place the cubes in a bowl and top them with thawed frozen strawberries (or any other fruit) and their juice. Aim for enough fruit to cover the top of the cake well. Let sit for an hour or so in the refrigerator so that the cake will absorb the juice. Top with sorbet, ice cream, or whipped cream before serving.

Try a Cake Mix

❏ Alternatively, you can whip up a batch of instant pudding, gently stir the pudding and cubed cake together, and then top with whipped cream. One small package (3¼ ounces) of pudding mix to one 9- by 12-inch cake will give you about the right proportions.

It's a Yoke, Get It?

❏ What do you do with the leftover egg yolks after you've made meringue? Simply place them in a bowl with enough water to cover and put the bowl in the refrigerator. The yolks will keep for two or three days that way. When you're ready to use the yolks (to make hollandaise sauce, for instance), just drain off the water.

White an Idea

❏ It's a waste of money to throw out perfectly good egg whites when you have a recipe that calls for the yolk only. Freeze the whites in an ice cube tray—one white per cube—then transfer them to sealable plastic bags. Add them (thawed) to omelets or add a couple of drops of water and use them as a glaze for baked goods.

EATING DILEMMAS

Fire!

❏ Your sinuses suddenly clear, and beads of perspiration form on your upper lip and forehead. Looking for a way to douse the fire of that spicy food you just ate? Reach for a dairy

Separation Anxiety

You've just separated a few eggs, and now you have some leftover yolks or whites. What exactly are you supposed to do with them? Here are some ideas.

Egg Whites

• Use three or four to make a delicious, cholesterol-free omelet. Just add a drop of milk, stir them up, and sauté as usual.

• Add ¼ teaspoon water to 1 egg white, stir well, and brush the mixture on a loaf of bread or pastry crust before you bake it to give it a shiny glaze.

• Drop the uncooked egg white into a clear broth—such as chicken soup—as it cooks. The white will add nutrition and texture.

• Make a lemon meringue pie or meringue cookies.

Egg Yolks

• Make some hollandaise sauce to top your broccoli.

• Add a yolk to the cheese mixture the next time you make lasagna. The yolk will add richness and flavor.

• Whip up a quick batch of egg custard.

product—yogurt, sour cream, or milk—which will neutralize the heat. Avoid water, which will only exacerbate the pain.

Don't Bite Off More Than You Can Chew

❏ If you're just starting out with new dentures, don't set yourself up with steak and corn on the cob at your next meal. You'll need to get used to all that new stuff in your mouth. What's appropriate food for a new denture wearer? Try soft foods such as mashed potatoes, pasta, or an omelet. After you learn to distinguish the food in your mouth from the artificial teeth, you'll feel more comfortable moving on to the harder stuff.

FEEDING A SICK PERSON

Hard to Swallow

❏ Trying to feed someone who's ill and has no appetite can provoke feelings ranging from frustration (if it's a child with the flu) to frightening (if it's someone seriously ill who needs to eat). One strategy is to offer the invalid small, frequent meals—a cup of soup, half a small sandwich, a fruit shake—throughout the day

ONE PERSON'S SOLUTION

Cold Day, Warm Oven

My kitchen is kind of chilly, so when I want to make bread on a cold day, it's hard to find a really warm spot where I can let the bread rise. In cool weather, I turn the oven to the lowest setting for about five minutes, turn it off, then let the bread rise in there.

—LORI BAIRD
Astoria, New York

rather than one or two large meals. Sometimes an invalid can comfortably finish something small when a large meal seems overwhelming and unappetizing.

Nutrition Booster

❏ If you're concerned that someone isn't getting enough nutrition because of a decreased appetite, try increasing the nutritional value of the food she does eat. You can double the protein in milk—whole, skim, or low fat—by adding 1 cup nonfat powdered milk to each quart of fluid milk. Pour the milk into a bowl, then slowly beat in the powdered milk. Store the milk in the refrigerator in an airtight container for a couple of hours before using it.

❏ You can increase the nutritional value of many other foods as well by adding nonfat powdered milk. Stir in 1 to 2 tablespoons powdered milk per cup of puddings, custards, mashed potatoes, or cream soups as you're preparing them.

Soft Serve

❏ When someone has a sore throat or a tender or sore mouth, he may not feel like eating. Try tempting him with soft but nutritious foods such as milk shakes, bananas, applesauce, watermelon, cottage cheese, custards, mashed potatoes, or scrambled eggs.

A Change of Taste

❏ Patients undergoing chemotherapy often find that foods, especially high-protein foods such as red meat, have an unpleasant metallic taste. One way to make meat more palatable is to marinate it in Italian dressing (enough to cover) for two to six hours before cooking.

❏ Alternatively, cut out the red meat altogether and get protein from chicken, turkey, and fish. Marinating will add flavor to those foods, too.

❏ Nausea is a common side effect of chemotherapy, and it's enough to turn the patient off from food. One

Feeding a Sick Person

way to combat nausea is to refrain from drinking liquids with meals. Beverages can cause a full, bloated feeling.

GIFTS OF FOOD

Too Pretty to Eat

❏ You've prepared a delicious chocolate sauce for the folks on your Christmas list, but now you're wondering how to get it from here to there. Inexpensive Mason jars (available at grocery stores) are terrific for all sorts of food gifts, from granola to soup. If you can't find single jars at your grocery store, check a kitchen supply store for small, decorative food jars.

❏ To make the jars fancier, purchase some stick-on labels from an office supply store, decorate them, and apply them to the jars. Enclose a gift card that lists the ingredients and reheating instructions, if relevant.

❏ For an extra-special touch, cut a piece of fabric or decorative paper in a circle or square about an inch larger than the jar top. Remove the screw-on band from the jar and center the fabric or paper on the lid. Replace the band, and you'll have a lovely decorative effect.

Packaging Is Everything

❏ Looking for a way to make your food gifts special? Line a basket with a pretty napkin, a fancy kitchen towel, or some wrapping paper. If the basket has a handle, wrap some yarn or ribbon around it. Then arrange your jars or wrapped baked goods in the basket. Include a tag that notes the ingredients and any reheating instructions.

BUYING WISELY
Shopping More and Spending Less

GROCERIES

They'll Catch Your Eye—And Your Wallet

❏ Looking for a way to save money at the grocery store? One good rule of thumb is to avoid buying items on shelves at eye level. Sure, they're easier to get to—and that's why grocers put them there! Better buys are usually found on the highest and lowest shelves.

❏ When you're trying to cut food costs, avoid those special displays at the ends of supermarket aisles. Many times, grocers doctor up those areas to make the items look as though they're on sale. The cans may be stacked in an elaborate pyramid, or cookie boxes may be arranged to form a beautiful arch, but that doesn't mean the stuff is on sale. Be sure to check the prices and signs, and if you're not sure whether the item is on sale, ask the store manager.

It's All the Same

❏ You've noticed that store brands are generally cheaper than the heavily advertised name brands, but you're still not sure whether to use them. Don't knock them until you've tried them. Many store brands are manufactured by the same folks who make your favorite name-brand product. The difference is not in the quality of the product but, especially with canned goods, in the uniformity. Maybe all the green beans aren't the same length, or perhaps the corn kernels are smaller than the name brand's. Check them out before you dismiss them; nine times out of ten, you'll be satisfied with the quality, *and* they'll save you money.

Be a Unit-arian

❏ When you're looking to get the best deals at supermarkets, you can't always assume that the best price is on the large economy-size package. So how do you know what's truly cheapest? When you compare prices, especially on nonfood items, always make sure to compare the unit prices (that's the price per pound, ounce, or other unit). Normally, the unit price is listed on the same shelf tag that lists the product price.

 DOLLAR STRETCHER

Cooperation

One of the best ways to trim the fat from your grocery bill is to join a food cooperative. Food co-ops are grocery stores run by their members. They generally offer better prices than their commercial counterparts, and unlike those larger stores, many co-ops sell certain foods—cereals, spices, flour, and grains—in bulk. That makes it easier to buy only as much as you need.

Co-ops are run on a membership basis. Some allow only members to shop there; others allow anyone to shop but offer discounts (around 10 percent) to members. Becoming a member isn't hard; most co-ops welcome newcomers.

To join a co-op, you need to pay a small fee, usually based on the number of people in your family. Some co-ops also require a refundable deposit. The amount varies from co-op to co-op, but it is usually no more than $100. You can generally spread out payments for both these fees over a year or more. Often members are required to work in the co-op—usually for no more than three hours a month. Jobs can range from stocking shelves to prepping produce to making signs (if you're artistically inclined). The best way to find out if your town has a co-op is to check the Yellow Pages under Health & Diet Food Products—Retail.

Get Tough!

❏ Save money on your food bill by opting for less tender cuts of meat—flank steak, for instance—and marinating it overnight before you cook it. The easiest
marinade you can use is a bottle of store-bought oil and
vinegar dressing. Place the meat in a sealable plastic
bag, pour in the dressing, squeeze out all the air, and
place the bag on a plate. Put it in the refrigerator for up
to 24 hours. The acid in the vinegar will break down the
tough connective tissue in the meat, tenderizing it.

Your Kids Will Never Know the Difference

❏ You can decrease your spending and increase the
iron in your diet by substituting chicken livers for more
expensive beef and calf liver. Chicken livers can cost
as little as one-fifth the price of beef and calf liver.

Fly through That Grocery Store

❏ Sometimes it can feel as if you spend half your life in
the grocery store. One way to reduce the amount of
time you spend food shopping is to pick one store you
like and always do your shopping there. Once you're
familiar with the layout of the store, you'll be able to
find what you need quickly. Knowing where to go also
decreases the chances of making impulse purchases,
the bane of the bargain hunter.

Play Supermarket Sweeps

❏ Once you've chosen a store, organize your shopping
list in the same way the store is organized. For instance,
if you walk into your store at aisle one and that aisle
has produce, put all your produce first on your list. If
aisle two has cereals and bread, put those products
next on your list, and so on. That way, you can whiz
through the store, going right to the aisles you need
and skipping the ones you don't.

❏ You can save even more time by keeping track of the
items you buy most often and writing or typing them
neatly on a list (again, in the same order you find them

at the grocery store). Leave extra space for adding items not on your standard list. Make copies at a copy shop. Rather than writing down each item each time you shop, you can simply circle it on your list. And if there's an item you need that's not on your list, you can enter it in the extra space.

Eat First, Shop Later

❏ If you have a hard time sticking to your shopping list, try eating just before you head to the grocery store. Shopping on an empty stomach makes everything look good. Your willpower is likely to be a lot stronger if you plan your shopping trip for after a meal.

 DOLLAR STRETCHER

Oh, Baby!

When it comes to kids, you can scrimp on haircuts, clothing, and toys. But one area where you shouldn't cheap out is with your child's safety, especially with car seats. Unfortunately, car seats can be expensive—as much as $100— and kids grow out of them. But here's a solution: In many communities, health care organizations rent car seats, sometimes for as little as a dollar a month. The best way to start looking for a rented car seat is by asking your family doctor or the staff in the administrative office of a local hospital.

Coupons: Double or Nothing

❏ Wondering whether coupons really save you money? It all depends. In many cases, the store or generic brand costs less than the name brand, even when you use a coupon for the name-brand item. But if the store brand just doesn't compare to the name brand, use your coupons. (You'll find them in your Sunday paper, sales flyers, and even at the grocery store.)

❏ To get the biggest savings with coupons, use them only where and when you can double or even triple them.

I Just Love Your Soap Flakes

❏ Having a hard time finding discount coupons for your favorite products? Check the package label. You'll probably find a toll-free number. Call the number and tell the service representative how much you love the product. Many times, after that person asks you a question or two about yourself (usually including your name and address, because the company likes to know who's buying its products), he'll ask if you'd like to receive some coupons.

MEDICINES

Rx for Savings

❏ When it comes to health, no one wants to take chances—but no one wants to waste money either. How do you find the right balance between savings and safety? When your doctor pulls out her prescription pad, ask if a generic drug will meet your needs. Many times, the generic will cost significantly less than the name brand, and the ingredients are exactly the same.

Mail-Order Medicines

❏ You don't need anyone to tell you that prescription medicines are expensive, especially if you're on a fixed income. One way to save money—sometimes more than 50 percent on name-brand (nongeneric) drugs—is to purchase them through the mail. Several services offer prescriptions by mail, including the American Association of Retired Persons (AARP). Here's how it works. You call the service and give the representative your prescription information, or you mail in the prescription form. The mail-order company's staff pharmacist contacts your doctor to confirm the information. The company then mails out your prescription and bill. To find the phone number for the AARP (you don't need to be an AARP member to use the service), dial 1-800-555-1212. Or ask your doctor about other such programs. This is a good idea if you use only one or two prescription medicines and if you're able to order them in advance. If you take a lot of medications, or if you like to get your refills at the last minute, you're better off sticking with your local pharmacist. In addition to serving you on the spot, he can keep track of all the prescriptions he fills for you and can alert you to any potential negative interactions among drugs.

CLOTHING

In the Swim

❏ In some parts of the country, you can spend more than $100 on a woman's bathing suit. That's criminal, since you're paying for little more than a yard of fabric. If you can't afford such prices, buy your new suit in the summer. By the time July rolls around, stores are looking to unload their bathing suits (and the rest of their summer stock) to make room for the fall clothing. Shopping for summer clothing when other folks are at the beach can save you 50 percent or more.

❏ Likewise, wait to shop for your winter gear—boots, coats, and sweaters—until the dead of winter. If you can make do with what's already in your closet until then, you'll find some hefty bargains.

Good Things Come in Small Sizes

❏ Tired of the meager choices and high prices for petite clothing at your local specialty or department store? Try stepping next door to the children's department. Often a size large boy's T-shirt or girl's jacket will fit just fine—and the price is likely to be a much better fit for your budget.

Mom! Gimme My Sweater!

❏ Even if you're not petite, you can take advantage of the price difference between women's and men's/boys' clothing. Search the men's and boys' department at your favorite store for great deals on basics such as T-shirts, polo and rugby shirts, and sweaters. And ladies, boxer shorts and a T-shirt make great pajamas for women.

Can I Interest You in a Howitzer?

❏ Are you in the market for inexpensive—but durable—clothing items such as sweaters, coats, and pants? How about a duffel or tote bag? A dead hand grenade? The answer may be just around the corner, at your local army/navy (aka army surplus) store.

Army/navy stores get their merchandise from big suppliers that buy surplus clothing (field jackets, woolen pea coats, and heavy woolen trousers) and equipment (canteens, knapsacks, and other camping stuff) directly from the government—and pass the savings on to you. To find an army/navy store, check the Yellow Pages under Army & Navy Goods.

 DOLLAR STRETCHER

Shop the Salvation Army

When you're looking to save money, the local Salvation Army thrift shop is a good place to start. You'll find used sporting goods (tennis rackets, golf clubs, and bowling balls); pots, pans, and dishes; furniture; even clothing. But "Sal's Place" is like the big retail outlets in one respect: Getting the best deals requires using the best strategies. For example:

• **Be a frequent visitor.** Because there is so much turnover in merchandise, you need to visit your local Salvation Army thrift shop regularly, even once a week, if you're in the market for a specific item.

• **Keep an eye out.** Just like regular stores, Salvation Army thrift shops run sales. Some have weekly specials, and nearly all hold holiday sales. Check your local newspaper to find out when the sales are, or call up the shop.

• **Be prepared.** If you can see that something is worth grabbing

(especially if it's furniture), so can everyone else. If you see a kitchen hutch you just have to have, buy it now; it probably won't be there tomorrow.

• **Buy off-season.** If you always wanted a seersucker jacket, shop for it in winter, when no one else is looking for one. And look for your winter coat during the dog days of summer.

• **Visit the wealthy neighbors.** Do you live near an upscale neighborhood? Head to that zip code's Salvation Army. Whose junk would you rather pick through, a rich person's or a not-so-rich person's?

Finally, a few caveats: The Salvation Army doesn't deliver—you need to take your purchases with you. All sales are final. Don't try to haggle. If possible, steer clear of upholstered furniture, as musty odors are nearly impossible to remove. Always dry-clean or wash clothing before you store it in your closets or drawers.

Clothing

Hey, Lady! That's My Coat!

❏ If you're looking to save some money on clothing, one place you may not have thought of checking is your dry cleaner. You know the line on your receipt that reads, "Not responsible for items left over 60 days"? Well, did you ever wonder what happens to that stuff on day 61? Many dry cleaners donate the clothing to charity, but some sell off, very inexpensively, the stuff people leave behind: winter coats, sweaters, dresses, trousers—and it's all clean! The easiest way to find out whether your dry cleaner sells abandoned clothing is to call and ask. You'll find dry cleaners listed in the Yellow Pages under Cleaners.

SPORTS AND HOBBY EQUIPMENT

Last Year's Model

❏ One way to save money on all sorts of products, but especially sporting goods (in-line skates, skis, hiking boots) and electronics (including computers and stereos) is to buy last year's models. Nine times out of ten, when a manufacturer introduces a brand-new style (usually in fall and spring for sporting goods, September and October for electronics), stores discount the old models to clear out their stock. If you can manage without the latest bells and whistles, you'll probably save money.

The Sporting Life

❏ Overwhelmed by the high price of sporting goods? A terrific place to buy recreational gear such as tents, kayaks, and skis is any store that sells *and rents* those items. Once a year, most of those stores inventory their rental stock to assess the equipment's condition. They sell off pieces that aren't rentable but are still in good condition for discounts of 20 to 30 percent or more. Stores don't always announce these sales, so if you're in the market, call the store periodically. You can find sporting goods stores listed under Sporting Goods—Retail in the Yellow Pages.

For That Budding Olympian

❏ Skiing is one of the most expensive hobbies going. And if you're a beginner, the cost of skis just might keep you off the slopes. One place to check for good deals on used equipment is your local ski resort, which may occasionally sell off its rental equipment. The equipment probably won't satisfy your 17-year-old downhill wizard, but it's certainly good enough for any beginner who doesn't want to spend a lot of money on new equipment. Keep in mind that these sales are usually final, so take a good look at the equipment before you put down your money.

Snow Deals

❏ If you're looking for a relatively inexpensive way to outfit a youngster (or anyone else) who's interested in trying a new winter sport, watch your local news-

---

Who Says Crime Doesn't Pay?

Crime is definitely one option to explore when you want to save money. Someone else's crime, that is. The government holds frequent auctions—free and open to the public—to get rid of property seized from drug lords, embezzlers, or people who have committed tax fraud. Items for sale aren't limited to bullet-proof Jaguars and diamond tiaras. (But if that's what you're looking for, a government auction is the place to go.) You also might find items such as artwork, carpeting, and clothing.

At government auctions, plan to pay for items on the day of purchase. The government doesn't deliver, so you need to be able to take your items with you.

There are a couple of ways to find out where and when government auctions take place. The first is to subscribe to the public auction newsletter, which costs between $25 (for a regional guide) and $50 (for the national guide). To subscribe, write to EG&G Dynatrend, Attention: Pal, 3702 Pender Drive, Suite 400, Fairfax, VA 22030. The second way to find out about auctions is to look at the Department of the Treasury site on the Internet. (Many libraries offer free Internet access and assistance.)

---

papers and the bulletin board at the grocery store for ads for community ski and skate sales. Generally run as fund-raisers by local organizations, these sales offer winter sports equipment that other children have outgrown. You can often get great deals here, and sometimes even some expert advice on choosing the appropriate equipment. If you're outfitting a child at a ski and skate sale, be sure to bring the youngster with you, since all sales are final. And remember that what you spend at these sales may not be the last money you'll have to cough up before Suzy hits the ski slopes. (You could end up paying more for new bindings, for example, than for the skis you buy at the sale.)

Tryouts

❏ Are you tired of signing up for an expensive hobby, investing in a lot of expensive equipment, and then finding it all consigned to the attic six months later? Next time you're considering skiing, tennis, sailing, or violin lessons, explore the option of renting equipment rather than buying. That'll give you the chance to try it out without investing a lot of money. If you decide a particular hobby isn't for you, you've lost nothing. But if you decide to invest in your own equipment, you'll be a more educated consumer.

BOOKS AND MAGAZINES

You Can Have Your Book and Read It, Too

❏ New hardcover books can cost $25 to $35 (or more) at a bookstore, and although most libraries do ac-

DOLLAR STRETCHER

Travel Insurance for Your PC

You've just poured a good chunk of your annual income into a new computer, and you want to make sure your insurance policy covers such an expensive item. Unfortunately, the standard homeowner's insurance policy offers very limited coverage for computers. It may not protect against certain accidents, such as a drink spilled on the keyboard; it may not cover lost or stolen software; and it may not protect computers away from home. The solution is a rider on your homeowner's (or renter's) policy designed to cover computers. These inexpensive additions are especially valuable for owners of laptop computers, which are frequently used away from home and are particularly vulnerable to theft. Talk with your insurance agent about the possibilities.

Tooling Around

I quit my construction job, sold my tools, and threw myself into touring with a band. But after two records even my friends didn't buy, I decided that maybe construction wasn't so bad after all.

I met a guy who restored historic buildings. He was about to start a big project and wanted me right away. There was only one problem: I needed my own tools, and on my frayed shoestring of a budget, I wasn't sure I would be able to buy any. I was afraid I was going to have to pass up that job.

I looked for cheap tools in the classified section of all the newspapers, because that's how I'd sold mine. And I visited the local thrift shops and tried every garage and yard sale I happened upon, with no luck. Finally, I took a walk to the local hardware store, just to see what a new drill and jigsaw might cost and if by chance I could afford to buy them. I couldn't.

But I did discover that I could afford reconditioned tools, which the store sold for a fraction of their original cost. The store manager explained that some of these tools were previously owned (that's used to you and me), but many were just discontinued models or had come from the manufacturer slightly damaged in shipping. Best of all, the warranties still applied.

This was just what I was looking for, and for the price of a previously owned bass guitar, I was in business.

—GERALD DONNELLY
Astoria, New York

quire best-sellers, if your tastes are anything but mainstream, you may have to wait a year or more for the book you want to hit the library. One way to get your hands on new titles for less is to share books with one or two friends or coworkers. Start by coming up with a list of books that everyone might be interested in reading. Buy one copy of each book and divide the books up. When folks are finished reading their books (you might want to set a deadline), they can exchange them. When all the members have finished with all the books, take them to a used bookstore, where you can either swap them for more books or sell them and put the money in the book fund. This strategy works best with only a few people, since larger groups may have trouble agreeing on a list of books.

Old Books Are Good Books

❑ Are you in the market for inexpensive books? Many libraries sell off books they no longer have room for. You may not find the latest best-sellers there, but such sales are terrific for unearthing cookbooks, children's books, older fiction, and all sorts of oddities. In some towns, too, local residents are encouraged to clean out their bookcases and donate *last* year's best-sellers to the sale. Prices can run as low as 25 cents for a paperback, somewhat more for a hardcover. Call your local library to find out if and when it may sponsor such a sale.

Down in the Dumps

❑ Many people are just looking for good homes for their old reading material; the problem is making the right connection. In small towns, a great source of used books and magazines is often the recycling center. Many centers set aside a small area where other folks' cast-off reading material is available for little or nothing. Next time you drop off your trash, take a minute to look through this section. You might find a women's magazine with some terrific recipes or a children's book that's just right for your youngsters.

Hair Today . . .

❏ Need a beauty treatment? The whole works—hair, nails, facial—at your local salon may cost upward of $100! If that's a little rich for your blood, take your business to the local beauty academy. For a fraction of what you'd pay the pros, you can get a haircut, a manicure, and maybe even a facial, all performed by eager students (with watchful instructors hovering close by). A note for nervous Nellies: It's less anxiety producing to get your hair cut at one of these places if you have

 DOLLAR STRETCHER

Art for Our Sake

Looking to get a good job done at a reasonable price? You or someone you know has probably hired a college student at some point for a job such as painting a house, tutoring the kids, or cutting the lawn. But the possibilities go well beyond those areas. There are lots of college kids out there with other, more technical skills. They're often eager and willing, and you can get their services for substantially less than those of a professional— especially if you're willing to spend a little time showing them the ropes or keeping an eye on their efforts. To find and hire these students, call a local university or college and ask for the career planning and placement office. Students in certain disci-

plines can be especially helpful in performing related tasks.

Art students. They're a gold mine for jobs such as hand-lettering wedding (or other) invitations and designing thank-you notes or place cards. Consider hiring an art student for help with home decorating projects such as decorative painting. Who better to touch up your molding or paint your wooden mantel to look like marble?

Drafting students. If you're remodeling your home, a drafting student can help you draw up plans.

Culinary students. Think about hiring the next Julia Child to help you prepare dinner for an upcoming gathering. Who knows, you may learn a thing or two yourself!

a fairly straightforward hairstyle. To find a beauty school, look in the Yellow Pages under Beauty Schools.

Tooth or Consequences

❏ Time for your semiannual dental checkup? Want to take care of that cavity without having to take out a loan? If you live near a university that has a dental school, you're in luck. No school offers free dental care, but all provide care at a reduced cost. And in most cases, you can get a full range of services, including general exams, cleanings, extractions, root canals, even dentures (which are particularly good deals). All of the work is performed by students, but there are always instructors close by, usually one per student. The downside is that because students are doing the work, procedures take a little longer. (For instance, if a dentist takes 30 minutes to fill a tooth, a student may take an hour.) To get in touch with a dental school near you, call a nearby university and ask to be connected to the school of dental medicine. (The best way to find out if there are any dental schools in your area is to head to

 Tips for Working with Students

Student help can be a windfall if you know what you're doing or a major aggravation if you don't. To get the best results from student workers, keep these rules in mind.

1. Call around and find out what professionals charge for these services before you work out a price with the student. Expect to pay roughly 30 to 50 percent less for a student's work, depending on the job. And be prepared to supply all the necessary equipment.

2. Be clear about what you want. A white cloud painted on a blue ceiling? Two hundred hors d'oeuvres?

3. Decide on a price ahead of time and agree on how the fee will be paid (all up front, at the end of the job, or in increments).

4. Set a deadline. Everybody needs them, but especially students.

5. Be reasonable in your expectations. You're paying less because you're *not* getting a seasoned professional.

your local library. There are several published guides to colleges and universities; Peterson's is one.)

APPLIANCES AND FURNITURE

Get It Yourself!

❏ When you buy a large appliance or piece of furniture that requires shipping, sometimes it seems as if the shipping costs more than the item itself. If you own a van or truck or have a friend who does, you might be able to pick up your merchandise yourself. Ask the salesperson where the warehouse is and what its customer pickup policies are. Keep in mind that some warehouses are open for customer pickups only a day or two a week.

Everything but the Box

❏ Looking to save money on an air conditioner, blender, toaster, or microwave oven? Keep an eye out for "open box" sales. Many electronics and appliance stores hold these sales to get rid of floor models, and they offer good discounts, sometimes 50 percent or more. The best part is that the manufacturer's warranty still applies in most cases, although the store sale may be final. Always inspect an item carefully before you pay for it. Ask to plug it in and give it a test run in the store before you leave.

Model Savings

❏ If you're trying to save money on furniture, take a closer look at the pieces on the showroom floor. Many stores sell these items, especially those that are no longer stocked or are being discontinued by the manufacturer, and sometimes they discount them 10 to 15

DOLLAR STRETCHER

Don't Take the Credit

At one time or another, you have probably overheard someone say, "I never pay retail." Where exactly are these people shopping? You probably can't walk into a chain electronics store and start bargaining on a $150 radio. But if you check out the smaller stores in your neighborhood, you may be able to negotiate a better price, especially if you're willing to pay cash. That's because credit card companies charge retailers money—usually a percentage of the purchase price—for accepting their cards. The owner of a smaller shop may be willing to split that difference with you on a cash purchase.

percent. Sales are usually final, so consider your purchase carefully.

❑ That showroom model won't be such a great deal if it arrives at your house damaged and the store refuses to take it back. How can you make sure that won't happen? Take photographs of the piece before you leave the store. Even though floor models are sold "as is," you may not have to accept an item that arrives at your doorstep more damaged than it was on the showroom floor. If it is damaged in transit, photos are your proof of the item's condition when you bought it.

The $100 Spray Can

❑ Some salespeople will try to sell you fabric protection—intended to protect your furniture from dirt and stains—when you purchase a piece of furniture. Such protection can cost up to $100, but you can save yourself some cash by purchasing a can of fabric protector (Scotchgard is one brand) at a discount store or grocery store and doing it yourself. Keep in mind that no fabric protection will keep a sofa clean forever, but it will buy you some time in cleaning up spills.

SHOPPING STRATEGIES

Charge It!

❑ How can you save money at a department, clothing, or specialty store? Ask a clerk what benefits you'll get by signing up for that store's credit card. Many offer an automatic discount (usually around 10 percent) off the price of items you purchase the day you apply. And some stores hold "preferred" customer sales, sending announcements for those sales to credit card customers only. But remember, the only way those sales really save you money is if you pay off your credit card balance at the end of each month and avoid interest charges.

Get a Rain Check

❑ You see a great sale on garden hoses at the local discount store. You jump in your car, drive frantically to the store, and pull into the parking lot—only to watch your next-door neighbor leave the store with the last sale hose. Are you out of luck? Not necessarily. Many stores will offer you a rain check—a promise to sell you the item at the advertised sale price once it's back in stock. In fact, many states require stores to offer rain checks on certain products. (You won't get a rain check on alcohol, tailored clothing, or large items such as cars, however.) Even if there are no signs about rain checks in the store, ask a salesclerk or the manager if you can get one.

And to All a Good Buy!

❑ Getting ready to remortgage your home to finish up your Christmas shopping? Don't move into that refrigerator box just yet. One way to save big on your holiday shopping is to do most of it—for either next year or the current year—during the few days after Christmas. Right after the holiday, department stores are looking to empty their shelves to make way for new

What's On Sale When

How do stores decide when to schedule their sales? One important factor is the release dates for new products. To make room for the new models, stores hold sales to get rid of last year's merchandise. Keep in mind, however, that stores often schedule sales at the drop of a hat, so although the following list notes the best times to watch for deals on these items, if you're in the market for a specific piece of merchandise, keep an eye out all year long.

TYPE OF MERCHANDISE	USUAL TIME OF SALE
Appliances (kitchen)	July–August, Columbus Day
Audio and video equipment	September–October
Cars	September–December, Presidents' Day
Cookware	August
Home textiles (linens, bedding)	January (white sales), Columbus Day
Lawn and garden tools	November
Washers and dryers	January

merchandise (or to make up for an unprofitable sea-son). Shop those sales, and you can get terrific dis-counts (50 percent or more) on winter clothing, shoes, appliances—probably most of what the store sells. This strategy works especially if you're buying for older (high school or college) children and other family members who can wait until after the big day to receive their gifts.

❑ Of course, everyone knows that Christmas cards, wrapping paper, and ribbon are all drastically reduced after Christmas—often at least 50 percent. So stock up for next year!

FACTORY OUTLETS

It's a Matter of Time

❑ One of the best things about outlet shopping is that you can get good prices all year round. One of the worst things is the crowds. If pulling into an outlet mall and seeing five tour buses parked out front gives you a queasy feeling, shop early in the day or later in the evening. Avoid weekends at all costs.

❑ Outlets have sales, too—winter sales in January, sidewalk sales in the summer. But how do you find out about them? Many outlets mail flyers to customers an-nouncing sales. Make sure to add your name to the mailing list when you visit the outlet.

Second Best

❑ If you're trying to find the best outlet bargains, don't shy away from seconds, or imperfect products. Inspect such pieces carefully to avoid unpleasant surprises when you get home, but you may find that the flaw in the item won't be noticeable to you or anyone else.

Size Up the Outlets

❑ Sometimes it seems that you can never find anything in your size at factory outlets. Try broadening your search. Check through the racks for *all* sizes, not just your own. When a lot of merchandise is packed in a small space, it's easy for a size 10 blouse to get misplaced with the size 16s. No one else is likely to find it there, so if you take the extra time, you could end up with a real bargain.

BUYING SECONDHAND

A Penny Saved

❏ If you're looking to save money on items ranging from bookshelves to winter coats, computers to car mufflers, you probably know that used items may be good bargains. But how do you find them? Publishers in many communities print directories filled with ads from people trying to sell their used stuff. These booklets are usually published once a week and cost around a dollar—a small investment if you end up finding that Davy Crockett coonskin cap you've been searching for. The easiest way to find out if one of these directories is published in your community is to ask your local newsstand dealer or bookstore clerk.

Sold! To the Shocked-Looking Gentleman

❏ If you're an inveterate shopper looking for a new place to find bargains, you may want to get in on the auction scene. When you read in the newspaper that a painting by Van Gogh sold at auction for $82 million, it may have scared you into thinking that auctions are for rich folks only. But that's not true. The vast majority of auctions are free and open to the public, and there are great deals to be found. Check out estate auctions, which are usually held when people inherit a relative's possessions—everything from clothing and jewelry to furniture and kitchen

DOLLAR STRETCHER

Tools: You Sometimes Get *More* Than You Pay For

Tired of cheap tools but don't have the money to spring for state of the art? Don't lose hope. Flea markets, yard sales, and auctions are among the best places to shop for tools, particularly cutting tools. Older tools were typically made from better steel than their modern equivalents. Old chisels, planes, and axes often hold a better edge, and saws often cut more cleanly. If you look around, you can probably pick up some of these tools for just a few dollars.

equipment—and want to liquidate it quickly. Even if you don't buy anything at an auction, it's an enormously entertaining way to spend a day or evening. You'll find estate auctions listed in your local newspaper, usually in the classified section. To find an auction house, look in the Yellow Pages under Auctioneers.

Demolition Derby

❑ Looking for a piece of stained glass for your living room window or a marble mantelpiece for your fire-

 DOLLAR STRETCHER

Going Once, Going Twice . . .
What's Going On?

An auction can be a great way to get your hands on a bargain—if you know how to play the game. Start by scouring your local newspaper's classified section under Auctions or Antiques. The ad should include information about when and where the auction will be, as well as a brief description of what's up for bid and a number to call for more information.

Find out when the "inspection" is—usually the auctioneer holds one a few days before the sale. That's your opportunity to take a close look at the merchandise—which is a good idea, since sales are final at many auctions. If you find something at the inspection you like and you think you might want to bid on it, you need to register, which entails filling out a form or two. That will entitle you to get a number or a paddle (that's what you hold up to bid). Most times you can register either the day of the auction or at the inspection. To be able to bid at the auction, you may have to give credit references.

During the auction, the item up for bid will be displayed at the front of the salesroom or shown on a slide. The bidding begins at a low price, usually set by the seller, and proceeds with the auctioneer calling out each bid. To bid, all you need to do is hold up your number or paddle.

Once you've been determined the "winner" of the item, you need to pay for it and make arrangements to take it home. Payment options vary but usually don't include personal checks. Plan to pay by cash, credit card, or certified check.

place? Some merchants are now making a business of buying up usable hardware, decorations, furniture, and building materials from demolition sites and selling them at a fraction of what they would cost new. If you're in the market for decorative molding, columns, flooring, chandeliers, or almost anything else for your home, check the Yellow Pages under Building Materials—Used or Antiques—Dealers.

YARD SALES

The Early Bird Gets the . . . Hummel

❏ Have you found that there's nothing but junk at the yard sales you go to? Maybe that's because you don't get there until 4:30 P.M. To get the best stuff and the best deals at antiques fairs and yard sales, you need to arrive early. Show up at the time the ad or poster says the sale *starts*.

All Yards Are Not Created Equal

❏ If you're unsure how to plan your route for hitting this weekend's yard sales, head first for the toniest neighborhoods, where the quality of the goods is likely to be highest. The secondhand clothing in those areas may be especially good, and you could find some real bargains.

How Low Can You Go?

❏ If you find a yard sale item that you love but it's out of your price range, don't be afraid to haggle. Remember, people usually hold yard sales to clean out the garage—the money is an added bonus. If a dresser costs $75 and you are willing to pay $50, pull out a $50 bill and say, "I really can't afford $75. How about $50?"

❏ Another good way to bargain at a yard sale is to offer to buy everything in a group. Ask the owner, "How much would you take for that whole box of books/puzzles/coffee mugs?" Often the owner will give you a good discount just to get rid of the lot.

THE HOME WORKSHOP
Tooling Up

ORGANIZATION

Tool Hang-Ups

❏ Circular saw blades can be easily nicked or dulled in storage. If you're looking for a way to protect them, try hanging them on the wall. Choose an appropriate-size dowel (say, one-half or three-quarters inch in diameter), then use a power drill to drill that size hole an inch or two deep into the wooden boards or studs of your wall. Pound the wooden dowel into the hole. Hang new blades on the dowel, then pound another dowel into the wall and hang used blades on it. (*Note:* This is not a good solution for a workshop with concrete walls!)

Small Items Require Proper ID

❏ Do you have trouble putting your hands on just the right size nail or washer? Whether you use tiny drawers, plastic boxes, old coffee cans, or glass jars to store your leftover nails, screws, washers, and nuts, no storage system works well unless the items are organized and easily identified. Creating a system ahead of time will save hours of needless searching and frustration down the road. Organize the materials in whatever way seems logical to you and works in your space: all nails on the top two shelves; wood screws on the left, sheet metal screws on the right; or bolts stored in cans in order of increasing size. Label all containers with masking tape and magic marker or use glass jars that let you see through to the contents.

Washers: Picture This

❑ It can be tough to find an efficient way to organize and store washers, particularly those in small sizes. Consider grouping them by size and storing them in discarded film canisters. Label the outside of each canister with masking tape showing a tracing of the washers inside.

Divide and Conquer the Toolbox

❑ Tired of lugging a heavy, overflowing toolbox to each work site, then having to search for the few tools you need for a particular job? If you do a variety of jobs around the house, chances are you can simplify your life by keeping specialized tools together in their own toolboxes. For instance, maintain one toolbox for carpentry, one for plumbing, and one for electrical work. Keep all your masonry and plastering tools—trowels,

---

ONE PERSON'S SOLUTION

The Can-Do Approach

I've always kept my nails and screws in coffee cans, but I could never remember exactly what was in each can until I took it down off the shelf and looked into it—often checking three or four cans before I got the right one. Then I thought of a better way to shelve them. I built a shelf that tilts forward just enough (about 45 degrees) so I can see into the cans at an easy glance. I put a

board along the front of the shelf to keep the cans from sliding off. That simple shelf has saved me a lot of trial and error over the years.

—HESTON SCHEFFEY
Hopkinton, New Hampshire

---

cold chisels, stone hammers, and the like—together in a five-gallon drywall joint compound bucket. Keep your chain saw files, goggles, ear protectors, and bar oil in a canvas bag.

SPACE SAVERS

The Fold-Down Workbench

❏ Every carpenter needs a workbench, but not every shop, cellar, or garage allows enough space for one. So-

For a workbench that's there only when you need it, start with a flat, solid door (A). Use hinges to attach two-by-fours for legs, and more hinges to secure the door to the wall (B). Add a hook at each end to hold the folded-up version to the wall (C).

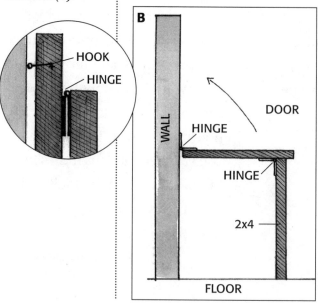

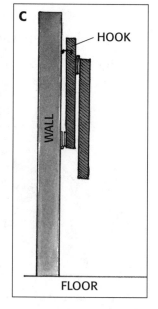

lution? Create a fold-down workbench by attaching a flat, solid door to a wall using large hinges. For legs, use a pair of two-by-fours hinged to the underside of the table. This type of bench also can make use of wall space otherwise lost to an opening door.

Double the Shelf Space

❏ If you've run out of shelf space for small items such as nuts, washers, and screws, here's an old-fashioned storage method that will double your space. Use glass jars with screw-top lids to store your items, then use a screw to attach the lids to the underside of the shelf. Use a lock washer to keep the lid secure even while you unscrew the jar. Choose your jars according to your space and what you're storing. Old Mason jars, jelly jars, peanut butter or mayonnaise jars, and baby food jars all work well.

Screwdrivers? Shelve Them!

❏ With so many different-size screwdrivers, it can be a chore to keep them sorted so you can quickly find just the one you need. Here's an easy and efficient way to store them. Drill a series of holes along the middle of a one- by three-inch board, making each hole just

TIME SAVER

A Penny for Your Tots

Once a job is done, it's all too easy to neglect sorting through all the leftover nails, bolts, and miscellaneous materials. But if you don't do it now, the clutter and disorganization seem to multiply. Here's a fast way to pick up. Throw all the leftover nails, bolts, washers, and such into a five-gallon drywall joint compound bucket. Empty the bucket on your workbench, sorting the materials into their proper cans or jars as you go. (If you have young kids, pay them to sort the leftovers for you. A penny for each piece is a time-honored wage.)

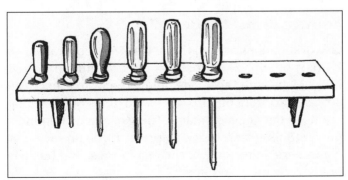

A simple one- by three-inch board, with holes drilled at appropriate intervals, makes a great way to organize screwdrivers.

wide enough to hold the shank of the screwdriver without letting the handle fall through. Mount the board to the wall with small angle brackets. Put your screwdrivers through the holes in ascending order. They'll be easy to see at a glance and won't take up any room in your toolbox or drawer.

Frame Your Windows

❏ Large, L-shaped framing squares are among the more awkward tools to store. An efficient solution is to cut a dado (a rectangular groove) into the top of a window frame and hang the square there. (One tongue of the square sits in the groove in the top of the window casing; the other hangs down next to the side of the casing.)

Get that framing square out of your way by cutting a groove in the top of a window frame (A), then hanging the square from there (B).

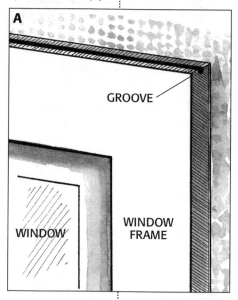

A

GROOVE

WINDOW

WINDOW
FRAME

B

Storage Below the Belt

❏ Workbenches and stationary power tools take up a lot of room in any shop. How can you minimize their bulk? Make sure the space below them isn't just dead air. Use it to store bulky or awkward items or those that are used only occasionally—things such as handheld power tools, generators, compressors, chain saws, gas containers, miter boxes, cartons of rags, and buckets holding cleaning supplies.

Nail thin boards across exposed studs to create the perfect home for piping, crowbars, shovels, and other large or awkward objects.

Fill Cavities (in the wall)

❏ If you're short on storage space and wall space, you may be able to use the space between exposed studs for storage. Nail or screw horizontal boards between the studs to create shelves. Nail up thin boards (or pieces of lath) to close in the cavity to a height of two or three feet off the floor. Use the space to store materials such as piping or molding and long-handled tools (splitting mauls, brooms, crowbars, iron bars, and sledgehammers). This often solves two problems at once: It creates additional space and provides a place to store awkward items.

FATIGUE

Hammers: Take a Load Off

❏ Does your arm get tired after a few hours of hammering? Perhaps you're using too light a hammer. Hammers come in different sizes, measured in ounces. A small 12-ounce hammer allows for good control and is appropriate for finish work, but it requires too many blows for heavier work such as framing. A 22-ounce or heavier hammer is recommended for driving large nails and spikes. You'll need fewer blows to drive the same number of nails, and the hammer will take much of the load off your arm, even though it's a bit heavier to lift. If you can have just two hammers in your toolbox, a 16-ounce and a 22-ounce hammer will adequately handle most of the jobs you'll take on.

Go to the Mat

❏ Are your feet tired from standing on hard concrete (as in a garage or cellar shop) for hours at a time? Consider laying down rubber "fatigue mats" in front of your work spaces. Plywood scraps, flattened cardboard boxes, and carpet remnants also work well and will save you money at the same time. (As a bonus, these mats can prevent damage to tools and materials accidentally dropped on the floor.)

PROTECTING AND MAINTAINING TOOLS

You Name It!

❏ It's easy to lose track of tools when you lend them to friends or share them on group projects. To protect against loss, make a habit of labeling all your tools. Engrave or paint your name or initials on each one.

Neon Orange Would Work

❏ Crowbars, iron bars, sledgehammers, and other heavy construction tools are easily misplaced and hard to find in dirty or overgrown areas. To reduce the chances of losing them, spray a wide band of bright paint on the handles. Use the same color on all the items. Not only will the tools stand out, but they'll also be immediately identifiable as yours.

The Top 10 Tools

If your shop could hold only ten tools, what would they be? It sounds like a parlor game, but if you're just starting to outfit a shop, the problem is a real one. Here's a list of ten that would be hard to beat.

1. Sixteen-ounce hammer with claw
2. Crosscut handsaw
3. Four-in-one screwdriver
4. Combination square or speed square
5. Four-foot level
6. Twenty-five-foot steel measuring tape
7. Sharp wood chisel
8. Utility knife
9. Circular saw
10. Three-eighths-inch-drive power drill

Rust Areas

❏ Rust can hurt the performance of saws. If a little rust has started to form on your saw, remove it by briskly rubbing the surface of the blade with medium steel wool. Keep the blade rust-free by occasionally applying a light coat of vegetable oil, silicone, or a lubricating oil such as WD-40.

❏ On jigsaw blades or other blades that do fine finish work, you don't want to add a coating that can leave a residue on the wood. Instead, apply a light coat of butcher's wax, then wipe the blade clean.

A Swell Idea for Hammer Handles

❏ Does one of your hammers have a loose head? If the handle is wooden, you can tighten the head by placing the hammer in a pail of water overnight. Remove the hammer, wipe it dry, and apply a thin layer of vegetable oil to the head. The wood in the handle will have swollen and will stay swollen for several weeks or more, holding the head in place.

PROBLEM PREVENTED

Go with the Grain

Wooden ax and maul heads are especially prone to breaking, but you can reduce the chances of breakage by choosing your tool carefully when you buy it. Look at the end grain at the bottom of the handle. Select only those handles whose grain is exactly perpendicular to the direction of the ax head—that wood is less likely to split by a misdirected blow. Some manufacturers paint the bottoms of handles, hiding the grain. Don't take a chance on those.

Tools to Keep Projects Moving

Some tools are especially good at saving time without compromising quality. Here's a partial list.

1. A utility knife with a quick-change blade saves the time of having to unscrew the housing, remove the blade, and replace the housing.

2. A four-in-one screwdriver has an adaptable head that allows you to change the type of screwdriver you have without having to carry or search for extras.

3. A combination square with level shows precise 45-degree and 90-degree angles along with level and plumb readings.

Stay Sharp! Bringing in the Sheaths

❑ Dull or nicked chisels can ruin the fine work they're intended for and can be dangerous, too. (Sharp chisels move more cleanly, requiring less force.) To protect a chisel blade, fold a piece of cardboard into a chisel-size pocket open at one end, then wrap the pocket tightly with duct tape. Slide your chisel into its sheath when you put it in your toolbox or take it to a work site outside the shop. A couple of times a year, give the inside of the sheath a light spray of a lubricating oil such as WD-40 to keep the chisel blade from rusting.

✔ PROBLEM PREVENTED

Power by Extension

Electric power tools, because they draw so much power, can be unsafe to operate using common household extension cords. Use only heavy-duty, grounded (three-pronged) extension cords of 14 gauge or larger. (The higher the number, the smaller the gauge.) Be careful not to use long lengths of extension cord with your power tools. These diminish the power reaching the machine and can damage or ruin the motor. If the motor sounds as if it has to labor to get up to speed, it probably isn't receiving enough power to run properly. Figure out a way to do the work closer to an outlet.

EVERYDAY FRUSTRATIONS

Paint Thinner: A Stretching Exercise

❑ Using paint thinner to clean up oil-based paint and brushes can be an expensive and environmentally hazardous proposition. Here's a system that gives you more thinner for your dollar and reduces the amount you ultimately need to dispose of.

First, cut an old paint thinner can in half horizontally and use the bottom half as a reservoir. After wrapping up a paint job for the day, pour an inch or so of thinner into the reservoir and clean your brushes. Then hold your brushes deep inside a five-gallon drywall joint compound bucket and finish cleaning them with a commercial brush spinner (available at paint and hardware stores). The paint will spatter the inside of the bucket but otherwise not make a mess. Pour the dirty thinner into the bucket, then hang the bucket up, out of reach, for a week or two. By the end of that time, the paint solids will have settled out, leaving relatively clean thinner in a layer on top. Use a funnel (a plastic quart-size oilcan works well) to pour the thinner back into its can so you can use it again later.

With care, you can use the same can of thinner for five or six times the number of jobs you could if you discarded the thinner after each use. The solids in the bottom of the bucket will slowly harden and build up, but it will take several years for them to build up to the point where you'll need to start over with a new bucket.

The Toolbox You Can Wear

❏ Especially when working on a roof, ladder, or some other inconvenient spot, simply getting the right tool in your hand can be a frustrating chore. The solution (and a good early investment for the home handyman) is a leather tool belt. Standard tool belts come with holders for hammers and measuring tapes, and good ones have pouch attachments that can be moved around the belt depending on what you store in them and how comfortable they feel. If you use one of the larger belts that carry more weight, consider adding a pair of suspenders to help support the belt. Tool belts are available at hardware and building supply stores.

To cope with a stubborn slotted wood screw, get extra torque with an adjustable wrench.

Delivered by the Torque

❏ If a slotted wood screw seems too stubborn to screw or unscrew, don't lose hope. Using as large a screwdriver as will fit the slot, tighten an adjustable wrench to the square shank of the screwdriver, then use the wrench to turn the screwdriver and simultaneously exert downward pressure. The added length of the wrench should provide enough torque to turn the screw.

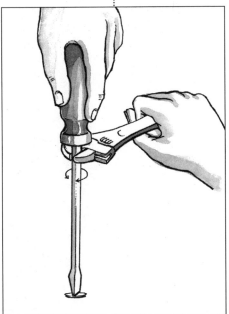

Big Jobs in Small Places

❏ How do you manage a large woodworking project in a small shop? The key may be in the design. Try to plan

Can the Paint

Few people want to paint every room in the house the exact same shade, but when you need a bit for touch-ups and are confronted by a row of half-full paint cans, how do you know which room was painted in oyster white and which in antique ivory? One solution is to mark the cans. Before storing a partially used can of paint, write on the lid all the vital information: the name or number of the paint formula (which identifies the color), the room in which you used the paint, and the part of the room where you used it. For example, your label might read "Sunshine Yellow, guest room, woodwork trim."

the project in units that can be assembled in place. Ideally, no unit should be bigger than a single person can lift. After you complete each unit, get it out of the shop before you start another. If you're building a project that involves drawers, cupboards, or boxes, sometimes you can nest smaller units inside larger ones to save space.

Shelves: A Test of Strength

❑ It can be tricky knowing how strong a new shelf has to be. In general, the heavier the load, the thicker, shorter, and wider the shelf should be. To estimate the strength of a planned shelf, place the shelf board between two chairs and stack the intended load on top of it. If the board sags, you'll need to shorten its span or go with a thicker and/or wider shelf.

Sag-No-More

❑ If an existing shelf sags under the weight of its load, you can reinforce it in any of several ways. Screw a strip of wood along the edge of the shelf. Screw or glue a board of equal size on top of the shelf, effectively doubling its thickness. Or add a support below the shelf at the point where the sag is the greatest.

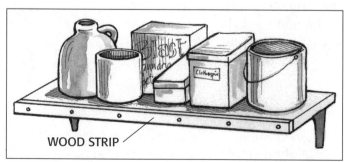

One of the simplest ways to bolster a sagging shelf is to screw a strip of wood along the front of it.

WOOD STRIP

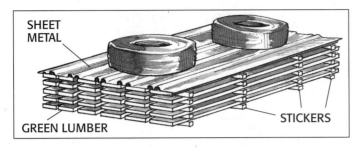

SHEET METAL

GREEN LUMBER

STICKERS

To keep things straight when it comes to drying lumber, insert stickers at even intervals between courses of boards. Top off the pile with scrap tin, and weight it down with old tires. This keeps the top dry and the air circulating through the pile.

Lumber: Don't Twist and Shout

❏ It's important to dry green lumber before using it, but it's also important to make sure it doesn't warp or twist in storage. To keep your boards straight until they're ready to use, be careful how you stack the lumber and make sure you use dividing spacers called stickers. Between courses of boards, place several long one- by one-inch or two- by two-inch boards (the "stickers") perpendicular to the boards being stacked. Use enough stickers so that the boards do not sag between them. Be sure to line up the stickers over each other so the boards will dry straight. And don't cover the stack with plastic sheeting. Instead, lay pieces of scrap tin or plywood on top of the stack to keep rain off it, while keeping the sides open to the air. The boards will dry faster that way. Plunk a couple of old automobile tires on top of the whole thing to keep the cover from flying off.

In One Door and Out the Other

❏ If you have to run a long board—say, 12 or 16 feet—through your table saw or planer, you may not have the necessary space on both sides of the tool. A solution might lie in where you locate those fixed tools. If you can, line them up in front of door and window openings. That way, you can run a long board in from outside the shop, through the machine, and back outside the shop.

DOLLAR STRETCHER

Buying Lumber: Material Savings

If you're framing a deck, shed, outbuilding, or other structure where a finished surface is not necessary, think about using rough-sawn wood from a sawmill rather than the more expensive dressed wood from a lumberyard. Rough-sawn wood is both stronger (because it measures larger for the same stated dimensions) and cheaper than dressed wood.

HOUSEHOLD REPAIRS
The Ceiling Is Falling!

WALLS

The Hole Story

❑ Sometimes you want to change the pictures on your walls without redecorating an entire room, but taking down the old artwork can leave unsightly holes. To hide them, apply a bit of Spackle with your finger or touch up the holes with a crayon that's a matching color. If you have paint that matches the wall, dab on a bit with a cotton swab.

❑ On a white wall, try covering the damaged areas with Elmer's glue. Or wipe some white toothpaste into the hole with your finger. It's a surprisingly unobtrusive filler, and any excess wipes away easily with a damp sponge.

Help for Problem Hairlines

❑ Hairline cracks frequently are a pernicious problem in plaster walls. Although they're usually only a cosmetic fault, they tend to be large, unsightly, and (most vexing of all) recurring. No matter how much you dig and fill the plaster, the cracks always seem to come back as soon as the seasons change. A good way to attack hairline cracks is to bridge them with drywall joint compound and tape. Paper tape will work, but fiberglass mesh tape is even better because it moves more. Apply a thin coat of compound over the crack, cover it with tape, and finish with another thin layer of compound. Be sure to feather the edges the same way you would

The Dior of Denim

Years ago, I worked for a contractor named Frank who was a country boy and a bit of a character (everything in his wardrobe was made from blue denim), but he was also a good carpenter and a clever builder. One day over lunch, he told the crew how he was remodeling the den in his own house. He was buying the cheapest sheet paneling he could find, then putting it up backward so that the finished side faced the wall. There were several jokes about Frank's refined sense of design—but a trip to the lumberyard showed me there was a method to his madness.

The grades and styles of four- by eight-foot paneling typically sold at home centers and lumberyards range from high-grade, real hardwood veneer (at $35 and up a sheet) to products so inexpensive that the "wood grain" is actually a photographic image printed and embossed on a common-grade paneling base. Yet cheapo paneling imported from the Far East typically uses a species of mahogany for its base material. If you comb the stack of paneling for sheets with uniform and unblemished backs, you can take home a product with a cabinet-grade wood surface for the price of cardboard (as little as $6 a sheet). I've used this method several times on projects as diverse as attic remodeling jobs and trade show booths. With a little clear finish, the results have always looked as if I'd spent about ten times the actual cost—thanks to Frank, the Dior of denim.

—GORDON BOCK
Lynnfield, Massachusetts

Your Four-Year-Old Could Help Install Paneling

When you're finishing a room with four- by eight-foot sheets of wood-grain paneling, you'll inevitably have vertical joints—and sometimes horizontal ones—where the sheets meet. As the wood expands and contracts with the moisture cycles in the building, those joints will develop unsightly gaps. You can keep the gaps relatively invisible if you anticipate them when you install the paneling. Before you put the paneling in place, paint the wall black or dark brown behind where the gaps will be. Even a large marker used for making signs will work.

complete joints in new drywall. Then simply paint over the patches.

DOORS

Swing Out!

❏ Doors get used hundreds of times a week, so when they don't swing right, they become a constant annoyance. Fortunately, many of the common causes of unruly doors can be traced to undermaintained hinges. For example, when a door repeatedly decides to close on its own, chances are it's off balance. To correct the problem, try moving the bottom hinge one-eighth inch to one side or the other. If the outer corner of the door catches on the threshold, check the top hinge. It may be loose and need longer screws to reanchor it to the jamb. If the top hinge looks OK, try setting it deeper in its mortise, shimming the bottom hinge, or swapping the top and bottom hinges. If the door is hung on three hinges and is hard to move, check to see if the hinges are aligned, then shim or remount the nonconforming hinge.

Get Sliding Doors Back on Track

❏ Sliding glass patio doors are a delightful way to enter a backyard, except when you have to arm-wrestle them open because they barely move. The reason most sliding doors stop doing their thing is that they're dragging on the track. To get them rolling again, try cleaning all the accumulated dirt from the track. Use a bent wire coat hanger and an old toothbrush to loosen the debris. Vacuum up the dirt, then wash with paint thinner.

❏ If a simple cleaning doesn't get the door sliding again, check the clearance between the bottom of the door and the track. The clearance on most doors can be increased by adjusting the rollers. Typically, you can do this by taking the weight off the door (say, with a screwdriver), then turning an adjusting screw located somewhere along the top or bottom rail.

Thanks, a Lock!

❏ Sliding glass patio doors have a tendency to lose their locking ability as they get older—an obvious security breach. You can create your own door lock without much effort. One way is simply to bore a nail-size hole through the rails of both doors where they overlap at the middle of the wall, preferably somewhere near the top. Then insert a nail when you want to lock the door. (Be careful not to drill all the way through to the outside, allowing a thief to push the nail out!)

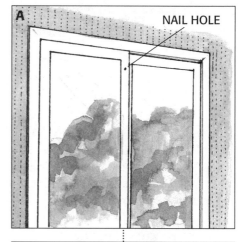

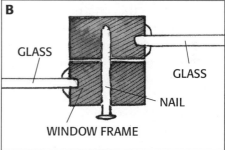

❏ Another gimmick is to attach a hinged length of strong hardwood or an aluminum bar (available at hardware stores) in the middle of the door on the fixed side. Measure the bar so it is just long enough to hold the sliding door shut when it's down but it hinges up out of the way to let the door slide open.

To lock a sliding door, drill a hole through the door rails (A), then insert a nail (B). Or bar entry (C) with a hinged length of hardwood (D).

Putty in Your Hands

Old, hard glazing putty can be murder to remove when you're fixing a broken window. Trying to dig the stuff out with a putty knife or chisel is a laborious job that often results in split or gouged wood—and possible injury if you slip as you fight the putty. A better way to clean out putty is to soften the material first. Apply heat from a heat gun, carefully controlled propane torch, or electric putty softener (available wherever they sell glazier's supplies). Move the heat source up and down the putty to soften it slowly and evenly; the goal is to make large areas pliable without igniting the paint. Work carefully to avoid cracking adjacent glass.

WINDOWS

The Pane of Broken Windows

❑ When a window gets broken—whether through accident, storm damage, or vandalism—it leaves the house vulnerable to rain, snow, insects, and animals until you can get the glass replaced. To make an emergency window repair, try covering the break or hole with the clear plastic tape that's sold for pasting up temporary interior storm windows. This two-inch-wide product has an adhesive that sticks readily to sash and glass, and it's heavy enough (six mils thick) to stand up to weather for months. To cover a large hole, just overlap strips of the tape.

Can We Open a Window in Here?

❑ Sticky sash windows not only make it difficult to get fresh air, but they also create a potential for damaging the window or the operator when you have to force them open by lifting delicate parts. If your windows don't open smoothly, avoid the temptation to increase their slip with spray-on lubricants or oils. Such treatments will swell the wood and make the situation worse. Instead, try waxing the channel with a candle stub or piece of paraffin. A swipe or two of this dry lubricant should do the trick.

FLOORS

They Make It Tough to Sneak in Late at Night

❑ Squeaks in floorboards aren't much of a threat to life and limb (unless they indicate an ongoing structural flaw in the building), but they *will* drive you crazy. A quick fix that sometimes works is to douse the offending area with talcum powder. Working it into the cracks may lubricate the wood enough that it will stop squeaking.

❏ Unfortunately, sooner or later your talking floor is likely to get worse if you don't address the source of the problem: boards, nails, or supporting joists that have shrunk or come loose over the years, allowing parts to rub against each other. If you have access to the underside of your problem floor—say, through an unfinished basement ceiling—you can usually tighten up a lot of squeaks. First, as you watch from below, have an assistant walk around the floor, locating squeaky spots. Look for moving boards—often unsupported ends of subfloors or spaces over joists. Mark these spots with chalk and return later to secure them. Use shims and glue where boards need more support over a joist. Short screws will pull the finish flooring back down to the subflooring.

CEILINGS

Surgery for Ceiling Embolisms

❏ Because plaster ceilings have to fight the force of gravity, as well as footsteps and occasional floods upstairs, they have a tendency to bulge and pull away from the structure that holds them up. A slight bulge may not even be unsightly, but it's a sign of a structural problem—broken keys that allow the plaster to separate from the supporting lath—that will only get worse until pieces of the ceiling start to fall to the floor. (Keys, the source of strength in plaster ceilings, are created in the building process when the wet plaster oozes through the spaces between the strips of wood lath.) If the bulge is not large—say, less than 18 inches in diameter—and the plaster moves readily back into

Ceiling need cosmetic surgery? If the sag is a small one, plaster washers (shown from the front and side views) may do the trick.

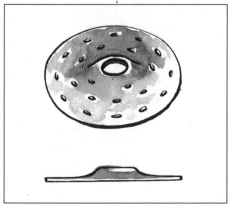

place with the pressure of your hand, try reinforcing the ceiling with plaster washers. These are half-dollar-size disks of thin metal (available at good hardware stores or from mail-order suppliers) that are counter-sunk to accept screws.

❏ To reinforce ceiling plaster with plaster washers, first mark the edges of the bulge, as well as any ceiling joists, with a pencil. This helps to define the work area. Have a helper push the plaster bulge back into place. Then, using a screw gun and long (1½-inch) drywall screws, secure the plaster to the joists with the washers in strategic places. (Stick with the joists or any similar solid nailing material as much as possible. Screw to lath only as a last resort.) When the plaster is back in place and all the washers are flush with the plaster, apply a skim coat of drywall joint compound to the repair.

Get on Top of the Problem

❏ If you're lucky enough to have access to the top of your ailing plaster ceiling—either because there's an unfinished room above or you can remove the floor up there—try another technique to keep your ceiling from falling to the ground. First, inspect the bulge from above and clean up the area as much as you can. Carefully pick up all broken keys and vacuum up dust and debris. Fish out particles from between the plaster and lath that will prevent the ceiling from moving back into place. Then gingerly test from below to see if it will return to its proper position. Once the work area is clean, inject flexible construction adhesive—the kind, made for paneling, that stays semisoft once it has cured—anywhere you can between lath and plaster. Work carefully, boring an occasional hole in the lath if it helps give you better access for injecting adhesive.

After you finish applying the adhesive, go below and place a sheet of plywood over the bulge. Cautiously push the bulge back into place while a helper watches from above. Perform this operation with great care; the only things that are giving the plaster a little integrity and preventing it from falling on your head are paint on the outside and perhaps some animal hair included in the base coat. When everything looks good, prop up the plywood with two-by-fours and mating wedges at the bottom for at least 24 hours, or until the adhesive has cured. (Mating wedges are two wooden wedges laid one on top of the other to make a rectangular block. Sliding them so they overlap more will increase the thickness of the block.) Remove the plywood carefully, preferably by twisting it off rather than pulling it down.

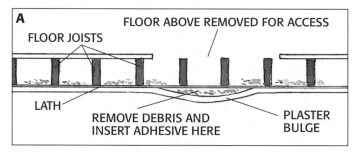

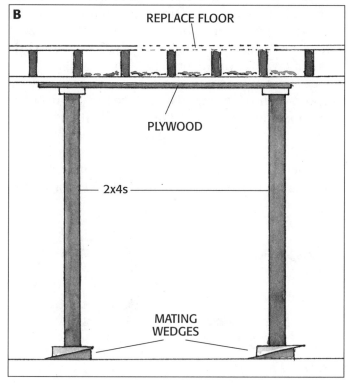

To fight the battle of the bulging ceiling, approach it from above. Clear out all debris, then inject flexible construction adhesive (A). From below, place plywood over the bulge and carefully prop it in place with two-by-fours and mating wedges (B). Wait at least 24 hours before replacing the flooring above and removing the supports below.

Ceilings

PLUMBING AND HEATING

Science (and a drain) in Action

❑ No one likes a blocked drain in a sink, tub, or toilet. Besides the fact that your fixture is unusable (and may be flooding), you're stuck with trying to get rid of the waste another way. A clog deep in the system may require a plumber's expertise and equipment, but if you can determine that the blockage is a simple one, it may be worth a try at clearing it yourself. To find out which is appropriate, test the drainage of all the other fixtures in the house by running water in them. If they all drain properly and the water level in the blocked fixture does not change, the blockage is affecting only that fixture and is not in some common pipe. Then it's appropriate to work on the drain yourself.

Sometimes You Have to Force the Issue

❑ If the clog is in a single fixture, you'll need to get your hands on a force cup—the old plumber's helper (plunger). (On toilets, you may want to use the kind made with flanges for an improved seal.) If you're working on a lavatory or tub drain with an overflow opening, be sure to plug this with a rag so it won't defeat the purpose of the force cup. Then place the cup over the drain opening and push down on the handle to expel air from the tool. Work carefully to avoid splashing. If you've done this right and the seal is tight, you'll create a vacuum under the force cup as you lift up the handle. This vacuum sometimes frees the blockage then

When a drain is clogged, get things moving again the old-fashioned way, with an ordinary plunger. The version on the left is best for toilets because it gives a better seal. The one on the right is for sinks.

and there. In any event, continue to pump the cup carefully. After about a dozen pumps, release the force cup. Either it will have cleared the drain or it will be time to stop and call the plumber. Don't use chemicals or compressed-air products. The chemicals don't always work, and if they don't, you're stuck with a fixture full of nasty liquids as well as a blocked drain. (Never use a force cup on a drain that you've already tried to unclog with chemicals. If you do and you get splashed, you can get caustic chemicals on your skin.) Compressed-air products have the power to explode old or weak plumbing.

When the House Smells Like a Sewer

❏ If your house suddenly starts to smell like a sewer, you have more than a cosmetic problem. Over and above being offensive to the senses, sewer gas is unsanitary and can even be explosive. When there is sewer gas in the house, suspect a loss of the water seal in one or more of the drain traps below sinks, tubs, and other fixtures. One of the ways this can occur is through evaporation. Fixtures that get regular use have a constant supply of water for the trap. However, traps in little-used areas, such as basements with old laundry sinks and floor drains or a toilet in a spare bathroom, will eventually go dry if left alone. If that's the problem, all you need to do is flush or run water and the problem will be solved.

❏ Another common cause of sewer gas is siphonage. Here, water flushing the drain of one fixture sucks the seal out of the trap in a nearby fixture. In this case, check the soil vent pipe going through the roof for blockage. You may find leaves, a bird's nest, or other debris that you can easily remove. Or call a plumber to see if the system is plumbed correctly.

If the Temperature's Falling

❏ If you suspect that your hot-water radiators aren't giving off the proper amount of heat or they feel only warm to the touch, try bleeding them to remove the

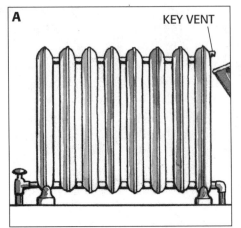

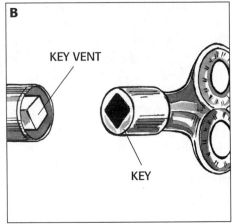

To bleed a sick radiator, place a bucket under the key vent (A), then open the vent with the key (B). When the air is released and water starts coming out, close the vent.

trapped air that's causing the problem. Place a container under the key vent at the top of the radiator column (there's no automatic vent) and open it slowly with the small key. Once all the air in the radiator is out, it will be followed abruptly by water. Close the vent as soon as water starts to come out.

ROOFS

Slipups Can Cure Leaks

"Weasel" metal slips in place to fix roof leaks quickly.

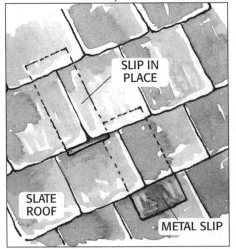

❏ Although slate and asphalt shingles make great, long-lasting roofs, sometimes they develop small leaks that cause damage inside the house. If the problem is not extensive enough to warrant a full-scale repair or replacement, try installing copper or aluminum slips anywhere roof slates and shingles are basically intact. Cut several metal rectangles, each roughly half the size of a slate, and slide them under slates and keys in the problem areas. Use a medium-size drywall taping knife to "weasel" them in as far up the slates as possible. Try a few slips at first, then be prepared to come back with more until the leak is fixed.

A Shingle-Minded Idea

❑ If your house has a cement shingle roof—any one of several products made from the 1920s to the 1950s to simulate slate or wooden shingles—that roof may have been originally colored red, green, or blue-black. Although the roof probably has plenty of life left in it, the color may be past its prime and somewhat unsightly, and the original manufacturer may be out of business. The solution? Repaint your roof. First, carefully wash it clean of all dirt and debris. Next, treat the surface with a masonry sealer. Finally, apply a good-quality exterior acrylic latex paint with a satin sheen.

DECKS

Space It!

❑ When you install a new deck, be sure it sheds water rather than bringing moisture in direct contact with the house. You can do that by slightly spacing the deck floorboards so that water and melting snow drain through them. But how do you keep the spacing even? You don't need a big gap; a space of about one-eighth inch or so will do, and that's about the width of a sixteenpenny nail. Just pound a couple of such nails into a piece of scrap wood. Hold on to the scrap wood to line the spacer nails up against the first floorboard and to keep them in place while you position the second floorboard. Repeat for the rest of the floor.

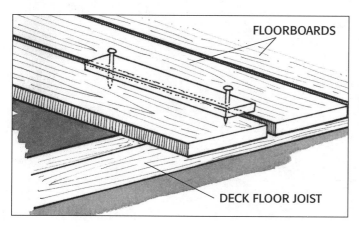

FLOORBOARDS

DECK FLOOR JOIST

To space deck floorboards evenly (so they'll shed rainwater), pound a couple of sixteenpenny nails into a piece of scrap wood. Use this gizmo to position each new floorboard evenly.

Decks

Pop Go the Deck Nails

❏ Probably the most common problem any backyard deck develops after a few seasons is a floor full of nail heads working their way out. Not only can these raised fasteners become dangerous toe stubbers, but they'll eventually stand in the way when you want to refinish the surface. The solution may be easy. If the boards are in good condition and the nails have never popped before, try using a nail set to drive the uppity nails deeper.

✔ PROBLEM PREVENTED

A Deck Should Never Become a Moat

A backyard deck makes a great addition to a home, but the pleasure will fade rapidly if your new deck leads snow and rain into direct contact with the house. To make sure your new deck sheds water, pitch the floor so that it slopes away from the house—say, a three-inch drop for every 10 inches of width.

Another way to block moisture damage is to make sure the deck floor header (the member that carries the joists) is separated from the house by an air space so it cannot trap water. To create this space, place a stack of washers on each lag screw that fastens the header to the house. The washers will keep you from getting the header too close to the house. A lag screw (available at hardware stores and lumberyards) is a big screw designed for wood. It has a hex head like that on a machine bolt so that it can be turned with a wrench.

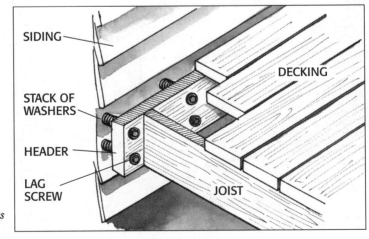

SIDING

DECKING

STACK OF WASHERS

HEADER

LAG SCREW

JOIST

A stack of washers creates an air space.

❑ If a deck nail pops repeatedly or the wood surrounding the nail has shrunk, pull the old nail and drive
a longer nail into the same hole but at a slight angle, so
it grabs new wood.

❑ If the nail popping is persistent or the deck lumber
is cupping, pull the offending nail and replace it with
a spiral-shank nail or a power-driven deck screw. (Both
of these fasteners are designed to resist pullout.)

Finishes: Try That Penetrating Look

❑ All wooden decks require some sort of protection
for the longest life and best look, but what do you do
if you can't seem to keep a coating on your deck? Don't
use paint, an opaque stain, varnish, or any coating that
forms a film on top of the wood. Although these films
are good protectors, they're not flexible enough to prevent cracking under the substantial expansion and con-
traction cycles of wood in an outdoor deck. Eventually,
water will get underneath them and cause peeling. Instead, use a penetrating finish—typically a semitrans-
parent stain or another, similar product made for this
purpose. These stains do not have the protective qual-
ities of opaque stains or paints (and have to be re-
newed more frequently), but they soak into the wood
rather than lying on top and thus are less liable to
crack.

CARS AND OTHER VEHICLES
A Brief Course in Driver's Ed

FUEL EFFICIENCY

When Miles Don't Bring Smiles

❏ If you think you should be getting better fuel mileage on a long trip, consider improving the aerodynamics of your auto by giving it a bath and a wax job. Surface dirt on the body can increase drag and cost you in gas and ease of driving.

❏ Switching to radial tires that meet the manufacturer's specifications also will improve fuel economy.

Pick Up the Efficiency of Your Pickup

❏ If you'd like to improve the fuel mileage you're getting with an open-bed pickup truck, try reducing its wind resistance by opening or removing the tailgate. Especially when there's no cover for the bed, this upright body part creates a significant barrier to moving air. If you are carrying articles in the bed, switch to a plastic open-mesh gate with holes that allow air movement through it. This is most appropriate, of course, when you're carrying articles that are large but relatively lightweight—not items that might break right through the mesh and fall onto the highway.

LOCKS AND KEYS

Hide, Don't Seek

❏ There are few thing more embarassing or frustrating than locking yourself out of your car. If you are prone to lockouts, it's wise to make a copy of your car door key and hide it someplace accessible on the vehicle. (Be sure you test the duplicate on the car before you leave the locksmith or store the key.) One possibility is to stash the key behind an easy-to-remove lens cover for a signal light. Although you may need to find a screwdriver or knife to remove the cover in an emergency, it will be much easier to break into the light cover than the passenger compartment.

For Door Locks That Don't

❏ If you have a door or column lock that sticks, treat it with a dry lubricant such as powdered graphite or another product made for this purpose. Follow the instructions on the container. Sometimes the dry lubricant comes in a little syringelike vial; other times it's in an aerosol can with a thin plastic tube or nozzle. Never lubricate the lock cylinder with a wet lubricant such as penetrating oil or grease. These liquids attract and retain dirt and metal filings that will ultimately foul the moving parts of the lock.

WINDSHIELDS AND WIPERS

Cut the Fog

❏ What's the best switch to hit on your dashboard when the windshield fogs up? Defrosters that operate off the heater are OK, but they do little more than warm up the moisture. Instead, run the air conditioner on Max A/C or Recirculating to remove moisture from inside the car. The air conditioner actually draws moisture out of the car and works with nearly twice the effect of the defroster. When you're trying to

---

The Princess of Grease

Because she wanted to make a contribution to the war effort, Britain's Queen Elizabeth II (then Princess Elizabeth) joined the Auxiliary Territorial Service in 1944—as a mechanic. Although she couldn't drive at the time and had to be picked up for duty every morning by her commander, the 18-year-old princess seemed pretty comfortable in greasy overalls. She learned to drive military vehicles and to strip and repair engines of all types. Although it's unlikely that she has needed to drive a jeep or a tank in all the years since, and she certainly hasn't had the opportunity to change the oil or replace the spark plugs in a vehicle, her reputation in Britain is certainly not hurt by the fact that she's known as the queen who was not afraid to get her hands dirty.

---

clear the windshield, avoid the Normal setting on the air conditioner—it brings in air from outside, whereas Max A/C or Recirculating recycles the inside air for greater effect.

Bubble Away Those Bugs

❑ Dead bugs can really impair your view through the windshield, and they seldom wash off with rain or an average car bath. But some tough windshield scum respond to a splash of cola. The carbonic acid (which causes the carbonation) actually helps soften scum.

Wipe Out the Problem

❑ When your windshield wipers aren't doing an ideal job, you may be able to improve the situation by wiping the wiper blades. Road dirt, oil, and other matter build up on the blades even when they are not in use,

 PROBLEM PREVENTED

Sure It's Out of Storage, but Can You Drive It?

If you are storing your vehicle for a long period of time, what should you do to make sure you can still drive it when it comes out of hibernation? Here's a checklist.

• Make sure that you keep clean gasoline in the tank, adding some gas line antifreeze in the winter.

• Disconnect the battery and store it in an area where temperatures are stable and above freezing.

• Remove tires and wheels to reduce flat spots, then store the car up on blocks.

• Wax and cover the vehicle with a breathable cover, such as an old bedsheet, rather than using plastic.

• On occasion, run the engine until the vehicle is fully warmed up. This reduces moisture in the tailpipe and muffler. (If the car is stored in a garage, you'll need to open the garage door or otherwise provide adequate ventilation first.)

• Run the air conditioner and then the heater to "exercise" these devices. You'll be warming them up, drying them out, and moving fluids around to maintain the seals.

• Run the lights for a while to avoid a buildup of condensation.

and those substances will prevent the rubber edges from making full contact with the glass.

THE EXTERIOR

Top This: A Quick Fix for Convertible Roofs

❏ You can repair a small hole in a convertible roof with a raft repair kit from a sporting goods store. Following the package directions, work from inside the roof and cut a patch that is at least one inch larger than the hole on all sides.

Ah, the Joys of Road Construction

❏ Scratches from road dirt, stones, and normal wear kill the gloss of an otherwise nice paint job. To remove light scratches, try buffing them out with compound wax—a mixture of automobile wax and a very fine abrasive. If just the top, clear-coat finish layer is affected, buffing with a regular, low-abrasive car wax will usually do the job.

Here's the Pitch

❏ Pine pitch or pollen on a car's exterior is very noticeable and gets harder to remove the longer it stays put. To get rid of it as soon as possible, apply hot water or a hot sponge to the affected area to soften the goo. Then follow up with a bug and tar remover (from an auto parts store) and/or a car wash. A good wax job will help protect the finish once it's clean and will make future cleanups easier.

TIRES AND WHEELS

Heads, Your Tread Is Dead

❏ How can you tell if a flat tire is worth repairing? Place the edge of a penny in the innermost tread in the tire; if you can see the top of Abraham Lincoln's head, your tread is dead.

The Bugs in Lug Nuts

❏ Who hasn't had occasional trouble loosening the lug nuts on a vehicle's wheels? Service garages use air wrenches that can really torque the nuts on tight if the mechanic isn't careful, and ordinary changes in weather can add a little corrosion that will seize the nuts in a season. Your best ally in getting nuts to budge is a good lug wrench. Put out to pasture the L-shaped tire iron that came with the vehicle and invest in a four-way, X-shaped lug wrench. Make sure the wrench socket fits snugly on the lugs; a sloppy fit encourages stripping. Although you'll put only one of the sockets to use (mark the correct socket with paint for easy identification), the cross arms will give you two-fisted leverage for "breaking" frozen nuts (versus one hand for a tire iron). Spend some money for a quality wrench that is forged at the intersection of the bars. Wrenches that are merely welded into an X will tend to break on a tough nut.

❏ When you're ready to remove the lug nuts on a wheel, how do you keep the wheel as stationary as possible? Instead of beginning by jacking up the car, "break" all four or five nuts while the wheel is on the ground (and the vehicle is properly chocked, of course). That way, you'll have the inertia of the vehicle to hold the wheel steady, not just a brake, and you'll get the maximum effect of your muscles.

OVERHEATING

Why You Might Want to Turn on the Heater in August

❏ If your vehicle is overheating or approaching the operating temperature limit, you run the risk of warping or fusing some of the critical parts of your engine. How do you prevent such serious damage? Turn on your heater as soon as you see the temperature start to creep up. Activating the heater will transfer heat away from the engine and give the cooling system an additional "radiator" to help with its job. (This is strictly a short-term fix to get the heat back to normal while you sit out a traffic jam. Should your car overheat in the course of normal driving, stop immediately and call a garage.)

It Runs Just Fine in January...

❑ What do you do about an older vehicle that tends to run on the hot side in warm weather but otherwise exhibits no gross problems with the cooling system or engine? Try removing the cooling system thermostat. It's typically bolted under a casting on the engine block, right where the top hose from the radiator is connected. This device is simply a valve that closes off the radiator to coolant flow until the coolant is good and hot—a strategy intended to speed warm-up of the engine and the heater in cold weather. You really don't need this advantage in the summer, however, and circulating coolant through the radiator at all times often helps the engine keep its cool.

Is the Temperature Rising?

Overheating can be a sign of serious problems—or it can mean that you need only to apply a quick fix. Once your overheated engine's temperature is back to normal, it's important to establish right away what caused it to overheat in the first place and to prevent that from happening again. Here's a basic list of components to check.

• **Coolant levels.** Open the radiator when it's cold and make sure it's full. Inspect for signs of leaks in the radiator, at hose ends, and under the water pump.

• **Oil/lubricant levels.** Crankcase oil cools and lubricates the engine, and when the oil is low, it can't do these jobs effectively. Use the dipstick to check your engine oil. If your vehicle has an automatic transmission, use the dipstick to check the level of the automatic transmission fluid as well.

• **Radiator debris.** Paper, plastic, or a massive number of bugs on the front of the radiator will block airflow and reduce the radiator's ability to transfer heat. If you find any of these, clean them off.

• **Thermostat.** If the thermostat is stuck or out of calibration, it won't open to allow for maximum engine cooling. Once you unbolt it from the cooling system, you can check the thermostat's performance by boiling it in a pan of water on the stove. Place a candy thermometer in the pan with the thermostat. When the water reaches the temperature stamped on the thermostat body (usually 160° to 180°F), the thermostat should open.

HEATERS AND AIR CONDITIONERS

Take the Chill Off

❏ If your car's heater never seems to get above luke-warm in the middle of February, try replacing the cooling system thermostat with one calibrated for a higher temperature. You can do this yourself or hire a mechanic for the job. You only need to go up five or ten degrees (say, 160° to 165°F) to improve performance.

DOLLAR STRETCHER

Upholstery: Eliminate the Age Lines

Leather vehicle upholstery takes a lot of wear and tear, and it's prone to cracking and fading as it ages. Commercial upholstery restoratives can be expensive, but you can rescue older upholstery by applying ordinary baby oil. Not only is it cheaper and more effective than many commercial upholstery products, but it also allows the material to breathe, rather than holding in the moisture that aids deterioration. Apply a light coat to the upholstery so that the oil will soak into the leather and not come off on clothing.

You're Getting Warmer . . .

❏ If a period of abnormally frigid weather is keeping your car too cold for comfort, you may be able to solve the problem by blocking off part of the radiator. Take some heavy corrugated cardboard and slip it between the front grille and the radiator. Try blocking about half of the radiator at first, then add more coverage if needed to keep the car warmer. Partially blocking the radiator means that less air will pass through it to remove heat, and it will stay warmer.

TOUGH STARTS

*Stay in Charge
of the Charging System*

❏ When you have trouble cranking your car or truck, it may be the charging system—not the battery—that is failing to do its job. This equipment (the alternator, the regulator, and their associated components) are likely culprits if the battery is relatively new and in good condition, but how can you confirm your suspicions? Test the output of the charging system with a simple voltmeter from a good hardware or electronics store. With the engine and all the accessories turned off and the voltmeter (or simi-

Get a Jump on a Dead Battery

Many times, a car with a dead battery can be started with jumper cables and another vehicle. However, it's important to jump-start a car correctly, or you risk a dangerous discharge of electricity or even an explosion. Before attaching the jumper cables to your dead battery, check to see if it's a maintenance-free, permanently sealed battery or one that must be filled periodically with water. If it has screw-on or snap-on caps, it's probably the latter. Remove the caps to vent hydrogen gas from inside the battery. Failing to do so could cause an explosion if either of the batteries sparks during a jump-start.

Turn off all the switches and lights in both cars to reduce the drain on the batteries and prevent possible damage to the electrical systems. Park the vehicles close together, but not touching. Now you're ready to make the connection.

As you connect the cables, be careful not to touch two of the clamps, or a shower of sparks may result. Attach one of the positive clamps of the jumper cables—always the red clamp—to the positive terminal of the dead battery, marked with a plus (+) sign. Attach the other red clip to the positive terminal of the healthy battery. Then attach a black clip to the negative terminal of the good battery, marked with a minus sign (–). Do not attach the other black clip to the dead battery—ground it instead by attaching it to a metal surface on the frame or engine of the car. You can improve these connections by twisting the clamps onto the battery terminals to cut through corrosion that might block the current.

Start the engine on the good car and run it at moderate speed for a few minutes, then try to start the dead car. It may take a few tries. Once the ailing auto is started, let both cars run for a few minutes to charge the dead battery. Remove the cables in the reverse order of how you installed them.

Be sure the second clip of the black cable is grounded.

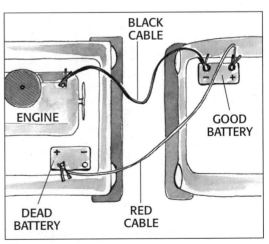

ENGINE

BLACK CABLE

GOOD BATTERY

DEAD BATTERY

RED CABLE

lar test equipment) set to DC volts, measure the voltage across the battery teminals. It should read about 12.6 volts. Then turn on the engine and measure the voltage again. It should be significantly higher—on the order of 14.5 volts—if the charging system is operating correctly and supplying power to the battery. If the meter remains around 12.6 volts or rises to only 13.0 volts or so, you can start looking for problems in the charging system—or ask your mechanic to do so.

Time for a Good Belt

❏ If you have isolated your electrical problem to the charging system, you'll want to make sure the problem isn't something simple before you take your vehicle to a mechanic to determine the specific component that has failed. And exactly how do you do that? Inspect the drive belt to the alternator. If the belt is worn and loose—that is, if it has more than a one-half-inch deflection at its midpoint—it may be slipping. If the al-

Instead of a mechanic, you may need nothing more than a new drive belt. Check the current one. If it's worn and loose, replace it.

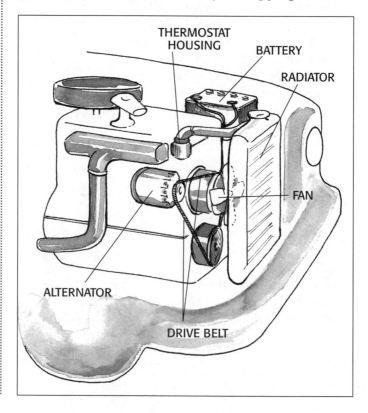

THERMOSTAT
HOUSING

BATTERY

RADIATOR

FAN

ALTERNATOR

DRIVE BELT

ternator is not getting maximum power from the engine, it cannot deliver maximum power to the battery. Tighten or replace the belt, and you may find the problem solved.

The Power of Good Connections

❏ How do you determine what else could be a simple cause of problems in starting your vehicle? Inspect the electrical connection between the battery posts and the cable terminals. Grossly corroded terminals are an obvious clue to a potentially bad connection, but even terminals that appear relatively clean can have imperfect electrical integrity. You can't really tell the quality of a connection by looking at it, but you can by testing it with a voltmeter from a hardware or electronics store. Set the meter to DC volts and, while the engine is running, place one probe on the battery posts and the other on the cable terminal clamped to it. (Really dig the probes into the lead so you get a solid contact with metal, not surface oxide.) If there is a good electrical connection between the post and the terminal, the meter should not move. If you get a voltage reading of any sort—even a fraction of a volt—that means the connection is imperfect and the electricity is seeking a path of lesser resistance through the meter. Clean the post and terminal to solve the problem, then repeat the test on the other side of the battery.

Batteries: Hold That Charge!

❏ Should you determine that your charging system is OK and it appears that the battery isn't holding a charge, what can you do before running to the auto parts store for a new battery? If you have an owner-maintainable battery (one with removable vent covers), inspect the fluid level in the battery. If the plates are not covered with fluid, the battery cannot take or deliver power to its full capacity. Remove the vent covers and fill the cells with distilled water up to the bottom of the cell tubes. Follow up by charging the battery with a charger or a long daytime drive, then see if it holds an improved charge.

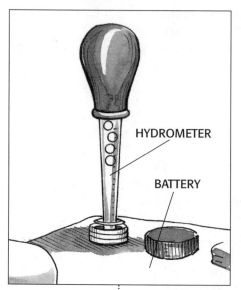

HYDROMETER

BATTERY

It looks like a turkey baster, but it's really a battery hydrometer. Use it to check the individual cells of your car's battery.

❏ You can test each cell of a battery with a battery hydrometer (available at auto parts stores). This device looks like a turkey baster and measures the specific gravity (and thus the level of charge) of the cell fluid. Follow the instructions that come with the battery hydrometer. If the battery has a cat's-eye charge indicator, blue or green means the cells are good; clear or yellow means the battery needs to be replaced.

False Starts

❏ Sometimes when a car has been parked outside for several days in bad weather, it won't start. This may be a classic instance of a high-voltage ignition problem. The ignition system has gotten damp, preventing the car from starting. In such a case, try spraying the cables and distributor with a water-displacing product, such as silicone spray or WD-40. This will drive off the moisture that is shorting out the ignition and keeping the spark plugs from firing. The car should start right up.

PARKING

Garage Parking: Know When to Stop

❏ Sometimes there's just barely enough room for the car in your crowded garage, and it can be tough to gauge when you've pulled in far enough without actually running into the back wall. Here's a simple solution. With a friend or family member guiding you, pull the car into exactly the position where you want to park it each time. Tie a piece of heavy-duty string around a tennis ball, then attach the end of the string to the roof of the garage so that the ball just hits the windshield of the car. Next time you pull into the garage, you'll know to stop when the ball hits the windshield.

At Your Leisure

Even when I'm not at work, I generally spend a lot of time thinking of good ways to solve problems.

Back before the Second World War, five friends and I got together and formed a model railroad club. Our trains weren't the toys you see today, but scale models that we built and ran ourselves. We rented part of an old barn—a space 80 feet long and 20 feet wide, with a 16-foot-high ceiling—and laid our tracks down there. Then I built a scaled-down switch tower, complete with small windows, a freight bell, and a dispatch panel that I could use to control the trains. I bought a good transformer to operate the thing and put the trans-

former out of the way underneath the panel. I had a lot of fun with that tower. At my best, I could sit there and run two trains of 20 cars each at the same time.

After World War II started and our club broke up, I went to the man who owned the building and sold him what was left of our setup for his kids. But I didn't forget about those trains or that transformer. When the kids had grown and taken what they wanted from the barn, their father told me I could have whatever was left. So I went up inside that tower, and, sure enough, the transformer was still there. I took it home with me and, years later, traded it for a new wet grinding wheel, which I have to this day.

From solving one problem—finding a power source for that railroad—I ended up with years of entertainment and was able to squeeze out some additional value as well. That's what problem solving is all about.

The next three chapters concentrate on problems that crop up just when you're trying to enjoy yourself. Turn to "Recreation and Hobbies" for ingenious ways to liven up dull camping food— and for a simple but effective way to thread even the tiniest of those pesky sewing needles. "Pets" tells you how to stop a dog from digging or a cat from jumping on counters, and it offers a no-fuss way to change the cat's litter box. And in "Travel," you'll find bright ideas for keeping your cool on long car trips, cutting vacation expenses, and making quick and easy emergency repairs. All three chapters are intended to keep minor annoyances from spoiling your fun.

RECREATION AND HOBBIES
Keeping Fit and Having Fun

HIKING AND CAMPING

Spice Up Your Meals

❏ Camping meals are notoriously bland, but you can perk things up with a simple spice kit that you keep with your camping gear. Wash empty photographic film canisters, then label them for salt, pepper, basil, ginger, curry powder, thyme, and rosemary. Fill each canister with the appropriate seasoning and throw the batch in a sealable plastic bag.

Grin and Bear It

❏ Bears are fun to see at campgrounds, but they can be scary visitors. They know food is available, and they are remarkably adept at getting it. To deter them, keep all food in the bear-proof lockers provided at campgrounds in bear country, or in the *trunk,* not the passenger compartment, of your car. Bears can identify food by sight as well as smell and may smash a window to get at it.

❏ No matter how sturdy it seems, don't trust an ice chest to keep your food safe; bears can easily open the latch. Also, don't leave any food scraps or wrappers around the campsite. Dispose of them right away in bear-proof trash cans.

Backpackers Prefer to Dine Alone

❏ When you're backpacking in bear country, neither a car trunk nor a special locker is likely to be available.

So how do you hang on to your food? By hanging it up. Almost no tree is entirely bear-proof. Some bears have even been known to climb a tree to the branch where food is hung, jump up and down to break the branch, and then fall to the ground with their dinner. A better solution is to hang the food from the top of a large boulder—the more difficult the climb the better, but make sure you can get down! Hang the food at the end of a six-foot stick, anchored on the boulder with rocks. As long as the bear can't reach the food bag from the ground, it's probably safe.

Foods to Pack When the Nearest McDonald's Is 50 Miles Away

Whether it's for a weekend car camping trip or a ten-day excursion into the backcountry, planning your food may take longer than planning your route! Here are some thrifty, tasty, space- and weight-saving ideas for your next trip.

• **Gorp or trail mix.** Make your own instead of buying the pre-packaged versions. Ounce for ounce, it's less expensive to buy the ingredients—raisins, dried apricots, seeds, nuts, maybe even some M&M's—separately.

• **Very thin pasta.** Lightweight and fast cooking, it's the perfect camping food.

• **Instant soup mixes** such as leek or tomato. They make terrific pasta sauces.

• **Homemade spice mixes.** Just because you're camping doesn't mean you have to eat blandly. Try a combination of garlic salt, Parmesan cheese, dried basil, and dried oregano to add an Italian accent to rice or noodles; cinnamon and brown sugar for bread and cereal; or cumin and chili powder for bean dishes. Pack the mixtures in small, clearly labeled spice bottles and add them to your campsite concoctions.

• **Bacon bits.** They weigh almost nothing, and they add crunch and flavor to almost any dish.

• **Chocolate.** It's a great high-energy snack, and if you buy M&M's, they'll melt in your mouth, not in your . . . well, you know.

• **Meat or chicken.** Freeze it well—until it's rock hard. It should thaw by the time you're ready for that first night's dinner.

• **Don't forget the marshmallows.** They're lightweight and fun to cook.

Bad Altitude

❑ Hiking in the high mountains provides some of life's greatest pleasures, but the thin air can be debilitating. When people first exercise in the mountains, they may feel the effects of altitude as low as 5,000 feet, and altitude sickness can be dangerous even at elevations of 8,000 feet. To ward off altitude sickness, travel to the base of the mountains you'll be exploring a day or two before you venture to higher elevations. Drink lots of fluids (at least two to three quarts of water a day); eat light, high-carbohydrate foods (bagels, crackers, cereal, or pasta with a simple, light sauce); and avoid tobacco, alcohol, and caffeine.

❑ Symptoms of altitude sickness include headache, dizziness, fatigue, dry cough, lack of appetite, and nausea. According to some experts, aspirin or acetaminophen (Tylenol, Anacin-3, and others) will help the headache. Avoid heavy exertion, but try engaging in light activity rather than giving in to complete rest or sleep. Symptoms should disappear within a day or two but may reappear as you move higher.

Time for a Downturn

❑ Unsteady walking, stumbling, drowsiness, apathy, or a bubbling or cracking sound from the lungs, in combination with the other symptoms of altitude sickness, are signs of potentially much more serious illnesses. In such cases, the only sure remedy is a prompt descent to lower elevations.

Holey Nets

❑ The fragile mosquito netting of tents often develops holes that could let nasty critters in. Fill these tears by putting a tab of masking tape on one side of the hole

DOLLAR STRETCHER

Better Bottles for Hikers

An expensive canteen or water bottle isn't necessary for hiking or camping. Plastic one- or two-liter soda or water bottles make lightweight and virtually indestructible carriers. For a larger water carrier, save the plastic and foil lining from boxed wine. These containers are very strong and refillable, and the foil lining helps keep liquids cool. Of course, you have to drink that wine first!

and dabbing some Seam Grip, a sealant available at most camping stores, on the other side. Once the Seam Grip is dry, pull off the backing tape. If the hole is a small one—say, up to one-quarter inch in diameter—this can be a permanent fix.

⏰ TIME SAVER

The Campfire Gourmet

Most folks don't associate camping trips with four-star dining. After all, time is generally short after a full day of outdoor activity, and who has the energy for anything but the most basic food preparation? The solution is to plan. If you're tired of the same old flavorless camping fare, liven things up a bit by preparing some ingredients at home before you head for the campsite. Try these camp food enhancers.

• Mix and pack tasty sauces or pesto for pasta.

• Dice fresh vegetables for a stir-fry or a side dish.

• Marinate meats or fish for a grill.

• Premix the dry ingredients of your favorite pancake recipe instead of packing a store-bought mix. At the campsite, just add the liquid, and you'll have instant flapjacks.

• Soak beans or lentils so they'll cook faster at camp.

• Precook potatoes or rice so all you'll have to do is heat them through.

❏ If the hole is a large one, the Seam Grip is still a good temporary solution, but you'll eventually need a sewn patch for the netting. Contact the tent's manufacturer to find out whether the company can repair the tent. (You'll probably have to send it by mail and pay a small fee.) Or ask your local sporting goods dealer to recommend a sewer in your area who specializes in outdoor equipment.

Down in the Dumps

❏ Even a small tear in a down sleeping bag or parka can lead to a virtual snowstorm of feathers. The best temporary fix uses Kenyon K Tape, an adhesive-backed nylon that comes in many colors. Clean the damaged fabric (use a swab with rubbing alcohol if you have it) and let it dry, then apply the tape, being sure to round the edges of the patch. To make sure that you always have repair tape when you need it, put a square of Kenyon K Tape in the pocket of your coat or vest and another in the stuff sack of your sleeping bag. The tape comes in both squares and rolls, and it has a backing paper so it won't stick to itself in your pocket.

❏ Since the Kenyon K Tape is a short-term solution, be sure to have the tear professionally sewn when you return from your trip. This is a job for the manufacturer or for a sewer who specializes in outdoor equipment. Ask your local outdoor-equipment store to recommend someone near you or to suggest a mail-order source for this kind of work.

Tents Don't Do Well on the Spin Cycle

❏ Washing machines can cause serious damage to camping equipment. So how *do* you clean a tent? The best way is to set it up in the backyard, shake or sweep out any loose dirt and sticks inside, and spray it with a garden hose to clean out zippers, netting, and hard-to-reach corners. Using a soft brush, scrub the tent with mild laundry detergent (such as Ivory Snow) and water. Let the tent air-dry completely before putting it away. Never leave a wet tent in its storage sack, or it will mildew.

Add Some Zip to Your Zippers

❏ Zippers on tents or sleeping bags get balky when they get dirty. A good field solution is to rub the zipper with a bar of soap or a candle. This should get it moving until you can clean it properly at home with a high-pressure blast from the garden hose.

Down and Dirty

❏ Sleeping bags lose some of their warmth when their insulation absorbs dirt and body oils. But washing a bag breaks down some of its insulating fibers. What to do? Wash a sleeping bag only if it becomes uncomfortably dirty or when the insulation is noticeably losing some of its loft—and then wash it very carefully, either by hand in the bathtub or in a front-loading

DOLLAR STRETCHER

Cheap Eats

Freeze-dried or dehydrated backpacking meals are lightweight, but they're also very expensive. With some imagination and careful shopping at the local supermarket, you can cut the cost of meals dramatically without adding much weight to your pack. Supplement those lightweight rice or pasta mixes with canned chicken or shredded beef jerky. Or pick up dried peas, carrots, and other vegetables at your local supermarket or health food store. Add these to powdered soups, and you have a meal.

commercial machine. Use a gentle soap, such as Ivory Snow, for a synthetic-insulation bag. For a down-filled bag, use a special soap formulated for down (available at outdoor-equipment stores). Soak the bag first, then wash it once with cold water on the machine's gentle cycle. Run it through a second cycle, this time with no soap. Remove the bag from the tub or machine, lifting it carefully from underneath to avoid ripping out the sewn baffles inside the bag that distribute the insulation.

✔ PROBLEM PREVENTED

Liner Notes
(for sleeping bags)

Frequent washing isn't good for your sleeping bag, but sleeping in a dirty bag isn't particularly good for you. Keep your sleeping bag clean and comfortable with a bag liner. A twin-size bedsheet, folded in half and sewn at the bottom and three-quarters of the way up the side, makes a simple liner that can be washed after every camping trip. Use the liner by itself on very warm nights or when you're staying at a hostel or hut that provides blankets. Some hostels require such liners.

A quick do-it-yourself sleeping bag liner.

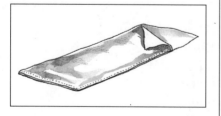

Dry Ideas

❏ Air-dry a sleeping bag by hanging it lengthwise on a clothesline with the zipper completely open. Or use the largest commercial dryer you can find and turn it to its lowest temperature setting. Don't let the nylon fabric get hot to the touch. Take the bag out of the dryer now and then during the drying process and de-clump the insulation. The drying may take as long as two hours.

❏ Never dry-clean a sleeping bag. The solvents used by dry cleaners can damage the insulation.

Impure Thoughts

❏ If you're not careful with your water purifier after a camping or hiking trip, potentially dangerous bacteria may thrive in the few drops of water left inside. How do you kill the hangers-on? Flush the filter with a mild bleach solution after every trip. Make a solution of 1 to 2 teaspoons bleach and 1 quart water. Pump it through the filter, then continue to pump the filter until all the solution is gone.

BOATING

If It's Not an Underwater Camera . . .

❏ Valuables such as cameras and binoculars are vulnerable to water damage on any boating trip. To keep them safe, put them in a "dry bag" like those typically used by kayakers and canoeists. These vinyl bags are available at canoeing and marine shops in many sizes. They seal with a twist that prevents water from getting in. As long as they are sealed and not loaded with extremely heavy gear, most will float if they fall overboard.

Look Ahead

❏ If you start to feel queasy on a boat, stay on deck, if possible. Stand near the center of the boat, where there's less pitching motion, and keep your gaze fixed on the horizon, not on the deck.

Tidy Boats

❏ Steel fittings, and even stainless steel parts, eventually corrode in salty air and water, and then they bleed orange on boat decks and in cabins. You can clean these stains off with any household cleaner, but the most effective ones—and the least abrasive to deck surfaces—are toilet bowl cleaners or cleaners designed for hard water, such as Vanish or Lime-A-Way. Follow the instructions on the bottle.

BICYCLES

April Showers Bring Rusty Bikes

❏ Riding a bike through puddles or streams can get water in the brake or gear cables, leading to rusty

PROBLEM PREVENTED

Bright Lights

The last thing you want when camping out on a dark night is for your flashlight to go dead. To prevent a scary situation, always remove a battery or reverse the batteries inside your flashlight when it's not in use. In addition, tape a spare bulb inside the flashlight housing (most have room behind the reflector). In cold weather, keep the flashlight warm by carrying it inside your coat. Warm batteries last longer and produce much more power than cold ones.

cables that may jam. You can't always stay out of the water, so if you suspect that these parts have gotten wet, stop rust before it starts. Grease the cables with cable lubricant (available at bike shops). Using the applicator on the bottle, put a couple of squirts into the upper cable housings and work the brake and gear levers a few times.

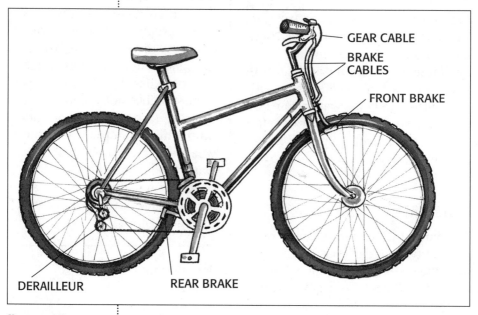

GEAR CABLE

BRAKE
CABLES

FRONT BRAKE

DERAILLEUR

REAR BRAKE

Keep your bike away from jam sessions by squirting cable lubricant into the upper cable housings anytime those parts may have gotten wet.

Tire Trouble

❏ A flat tire will ruin your bike ride if you're not prepared. You can handle the problem easily, however, if you have the foresight to carry a standard patch kit. (Available from any bike shop, these weigh only a few ounces and can salvage a potentially disastrous situation.) If your bike's wheels don't have quick-release levers, you'll also need a wrench. Begin by removing the wheel and releasing any remaining air in the tire. If the tire is difficult to remove from its rim, use smooth plastic or metal tire irons to work it off; never use a screwdriver or other sharp tool, or you risk further damage to the tube. Locate the puncture, then use the sandpaper or abrasive in the patch kit to roughen the surface of the tube in that area. Apply a thin film of adhesive, wait a couple of minutes for the adhesive to dry, and firmly apply the patch. Now you're ready to replace the tube—almost. First, inspect the inside of the tire carefully, looking for a thorn or shard of glass that might have caused the original problem and could repuncture the tube. Then sprinkle some talcum powder in the tire to act as a lubricant and to help the tube fit properly in the tire. *Now* replace the tube.

Bubble, Bubble—There's the Trouble

❑ If the puncture in a tube is tough to locate, try immersing the lightly inflated tube in water. Bubbles will pinpoint the hole.

SKIING

Stymie the Ski Bums

❑ It's not particularly difficult for anyone to walk off with your valuable ski equipment while you're taking a break from the trails. A simple way to deter ski thieves is to separate your skis when you go into the lodge. Put one ski and pole on a rack at the front of the lodge and the other ski and pole around the corner. If possible, keep one half of the pair in sight while you rest and eat.

Time to Rewax

❑ Waxing cross-country skis is tricky, and conditions often change during the day, requiring you to rewax. If your skis seem to be slipping, try applying a warmer "kicker" wax to the sections under your feet and a bit beyond—the swath of wax on each ski should be about two to three feet. If you're sticking, scrape the bottoms of your skis to remove any ice and excess wax, then apply a wax for cooler temperatures.

✔ **PROBLEM PREVENTED**

Snakebit

It's tempting to lower the tire pressure on a mountain bike for trail riding because doing so can improve your traction. If you let too much air out, however, you can get snakebites—twin puncture marks like those made by the fangs of a rattlesnake—when the underinflated tube pinches on the rim as the bike goes over a sharp bump. To prevent this, keep the tire pressure near its prescribed level.

When Groovy Isn't Good

❏ Unless you always ski on perfect snow, you'll occasionally hit rocks that leave small grooves or dents in the bottoms of your skis. Fix these with P-Tex "candles." (About the size of licorice sticks, these candles are available from any good ski shop.) Place the damaged ski, bottom up, on some old newspaper. Hold a flame to one end of the candle for a few seconds until it begins to burn on its own. Aim the candle so that it drips into the groove or hole in your ski and the plastic fills every crevice. Wait until the P-Tex on your ski is cool to the touch, then use a metal scraper to remove the excess plastic and smooth the surface.

Snowy Shoes

❏ In warm conditions, snow frequently balls under ski boots or ices up on bindings, making it difficult to get in and out of the bindings—and possibly preventing them from releasing properly. To prevent this, spray a light coat of silicone lubricant (available at hardware and automotive stores) on the skis and bindings at the start of the day.

Backcountry Fixes

❏ If a ski pole breaks when you're out on the trail, splint it with a green stick and duct tape or hose clamps.

❏ For emergency repair of a broken ski tip, try taping or clamping a metal wax scraper across the break. You won't set any speed records skiing out, but at least you'll get home.

HOME EXERCISE

Space Invaders

❏ Home exercise equipment is expensive and takes up room in the house. But you don't need fancy equipment to get a workout. Stairs are the place to do calf raises. A couch will anchor your feet for crunches or sit-ups.

You can do pull-ups on sturdy door or window frames. Any carpeted area is suitable for stretching or light aerobics. Light hand weights can be used anywhere, and you can use a loop of surgical tubing attached to a doorknob for stretching and strength building. (You can get surgical tubing—it may be labeled as rubber tubing or rubber hose—at a hardware store. Look for the kind of hose that's especially stretchy, like a rubber band.)

Follow the Children

❑ If you're looking for a low-cost alternative to home exercise equipment, head to the neighborhood playground. With a little imagination, you can find all sorts of ways to use children's playground equipment for an adult workout. For starters, try pull-ups on the top bar of a swing set, climbing on the underside of a slide (the back of the surface a child would slide on), or swinging across the monkey bars. Walk briskly or jog to get to the playground and back, and you'll get in an aerobic workout, too!

OTHER RECREATION EQUIPMENT

"Leaky" Gore-Tex

❑ After a couple of years of use, Gore-Tex garments may appear to leak. The outer layer of such clothing gets saturated when its water-repellent treatment ages, and this can lead to condensation inside the garment. Properly washing and heating the garment may restore its water repellency. Use a washing machine on the gentle cycle and a mild powdered laundry detergent (such as Ivory Snow). Rinse twice, then dry the garment in a clothes dryer on the lowest setting. The heat is neces-

---

✔ PROBLEM PREVENTED

Seams Good to Me

Many "waterproof" garments and tents are not truly waterproof when they come from the store, and you can spend some wet nights under the stars if you don't do something about that. Unless the needle holes in the seams are covered with one-inch-wide nylon tape—easily visible on the inner layer—you need to do the job yourself. Seam Grip, a sealant that comes in a tube and is available at most outdoor-equipment stores, is the right stuff for this task. Place a thin layer of Seam Grip on the inside of the seams, and you'll plug any gaps.

Other Recreation Equipment

sary, but you must keep an eye on things. Don't let the garment stay in the dryer too long or get too hot, or you're likely to harm the fabric.

❑ Don't clean a Gore-Tex garment with a liquid detergent that isn't made for Gore-Tex. The liquid's surfactants will prevent water from beading up and rolling off the garment, as intended. And never dry-clean a Gore-Tex garment. The chemicals will strip off the water-repellent treatment.

Hard Balls, Soft Gloves

❑ New baseball and softball gloves usually come from the store as stiff as boards—definitely not ideal for catching a hard line drive. To break in a glove, rub the leather thoroughly with several thin coats of neat's-foot oil (available at shoe stores) or special glove oil from a sporting goods shop. Then put a ball in the pocket of the glove, wrap the glove with rubber bands or string to hold it shut, and put it under a mattress for a day. This will help shape the pocket into a "vacuum cleaner" for ground balls. Whenever the leather appears stiff or dry, just reoil the glove.

INDOOR GARDENING

Who's Gonna Water Us?

❑ Keeping your plants watered when you're away from home can be a real challenge, especially if there's no one else around to care for them. One way to make sure your plants get enough water when you're gone for two or three days is to soak some sphagnum moss with water and place it on the soil in the pot. You can buy the moss from any plant store or florist.

❑ Alternatively, if the plants are small, water them well. Then place a large, clear food storage bag over each and poke several holes in the bag. Secure the bag around the pot with some twine or rubber bands. You may need to insert some sticks around the plant to keep the bag from touching the greenery. The bag acts

Indestructible Houseplants

I s your thumb decidedly not green? Do plants visibly recoil when you walk into a room? Fear not, there are some even you (probably) won't kill. Following is a list of some of the easiest plants to grow, along with their basic requirements. The easiest way to feed them is with plant spikes—fertilizer sticks that you insert into the soil and that release food automatically when you water the plants. You can find these spikes at flower shops, garden centers, and many grocery stores. If you prefer to use liquid or powdered plant food, follow the directions here.

PLANT	LIGHT REQUIREMENTS	WHEN AND HOW TO WATER	FOOD REQUIREMENTS
Aloe vera	Medium to high	Water well, then let soil dry out	Twice a year, in April and July
Aluminum plant	Medium	Frequently; keep soil moist but not soaked; mist regularly	Every two weeks during spring and summer
Cacti	High	Occasionally in spring and summer; tapering off in fall; rarely, if ever, in winter	Every three to four months
Cast-iron plant	Low to medium	Occasionally, then let soil dry out	Twice a month in spring and summer
Grape ivy	Medium	Water well, then let soil become barely moist	Every six months
Rubber plant	Medium	Water well, then let soil dry out	Every two weeks in summer
Spider plant	Medium to high	Frequently; keep soil moist but not soaked	Every two weeks in summer

as a sort of greenhouse, sealing in moisture. Leave the plants in an area where they will receive less than their usual amount of light. This method is best if you're going away for less than three weeks.

❏ For a larger plant, water thoroughly, enclose the whole thing in the ventilated bag, and seal the bag around the plant's stem.

Fear of the Dark

❏ Wondering if there's enough daylight in a particular spot to support a houseplant? Here's a rule of thumb: If there's enough light to read by, there's probably enough light for a plant.

❏ Sometimes the rooms where you'd most like to keep plants (the living room or dining room, for instance) don't get enough light to grow anything well. But that doesn't mean a plant can't drop by for an occasional visit. Place a healthy plant in the dark area until it begins to droop. That will happen in about a month. When it does, return the plant to its original location and move another plant to the unlit spot. Visitation rites like this can add a touch of greenery to even the darkest rooms.

❏ If the amount of available light in a particular room is borderline for growing plants, make the most of what you have. Try placing a mirror behind a poorly lit plant for a few hours each day. Or simply hang a decorative mirror behind the plant. The mirror will reflect the light in the room back onto the plant.

It's Not the Heat . . .

❏ It's difficult to keep plants with high humidity requirements in your home, especially if you live in a dry climate, but one approach is to purchase a window box drainage tray (available at any garden center or discount store with a garden department) that is large enough to accommodate all the plants. Pour in two to three inches of gravel or pebbles, then add enough water to almost, but not quite, cover the drainage material. Place

Place gravel in the drainage tray and add water. Insert house-plants in their pots, and you have a great way to keep your plants supplied with all the moisture they need.

the plants—in their pots but without the saucers—on top of the gravel or pebbles, making sure they are not sitting in water. The water will evaporate, ensuring that the plants will always have enough moisture.

I Don't Want a Bath

❏ Some plants, like African violets, form wet, brownish spots anytime water touches their leaves. That makes watering a bit tricky, so how do you manage it? The best way is to pour water into the saucer and let it sit for 15 to 20 minutes. Make sure to pour the excess water out, because sitting in water encourages root rot. Use only tepid water; cold water will turn the leaves brown.

Stop Buggin' Me!

❏ When you notice bugs on your houseplant, don't reach for the commercial pesticide right away. Spray the plant with some ice water (or about 1 quart cold water mixed with 1 to 2 tablespoons skim milk or beer). Sometimes that's enough to get rid of the bugs. Repeat the spraying every three or four days.

❏ Here's another home remedy for pests. At the first sign of bugs, crush a clove of garlic and put it in one-half gallon of water. Let the water sit for two (or more) hours, then strain out the garlic. Put the garlic water into a spray bottle and mist the plants every three or four days.

Indoor Gardening   197

KNITTING AND CROCHETING

Get Those Needles out of the Haystack

❏ If you have a large collection of knitting needles, it's a challenge to keep them all organized and accessible. Store-bought needle cases can be expensive. An easy alternative is to stitch up your own case. Start with a piece of felt that measures approximately 18 by 33 inches. Position the fabric with the 18-inch side facing you, then fold the right side of the fabric back on itself to create a pocket that's 14 inches deep. Pin or baste the fabric in place, then use a decorative stitch

For a needle case that's a cinch to make, fold the fabric back on itself to create a pocket (A), then use a decorative machine stitch to divide that into smaller pockets. Fold the top flap over the needles to keep them in place (B), then roll the whole thing up (C) and tie with a ribbon.

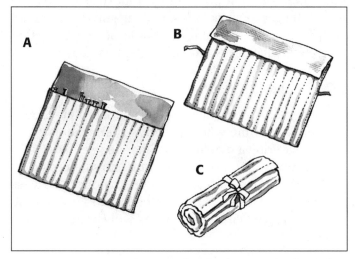

on your sewing machine to divide that one long pocket into a series of narrower ones, each approximately 1 inch wide. Insert a pair of needles in each pocket, fold the top flap down over the needles to keep them from slipping out of place, roll up the entire case, and tie it shut with a pretty ribbon. (To hold shorter needles, follow the same procedure on a smaller scale.) The next time you're looking for the right size needles, you'll be able to find them in a jiffy.

Here's the Hook

❏ If you store your crochet supplies in drawers, one good way to keep them organized is with utensil trays from a discount store or kitchen supply store. A wide variety of sizes and shapes are available, and you'll have spots for all your crochet hooks as well as a pair of scissors.

Plastic Needles: Avoid Time Warps

❏ Plastic knitting needles are extremely heat sensitive and warp easily—which can be a real problem if you like to take your projects with you when you travel. Leaving plastic needles in a hot car can lead to disaster. Here's the solution. Invest in an inexpensive picnic cooler. Keep it in the trunk—filled with ice, of course—and leave your needles there.

If the Eyes Have Had It

❏ If you notice that your eyes get tired after you've been knitting for a while, occasionally change the color of the needles you use. Sometimes the color combination of the yarn and the needles can cause eyestrain.

SEWING

Quit Needling Me

❏ Threading tiny needles can be difficult, especially if your vision isn't the best. You'll have an easier time threading a small needle if you cut the thread on a slant. That way, you'll have a point to guide through the eye.

❏ Another trick for threading a needle is to hold the needle and thread in front of a contrasting background—say, a piece of white cloth or even an off-white wall when you're working with colored thread. Try this technique with sewing machine needles, too. The needle and thread will stand out against the white, making it much easier to accomplish your task.

Coming Through!

❏ If you're having trouble pushing your needle through thick fabric such as canvas, even though you're using a thimble, keep a small block of paraffin (available at hardware stores) nearby. Run the tip of the needle over it a few times, and the needle should glide right through the fabric.

A Thread and Bobbin Caddy

❏ Keeping bobbins and spools of thread organized can be a real headache, and it seems as though the sewing boxes for sale in stores never have enough spindles to hold all the thread you have. With a few inexpensive ma-

---

ONE PERSON'S SOLUTION

A Magnetic Idea

One day several years ago, while I was at my sewing machine making a comforter cover for a friend, I turned to grab my scissors and accidentally hit the box of pins that was sitting on the edge of the table. A thousand pins (the economy-size box) cascaded to the floor. I spent the next hour and a half on my hands and knees, picking pins out of the carpet. And I was still stepping on pins for weeks afterward.

About a month later, I was in a hobby shop when I noticed magnets for sale. A little light bulb went off in my head, and I bought the smallest one, not sure my idea would work. I got home, and, sure enough, the magnet picked up the pins like a charm. Now I always keep a magnet tethered to my machine, and not just for spills. It's terrific for picking up pins that roll around and get caught in the crevices between my sewing table and the machine.

—LORI BAIRD
Astoria, New York

---

terials, you can easily make a thread and bobbin organizer. You'll need a piece of plywood at least one-half inch thick and large enough to accommodate all your bobbins and spools, a batch of one-quarter-inch-diameter dowels (they come in standard lengths), a saw, a drill with a quarter-inch bit, and some wood glue. You should be able to find all these materials at any hardware store that sells lumber.

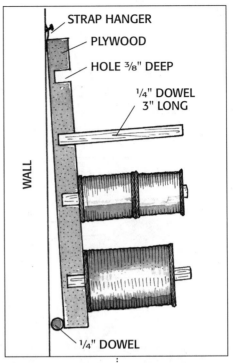

To start, drill three-eighths-inch-deep holes in the plywood (wrap a small piece of tape around the bit at three-eighths inch so you know how deep to drill), leaving enough space between the holes to accommodate either spools or bobbins. Cut the dowels into three-inch-long pieces. Place a drop of glue into each hole, then insert a dowel. Next, cut a length of dowel as long as the width of the bottom of the board and glue it, horizontally, on the back bottom. This allows the board to sit at an angle away from the wall and keeps the spools from falling off. Finally, purchase some strap hangers from a hardware store and attach them. Once the glue is dry, you can sand and varnish or paint the organizer if you want a more finished appearance.

For a spool-hardy storage rack, drill a vertical row of holes three-eighths inch deep into a piece of plywood. Glue and insert a three-inch length of dowel in each hole. Glue another dowel onto the back of the plywood, at the base. Add strap hangers and spools.

Extra! Extra!

❏ Are your favorite sewing patterns getting so worn that they're hardly usable anymore? If your town has a local newspaper, you may have a terrific solution at hand. Go to the newspaper's office and ask for a newsprint roll end. (It's the cardboard core that's left over after a newspaper has been printed.) There's actually a lot of paper left on the roll, and it's perfect for transferring old beat-up patterns (it takes transfer marks beautifully). Newspaper publishers often give the rolls to schools for projects, so you should be able to get one, too.

Sewing

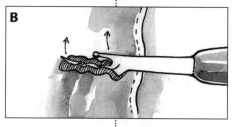

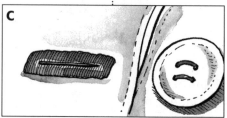

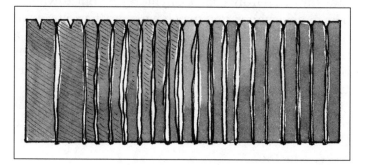

To open a buttonhole, insert a seam ripper at one end (A), then bring it up through the other end (B). Pull up, and you've got the hole thing done (C).

A child could easily make this embroidery thread holder. Just cut notches in a long strip of cardboard and use the notches to secure the threads as you wrap them.

Holy Buttonhole!

❑ Opening a buttonhole with a seam ripper can be tricky, especially if the ripper is new and sharp, because it's very easy to rip completely through the hole. Next time you need to open a buttonhole, insert the tip of the ripper into the fabric at one end of the buttonhole. Without ripping through the hole, bring the tip of the seam ripper back up through the fabric at the other end of the hole and pull up. The hole should open right up, and you won't risk ripping your garment.

EMBROIDERY

Don't Forget the Floss

❑ If you're looking for a way to keep different colors of embroidery floss organized and dust-free, start by making your own organizer. Take the cardboard backing from an 8½- by 11-inch pad of paper, cut it in half lengthwise, and discard one of the halves. Cut a narrow V-shaped groove one-half inch deep roughly every half inch along the length of the remaining strip. Arranging your threads by color, anchor each hue in one of the grooves, then wrap the remaining length of that hue around the cardboard. Store the whole thing in a child's clear plastic pencil case (available at discount stores and office supply stores).

See Spot Run—
Right in Front of That Car!

PETS IN GENERAL

New Pets: I Want My Mother!

❑ If your new puppy or kitten cries at night when you first take the animal home, the young pet probably misses his mother. To comfort the animal, wrap an old clock in a towel or blanket and put it in the animal's bed. The ticking sound will soothe your pet.

❑ Another way to comfort a new pet at night is to put a hot-water bottle in the bed to keep your pet warm and cozy.

Get Those Fleas to Flee

❑ Fleas love pets, but pets don't like fleas. The itchy critters cause dogs and cats untold misery, and an animal's scratching can damage his skin. A flea infestation also can spread throughout a house and to the people in it. A good natural flea fighter is vitamin B_1. To keep the pests at bay, sprinkle ½ to 1 teaspoon brewer's yeast (which contains large quantities of the vitamin) on your pet's food every day. Or crush a 25-milligram tablet of vitamin B_1 on the food. You can get vitamin B_1 at pharmacies and brewer's yeast at health food stores and pet stores.

DOLLAR STRETCHER

Kill Fleas without Getting Fleeced

It's not necessary to use an expensive flea shampoo to rid your pet of fleas. Any human shampoo will work as long as you let the lather soak in for at least five minutes. Technique, however, is important. The shampoo works by drowning the fleas, and you must work it into every nook and cranny of your pet's hide for it to be effective. Be sure to get the areas under the legs and tail, the snout, and the tail itself.

❑ To help keep your pet free of fleas and ticks, add 1 teaspoon vinegar to each quart of the pet's drinking water.

Not in My Backyard

❑ If you don't rid the house and yard of fleas at the same time you treat your animals, the pests will soon be back. To kill fleas in the yard, sprinkle the ground with diatomite (also called diatomaceous earth), a powder that has tiny, sharp crystals that are lethal to fleas. It is available from building and pool supply stores. Spread the diatomite over the entire yard, especially in shady and sandy areas and in places your animals frequent. This substance can be harmful to humans if inhaled. Spread it on a calm day and wear a mouth and nose filter, such as the ones used by painters. Also, stay out of the yard (and keep your pets out of it) for a couple of days, until the stuff has settled. Repeat this process every couple of weeks for a total

Many Problems, One Solution

It's not often that a single solution solves multiple problems, but here's the exception. Do you know what single action on your part will have all these benefits?

• Your pet will be healthier.

• The animal will be less likely to roam and become lost.

• The animal will be calmer and easier to train.

• In many areas, your pet will be cheaper to license.

• Your cat will be less likely to spray or attempt to mark his territory.

• Your female dog will be much less likely to develop the life-threatening uterine infection called pyometra.

• Your female dog won't stain the house with her discharges.

• Your male pet will be less inclined to howl, scratch, fight, and become involved in embarrassing sexual displays.

The answer? Having your pet neutered, of course. In addition to all the above benefits, neutering is the most effective way of keeping the pet population under control. Unless you're planning to breed the animal, you should have your pet neutered as soon as your vet recommends it.

of at least three times. Fleas hatch new young every two to three weeks, so the process must be repeated to catch young fleas between cycles.

What a Place for a Catnap

❏ Cats and dogs often sleep where you don't want them—on beds, couches, or upholstered chairs, for instance—leaving tufts of fur behind. But pets are very particular about their sleeping spots, and sometimes you can dissuade them just by putting something in the way—a box on a couch, for example. Once they get out of the habit of using a particular spot, they may find another favorite place to nap.

❏ You can encourage pets to choose a suitable resting place by folding up a comfortable blanket or towel in a good spot. Praise the animal for choosing this spot.

❏ If all else fails and you can't keep a pet off the furniture, cover the animal's favorite napping spot with a blanket. At least your pet will confine herself to only one part of the furniture, and you can clean a blanket more easily than the upholstery.

Don't Shed on Me!

❏ Longhaired pets that shed their fur can make a mess of your house. To minimize the flying fur, brush the pets frequently during shedding season, then use a damp cloth to blot loose hairs from their coats.

Missing in Action

❏ Pets sometimes stray from their homes, and they may become lost for good—through accident, theft, or destruction by animal control officers—if they aren't

---

☑ PROBLEM PREVENTED

Uneasy Riders

Dogs like to ride in the open bed of a pickup truck, but it's estimated that 100,000 dogs die each year from falling out of trucks at sudden turns or stops. That's why the practice is illegal in many states. Riding in the back also exposes dogs to sun, rain, and cold, and in summer the hot metal truck beds can burn their paws. And although dogs love to feel the wind blowing in their faces, prolonged exposure to such high-speed breezes can irritate the mucous membranes around an animal's eyes, nose, and mouth and may blow debris into the dog's eyes or nasal passages. It's best to keep your pet inside the car or truck.

---

found quickly. As soon as you discover that a pet is missing, contact your local Humane Society; be prepared to provide a complete description of the animal. Also, post signs around your neighborhood with a description and, if possible, a photo. Don't hesitate to offer a small reward for the animal's return.

❑ A classified ad in the local newspaper is another way to turn up leads on a lost pet.

PROBLEM PREVENTED

Hot Dogs

A dog can suffer heatstroke and even death if left in a hot car for even ten minutes. *Never* leave a dog unattended in your car in warm or even mild (70°F) weather. If you must leave the animal in the car on a cool day, crack the windows, park in the shade (anticipating the sun's movement), place a cardboard sunscreen across the windshield, and, if possible, leave some water for the animal to drink. Most important, don't forget that your pet is in the car!

The Death of a Friend

❑ The death of a pet, whether from old age, accident, or euthanasia, can be a traumatic experience for the human family. Many people benefit from support groups and the counsel of pet owners who have had similar experiences. To locate such support in your area, try contacting your local Humane Society or the Delta Society, which offers an extensive resource library with educational literature and videotapes. You can reach the Delta Society at 289 Perimeter Road East, Renton, WA 98055-1329.

DOGS

Dry-Clean Your Dog

❑ Washing your dog too often will dry out the animal's skin, but it's no fun to spend time in the company of a pet that's starting to smell. To deodorize your dog's coat between baths, sprinkle it with baking soda. Work the soda into the fur with your fingers, then brush it out. The baking soda will neutralize the odor and gently clean the fur.

Dog Baths: Who's Washing Whom?

❑ Giving your dog a bath can soak both you and the animal. To keep the splashing to a minimum, wash all other parts of the dog first, then finish with the head. The dog will shake when his head gets wet, so stand back.

If Fido Is All Ears

❏ If your pet develops a sudden, strong odor, particularly around the ears, the animal may have an infection. Take the pet to the vet.

Break 'Em In Easy

❏ If you're having problems housebreaking a dog, try feeding the animal at the same time every day. Leave the food out for half an hour, then pick it up even if the dog hasn't finished. That way, you'll be better able

---

If It's Brown and It Moves, It Must Be a Deer

Deer-hunting season can be hazardous to the health of domestic animals. It's not uncommon for hunters who get too close to rural homes to mistake large dogs for deer. Dogs that are allowed to run loose and end up chasing deer are in particular danger. The pets may get lost, or they may be shot by hunters or animal control officers. Moreover, as the owner of a deer chaser, you may be fined for harassing wildlife. To minimize the danger to your dog at this time of year, take these preventive measures.

• **Play dress up.** If you live in a rural area, keep confused hunters from taking aim at your favorite pet by tying a brightly colored kerchief around the dog's neck anytime you let the animal outside the house during hunting season. Deer rarely wear neckerchiefs, so that should be enough to make anyone look twice before shooting.

• **Encourage pet stay-at-homes.** During hunting season, deer often wander into areas where they are not usually found. To prevent deer-chasing problems during this time, leave your pets at home when you're out in the woods, and make sure you keep your dog inside or tied up at all times.

• **Don't let your dog walk alone.** If you must bring your dog along on a hike, stop the animal from going after deer by keeping her on a leash at all times.

Dogs

Doggy Discipline

No matter what you're trying to teach a dog, certain principles apply to all effective discipline. For example:

1. Always discipline the dog immediately. The dog won't understand why she's being punished if you hold off even a moment.

2. Never call a dog to scold him or yell, "Fido, get over here!" Calling a dog so you can punish the animal will make him reluctant to obey the command to come. Go *to* the animal to scold or punish him.

3. Never correct a dog for more than five to ten seconds. After that, the animal will have forgotten what she did wrong.

4. Reinforce good behavior right away with effusive praise and perhaps a treat.

to predict when the animal will need to go out, and she'll go out fewer times overall.

❏ In severe problem cases, give the dog water only at mealtimes. Take up the drinking water at night and when you leave the pup alone in the house.

Dogs Prefer Clean Latrines

❏ It's a good idea to designate one place for a dog's toilet area, rather than the whole backyard, and to reward the pet with much praise for using this area. But what do you do if a dog refuses to return to a designated area? Clean it up. Dogs prefer areas that have been used but not overused.

Chew It Over

❏ Chewing on things is a natural habit of most dogs, but it can be destructive. You can encourage your pet to stay away from your heirlooms if you provide the animal with good alternatives, such as solid chew toys. Make sure the toys can't break into dangerous pieces and be swallowed. Larger dogs love to gnaw on old tennis balls. Change the toys every week or two—or whenever a toy is destroyed—to keep the dog interested.

Gnawing Problems

❏ Young dogs go through teething, which can irritate the gums. To ease the irritation, offer your pet one of the rough-textured chew toys available at pet stores.

❏ Alternatively, soak an old washcloth in water and freeze it, then give it to the dog to gnaw on. This should make the animal's gums feel better.

Stool Pigeons

❏ If a dog's stool is loose, reduce the animal's amount of food by 10 percent to correct the problem. If it seems dry, increase the amount of food by 10 percent. If the problem persists, call the vet.

Johnny-Jump-Ups

❏ Dogs, especially puppies, are just trying to be friendly when they jump up on visitors. Here's a way to teach your pet better manners. Cut a slit in the top of an old soda or juice can, then squeeze a few coins into the can through the slit. The next time the dog gets a little too friendly, shake the can. The rattling noise will scare the animal and get her to back off.

Hot Diggity Dog

❏ Dogs like to dig, and the backyard of a dog owner sometimes looks as if a family of prairie dogs has moved in. One cause of digging is boredom. Try playing more with your pet and allow the animal into the house when you're there.

A piece of broomstick tied to a dog's collar is a bewitching way to keep the animal from chasing cars.

❏ If the digging persists, crumble a cake of toilet freshener on the ground where the dog likes to dig. Most dogs can't stand that lemon-fresh smell.

Follow That Car!

❏ Many dogs like to chase cars—a phenomenon that can be annoying to drivers and dangerous to the dog. The obvious solution is to keep the dog on a leash or dog run when the animal is outside. For more mobility, try this low-tech, low-impact hobble. Cut a one-foot length off an old broomstick or hockey stick, then drill a hole through it at the mid-point. Tie a short cord through this hole and tie the other end of the cord to the dog's collar, so the stick hangs at about knee level. The stick will allow the dog to walk comfortably, but the animal won't be able to run without tripping.

Fencing Lessons

❏ Big, aggressive dogs may climb or jump over even seemingly impregnable fences. To discourage dogs from climbing, string soda cans on a cord—like popcorn on a Christmas tree—and hang this contraption along the fence. Some dogs will shy away from the noise that climbing over these cans will make.

❏ Another deterrent is short lengths of plastic piping strung on a horizontal cord in front of the fence. The piping will spin under the dog's paws if he tries to climb.

Burr Dog

❏ Burrs tenaciously latch onto dog fur. To remove burrs, crush them with pliers or soften them up with shampoo or vegetable oil, then comb them out.

CATS

Just-in-Time Discipline

❏ If your cat seems to be ignoring your teaching attempts, your timing may be off. The first principle of successful training is to discipline a cat only if you catch the animal in the act of misbehaving. If you punish a cat after the fact, the only thing the animal will learn is to distrust you.

If Tabby's a Terror

❏ One proven way of stopping a cat that's misbehaving is to squirt the animal with water from a water pistol or spray bottle.

DOLLAR STRETCHER

The Skunk Solution

When a curious dog gets sprayed by a skunk, a tomato juice bath is the traditional way to rid the animal of odor. For a less expensive and neater solution, try giving the dog a bath in a tub filled with half water and half vinegar. Or mix up two packages of Massengill Douche Powder (available at drugstores and grocery stores) and wash the dog with this. It's more effective in breaking down the skunk's oil, and it's not as messy as tomato juice.

❏ Another cat deterrent is to make a sudden loud noise. When you catch your pet in the middle of unacceptable behavior, try clapping your hands sharply or loudly saying "No!"

Litter Lessons

❏ Once a cat finds a place other than the litter box to urinate, the animal will keep coming back to that spot. The problem with just cleaning up the mess is that doing so may only mask the odor. To prevent repeat offenses, you must neutralize it. Using a mixture of equal parts white vinegar and baking soda, wet the problem fabric, carpet, or wall thoroughly. Repeat if the cat does.

❏ Another way to discourage repeated urination in a bad spot is to soak a cotton ball in lemon extract and put it in a tea ball. Hang the ball where the cat has been urinating. The smell should keep the animal away.

❏ Some cats like a little privacy when they do their business. If your pet has been avoiding the litter box, try putting the box in a closet with a door that's wedged partially open, or try using a hooded litter box (available at pet stores).

PROBLEM PREVENTED

All Choked Up

A simple choke chain or slip collar can be dangerous if it catches on something while a dog is running or playing. These collars are designed only for training and should never be left on a dog when the animal is unattended. For general use, switch to a sturdy, buckle-on collar with the dog's identification tags.

A Litter Box Deodorant

❏ When the smell of a litter box gets too strong, sometimes emptying it isn't enough. In that event, deodorize the box by sprinkling the bottom with baking soda before filling it with fresh litter.

Litter Box Wipeouts

❏ Litter boxes eventually get dirty even if you change the litter frequently. How do you keep them sanitary? Clean the boxes once or twice a month, then disinfect them by wiping them down with a solution of ½ cup bleach and 1 gallon warm water. Rinse thoroughly.

❏ Never use pine oil cleaners to clean a litter box. These can be toxic to cats.

Pan Case

❏ Changing kitty litter is a dusty, stinky job. A good way to make it easier and to keep the pan itself cleaner is to slip the box into a plastic garbage bag before filling it with litter. Dump the litter in on top of the bag. When it's time to change the litter, just peel the bag over the box, turning it inside out as you fill it with the dirty litter. Slide the full bag into another trash bag before carrying it out of the house, as the cats may have punctured the first bag with their claws.

Finicky Felines

❏ Some cats are notoriously finicky eaters. If this is true of your animal, make sure the cat is really hungry when you feed him. Don't leave food out all the time; instead, put it out only at regular intervals—once or twice a day—and remove the extra food when the cat is done eating.

❏ If you've been feeding table scraps to a finicky cat, stop! An animal that becomes accustomed to people food is likely to disdain cat food.

What, No Milk?

❏ Cats occasionally suffer from diarrhea, and usually something in the diet is behind this illness. Milk is sometimes the surprising culprit, as many cats are lactose intolerant. If your cat has been having problems since you started occasionally setting out a bowl of milk, try eliminating the milk from the animal's diet.

My Cat's a Goddess

Cats are natural rodent killers, and it's likely that pest control was behind their domestication. The first people who settled into agricultural communities found their barns and grain bins inundated with mice and rats, and they soon discovered that cats were the solution.

There's no record of exactly when cats were first domesticated, but as long ago as 3000 B.C. in Egypt, felines were regarded so highly that a human could be put to death for killing one. When a cat died of natural causes, people went into mourning. (For some reason, removing one's eyebrows was part of this grieving process.) The feline body was embalmed and buried in a mask and coffin in a special cemetery. The Egyptians even had a cat goddess, Bastet, who was honored at a festival that drew hundreds of thousands of celebrants each year.

And you thought *your* cat acted like a princess!

Save the Birds

❏ Cats are natural predators, and small mammals, moths, and birds are frequent victims. In addition, cats often drag their bloody victims into the house, staining carpets and furniture, and they may vomit or suffer diarrhea after eating the animals. One way to protect wild birds and animals—as well as your house and the cat's digestive system—is to attach a small metal bell to the cat's collar. The tinkling of the bell may give the prey enough warning to escape before the cat pounces.

Save the Houseplants

❏ Cats love to explore houseplants, but their attention can be destructive. They may chew on the leaves or dig and urinate in the soil. To deter pets from chewing, spray your plants' leaves with Bitter Apple or Bitter Orange (available at pet stores). To discourage digging, spread gravel over the dirt in the plants' pots.

❏ Another way to stop a cat from snacking on houseplants is to sprinkle a little cayenne pepper or a drop

Landing on All Fours

Can a cat land safely when it falls from a fourth-story window? I *know* it can. A few years ago, I was house-sitting a friend's apartment, and taking care of his cat was part of the bargain. I like cats, but this one kept jumping up on the bed at night. I got in the habit of tossing the animal off in my sleep.

After a few weeks in the apartment, I rearranged the bedroom so I could sleep closer to the window. The first night in this new arrangement, my friend's cat jumped onto the bed, and I tossed the cat off as usual. Only this time, there was an open window by my bed, and the cat went sailing through it. The animal's yowls woke me up, and, realizing what had happened, I ran downstairs in my pajamas, contemplating how I would tell my friend about his cat's demise. At the front door, the cat was waiting to come in, seemingly no worse for the flight. Sheepishly, I let him in and went back to bed—this time with the window shut.

—JOHN SMITH
Peoria, Illinois

or two of Tabasco in a quart of water. Let the solution sit for a couple of hours, then mist your plants with it. (You may want to move the plants to a bathtub or sink so that you don't wet everything around them.) The smell alone should keep animals away, but one taste definitely will.

Open Sesame!

❏ A cat door cut into a full-size door or wall is a convenient way for outdoor cats to get in and out of the house on their own, but it can also become an entrance for other critters, especially food-foraging raccoons. If this is a problem (or a potential problem) in your area, try installing a lockable cat door that can be closed at night, keeping the cat in and the critters out. Lockable cat doors are available from pet stores.

❏ Most cats will resist using a cat door at first. To teach your pet to use the door, try putting a little food on the other side of the door at mealtime, then hold the door partly open until the cat gets used to going in and out.

Counter Waits

❏ Cats like to climb on countertops or tables to look for food—or just to be around people. To discourage them, try stacking some lightweight pots, kitchen utensils, or empty aluminum cans at the edge of the counter. When the cat jumps up, the surprise and loud noise of the metal pieces will make the animal wary of jumping up again.

Oh, No! Not the Grand Piano!

❏ Scratching is natural behavior for cats, but it can be a nightmare if the cat scratches your prized ottoman

---

✔ PROBLEM PREVENTED

Cat Collars: A Breakaway Sensation

Cats are natural explorers, and they like to slink into tight-fitting places. A dangerous problem can arise when a cat's collar catches on something, trapping the animal. To prevent this, use the breakaway collars available at pet stores. These collars have plastic clips that hold them securely in place during normal use but will release if they catch and the cat tugs to get away.

---

or Oriental rug. Discipline the cat by spraying her with water (from a squirt gun or spray bottle), but only if you catch the animal in the act.

❏ To keep a cat away from wooden chair legs or woodwork, treat the area with a cat-deterring spray such as Bitter Orange or Bitter Apple (available at pet stores).

❏ A scratching post will provide the cat with a good alternative to scratching your furniture. Rope-covered scratching posts are available at pet stores. Put them near the furniture or carpet that kitty likes to scratch, and rub a little catnip on the post to encourage its use.

❏ If your cat is scratching a carpet, she may be learning that behavior from a carpet-covered scratching post. Try switching to one covered with natural-fiber rope.

✔ PROBLEM PREVENTED

Cozy but Dangerous

Cats love to curl up in warm, cozy places. Unfortunately, some of these can be dangerous. To prevent a tragedy, always check for cats inside your clothes dryer before loading wet clothes, and bang on the hood of your car to scare cats away before starting the engine.

What Was That Masked Odor?

❏ When you move into a new house, a cat's litter box behavior may be affected by the odors of animals that once lived in the house. To get your pet to go back to using the litter box, you'll need to clean and deodorize (with Lysol or another strong cleaner) all areas that any previous pets may have frequented. Such areas might include the kitchen, litter box locations such as closets, and entryways. To avoid poisoning your pet, be sure to rinse off all traces of the cleaner you use.

Your Friend the Vet

❏ A cat's anxiety level rises when he visits a waiting room filled with strange animals, most of whom are themselves fearful. To decrease a cat's fear of veterinarians, look for a cats-only vet or one who makes house calls for routine care.

❏ Another way to minimize a cat's nervousness around vets is to train the animal from a very early age to accept the vet's treatment. To do this, start early to handle your pet in the way a vet will. Check the animal's eyes, ears, nose, and mouth; lift her tail to look at the anus; and check her paws individually. Regular inspections such as these will teach you the signs of a healthy cat, and you may notice changes that could indicate an illness.

FISH

Go Fish!

❑ Moving with fish requires planning and some special equipment. The problem isn't providing enough water, but ensuring that the fish get enough oxygen. One solution requires a small battery-operated air tank (also available at pet stores). Run a short hose from this tank into a heavy-duty plastic bag designed for moving fish (available at pet stores). Fill the bag about one-quarter full of water, put the fish inside, and seal the bag tightly around the oxygen hose. Now fill the bag with oxygen, remove the hose while twisting the bag tightly shut so that no oxygen escapes, fold the twisted top over, and seal the bag with heavy-duty rubber bands.

Waste Not . . .

❑ Waste from the fish will generate ammonia during transit. This isn't a problem unless the fish will be in their travel bag for more than 24 hours. In that case, you can neutralize the ammonia by treating the water with AmQuel (available at pet stores and aquarium supply stores) before putting the fish in the bag.

❑ Reducing the fish's food supply for several days prior to the move will cut down on the ammonia produced during the trip.

Starter Fish

Caring for tropical fish might seem like a fairly simple, low-maintenance hobby, but when you walk into a pet store, the choices can be overwhelming. If you're a first-time fish owner who's looking to fill a small aquarium, you need fish that are hardy and easy to care for. Try starting with any of the following types.

- Danio
- Gourami
- Guppy
- Swordtail
- Tetra

TRAVEL
You Can't Get There from Here

DAY TRIPS AND WEEKEND TRAVEL

Navigator or Navi-Guesser?

❏ If you're traveling an unfamiliar route on a car trip, what's the best way to keep from getting lost? Trace your route on a map with a highlighter (you can find one in the stationery department of discount stores, drugstores, or grocery stores; in art or office supply stores; or stationery stores). That way, your front seat passenger will know the exact directions, allowing you to concentrate on the road, not the road signs.

Smoke Gets in Your Car

❏ If you travel with a smoker, the mess in your car's ashtray may be nothing compared with the odor of stale cigarette smoke. Cope with both by filling a three-pound coffee can with a mixture of sand and baking powder (use about three parts sand and one part baking soda). The smoker can extinguish his cigarettes in the sand, and the baking soda will absorb much of the odor. (The weight of the sand will keep the homemade deodorizer from tipping.)

Gym Class on the Road

❏ Getting overtired when driving for long stretches is not only annoying, it can be downright dangerous if the driver falls asleep at the wheel. One of the best cures for tiredness on a long drive is an exercise stop. On your next trip, throw into the trunk a ball and some baseball gloves, a jump rope (terrific aerobic exercise for adults and children), a driver and some Wiffle golf balls (which don't go very far), or even some badminton rackets and a shuttlecock. None of these takes up much room, and they'll come in handy when you find a highway rest stop that has a grassy area.

When Did Everyone Turn Blue?

❏ One of the pleasures of travel is taking lots of photos as souvenirs of your trip. If the film is exposed to excessive heat before it's developed, however, the colors of your photographs can be dramatically affected. What can you do to prevent heat damage when traveling? Process exposed film promptly and avoid leaving any film in a hot car. When camping, keep your film in a resealable plastic bag in the cooler to protect it from heat.

WHAT AND HOW TO PACK

Pack in Haste, Repent at Leisure

❏ Most of us have had the experience of packing in a hurry for a trip and then leaving with the uneasy feeling that we forgot something. Then, sure enough, three days later we reach for a bathing suit, an address book, or a pair of gloves, and it's not there. The best way to make sure you have everything you want and need is to start a packing list days, even weeks, before your trip. Post it on the refrigerator, the bathroom mirror, or some other place where you can see it. Add items as you think of them rather than hurriedly trying to remember what to pack at the last minute.

❏ Another trick for compiling a complete packing list for your next trip is to run down your day, mentally listing what you do (take vitamins, brush teeth, shower) and what items you use for those activities (vitamins, toothbrush, toothpaste, soap, shampoo), taking notes as you go. Start with your morning and continue through until bedtime, and you'll never forget the essentials.

❏ Alternatively, make a list of the standard items you need for virtually every trip (toothpaste, deodorant, change of underwear) and store it in your suitcase. That way, at least you won't forget the basics.

Weight Watchers

❏ Looking for a way to minimize the aches in your feet and back when you travel? Pack light so you have less to carry. To keep your load at a minimum, take along the fewest items of clothing possible. You're traveling— who's to know if you wear the same shirt twice in one week? Whittle your wardrobe down by choosing only those items you can wear with every other item. That means every shirt should match or coordinate with every pair of trousers and/or every skirt and vice versa. And select low-maintenance clothing—pieces that are wrinkle resistant, hide dirt well, and are of neutral color (or patterned).

The Short List: 11 Items No Traveler Should Be Without

1. Swiss Army knife. Indispensable. Depending on the model you choose, you'll get scissors, tweezers, a toothpick, a corkscrew, a bottle opener, a can opener, a screwdriver, a ruler, a file, a magnifier—and a knife.

2. Copies of medication and eyeglasses prescriptions.

3. Spare eyeglasses or contact lenses.

4. Sunglasses. Even in winter.

5. Shower sandals. For icky shower stalls and to prevent athlete's foot.

6. Address book.

7. A personal cassette player or a book.

8. A deck of cards. For rainy days or extended layovers.

9. Rain gear.

10. Important phone numbers. Be sure to include numbers to call if your credit cards or traveler's checks are lost or stolen.

11. A sewing kit with safety pins. Don't forget to bring the right color thread; four mini spools of white aren't any good if your entire wardrobe is navy blue. Safety pins come in handy for torn hems, broken luggage straps, popped buttons, snapped swimsuit straps, and curtains that won't stay closed.

What and How to Pack

If You Must Carry the Weight of the World

❑ Another way to reduce back strain when traveling is to carry a travel pack—a large bag that resembles a backpack and is designed to be carried on your back. Properly fitted, these reduce the stress and strain on your back and offer the added bonus of keeping your hands free. You can find these packs at most outdoor-equipment stores and luggage stores.

❑ If you go the travel pack route, you can further reduce the strain on your back by always packing the heaviest items—shoes and guidebooks, for instance—at the bottom of the bag.

A Reducing Plan

❑ If you really want to reduce the amount of weight you're lugging around, follow the lead of backpackers, who make a science out of traveling light. Head to your local outdoor-equipment store and stock up on items

6 Items Every Carry-On Bag Should Contain

Your carry-on luggage can bail you out of some annoying situations—if you know what to pack. Since most airlines allow passengers *two* pieces of carry-on luggage, there's no excuse for not having the essentials.

1. Important phone numbers and addresses. If you have made arrangements for someone to pick you up at the airport or if you have a meeting, you'll need to make some calls in the event of an unscheduled layover.

2. Anything you'd need for an overnight without your luggage. Prescription medicines, tooth-brush and toothpaste, a change of underwear, contact lens solution and glasses, and perhaps a fresh shirt.

3. A pack of cards, a travel game, or a book to combat boredom in case of a delay or layover.

4. Your wallet with a photo ID, money, traveler's checks, and credit cards. Never, ever check your wallet or any of these items.

5. Snacks or hard candies.

6. Finally, even if you're flying to a warm climate, take along a **lightweight cotton sweater.** Like movie theaters, airplanes can get awfully chilly.

ranging from travel packs to freeze-dried foods to soap that does triple duty as shampoo, laundry detergent, and toothpaste.

Clean, Dry, and Wrinkle-Free

❏ It's no fun to carefully press and pack your entire travel wardrobe, only to arrive at your destination and find a bag of wrinkled clothing. To avoid that mess, pack your clothes in the plastic garment bags in which they came back from the dry cleaner. They'll stay neat, clean, and perfectly pressed.

The Portable Office

❏ How can you make it easier to keep track of post-cards, tickets, stamps, and your address book? Just take along a portable office when you travel. Use a seal-able plastic bag or a zippered pouch, and fill it with stamps, your address book, a small pocket calculator, a pen and pencil, a small pair of blunt craft scissors (if you don't have a Swiss Army knife), and a glue stick (for affixing small souvenirs in your journal).

If It's Tuesday, My Bags Must Be in Belgium

❏ One of the worst feelings in the world is standing at a deserted airport baggage claim, realizing your bags are probably winging their way to Reno. You can't stop the airline from losing your luggage, but you can make sure that you get it back as soon as possible. Before you leave, label each piece, both inside and out, with your business address and phone number as well as the address and phone number of the place you'll be staying during your trip. (Avoid listing your home address, which could be an invitation to burglars while you're away.) Use a good, sturdy tag for the outside, then write your vital information on a piece of athletic tape (available at sporting goods stores and some drug-stores) or fabric tape (available at fabric stores). Apply it somewhere on the inside of your suitcase or bag. Make sure to use a permanent marker and let it dry before you finish packing so that the ink won't rub off on your clothes.

What and How to Pack

...And All I Got Was This Lousy T-Shirt

❑ Souvenir hats, T-shirts, and other items can pile up quickly when you're on vacation, and before you know it, you don't have enough room in your bags to bring them home. If you know you're likely to purchase lots of gifts and souvenirs and are concerned about how

---

ONE PERSON'S SOLUTION

How I Got Stuffed

A few years ago, I was going on my first overseas trip, a three-week vacation to Europe. I'd never had to pack for such a long trip before, and I was having trouble finding a way to keep all my gear organized. I came up with the idea of putting everything into seal-able plastic bags I got at the grocery store. It was a perfect (and inexpensive) solution.

I put larger objects and sharp things such as pencils in freezer bags, which are made of heavy-duty plastic, and my film, sewing kit, and deck of cards in regular smaller bags. Since they're transparent, I didn't have to fumble around in my suitcase to find what I was looking for, and the bags kept every-thing clean and organized. I got a little carried away and brought a handful of extra bags with me. It turned out to be a good idea be-cause I ended up giving most of them away to the other women in my tour group. They used them for makeup, damp washcloths, even papers they wanted to keep dry.

—Nina Gannon
Contoocook, New Hampshire

---

you'll transport them, pack a spare bag in which to bring them home. Choose a large, soft bag (preferably one with a zipper top) that you can crumple or flatten and stuff into your suitcase.

The Big Squeeze

❏ Looking for a way to squeeze more items in your suitcase? Take advantage of every nook and cranny. Stuff socks into shoes. Tuck underwear and scarves into corners and into the sleeves of shirts and blouses. Remove the cardboard tube from a roll of toilet paper and crush the roll. Take vitamins and aspirin out of their heavy glass bottles and repack them in sealable plastic bags.

❏ Another way to save space in your suitcase is to avoid folding clothing if possible. A folded sweater, for instance, takes up more room than an unfolded one, so pack garments flat whenever you can.

One Sheet to the Wind

❏ You have to pack your dirty laundry somewhere for the trip home, but you don't want it to stink up your fresh clothing and your good suitcase as well. To keep everything smelling fresh, place a fabric softener sheet in the bottom of your luggage before you leave on the trip. The scent will offset any odor from the dirty clothes, even if the softener sheet is not right next to the laundry.

Keep your chain gang in place! To prevent tangles, wrap gold and silver chains around an old toilet paper roll, then tape them in position.

Wrap 'n' Roll

❏ When gold and silver costume jewelry chains are packed loosely in a jewelry case for traveling, they often arrive on the other end in one tangled mass. To conquer this packing dilemma, wrap the chains around the cardboard from a roll of toilet paper and secure them with tape or bobby pins.

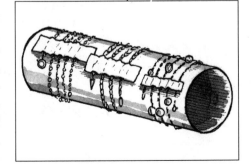

What and How to Pack

Oh, the Cologne

❏ It seems that no matter how tightly they're sealed, perfume lids leak. Putting the bottles in securely sealed plastic bags keeps the perfume from leaking on your clothes, but it doesn't save your expensive perfume, which still trickles into the bag. Here's a solution. Seal the lids with a little clear nail polish, which will form a tight enough seal to stop drips but won't prevent you from opening the lid easily. Take along some extra nail polish to reseal the lids after you use the perfume.

Polish Remover for Lightweights

❏ If you know you'll need nail polish remover while you're on vacation but don't want the weight of a whole bottle (let alone the smell if it should break), soak a few cotton balls in the remover and seal them in an airtight plastic bag. That way, you can bring only as much as you need.

Sole Survivor

❏ Credit card numbers. Traveler's check numbers. Phone numbers to call if your credit cards or traveler's checks get lost or stolen. Aunt Sally's address. How can you keep all your most important information safe and secure? Store it in your shoe! Write the information clearly on a *small* piece of paper (this is going into the bottom of your shoe), fold the paper, and place it in a plastic sandwich bag. Remove the insole from your shoe (nearly all shoes, but especially sneakers, have removable insoles), place the bag inside, and then replace the insole. You may have to make some adjustments to the paper or bag, but once it's all set, you'll always have your important information with you (or at least in a spot most thieves wouldn't dream of checking). And it'll always be safe and dry, even in the rain.

I Made Connections, but My Jacket Didn't

❏ When you travel by plane, keeping track of all your carry-on possessions can be tough, especially if you're rushing to make connections. To avoid leaving any-

Travel Smarts: Leave Home without It!

Just as you wouldn't pack mukluks for a trip to Miami or a surfboard for St. Louis, there are some items that don't belong in your suitcase when you take *any* trip.

1. Expensive jewelry. If you're not willing to lose it or have it stolen, leave it at home.

2. Originals of important or hard-to-replace documents such as birth certificates. To be on the safe side, bring copies instead.

3. Shoes that look terrific but feel horrific. If they're not comfortable at home, they won't be comfortable on vacation.

4. High-maintenance clothing. You should be able to wear almost everything you bring for two days in a row without having to wash or iron it.

5. Large amounts of cash. In these days of nationwide automatic teller machines, traveler's checks, and credit cards, there's absolutely no reason to carry more than an afternoon's worth of cash.

6. Blue jeans. Jeans are relatively heavy and take a long time to dry if they get wet or you launder them.

thing behind, take a count of how many items your family carries onto the plane (and how many pieces of baggage you check). Then make sure you leave with the same number.

❏ If you remove your heaviest clothing for comfort during a plane trip and are concerned that you won't remember everything when you land, try this: Before stowing your jacket or overcoat in the overhead compartment, take a minute to tuck a business card (or a scrap of paper with your name, address, and phone number on it) in an inside pocket. If you leave the plane without your coat, at least you have a chance of retrieving it. (If possible, it's best to list a business address rather than a personal one. A home address could be an invitation to thieves while you're away.)

FINANCIAL CONSIDERATIONS

Boondocks Bargain

❏ Lodging is usually one of the biggest expenses for vacationers. You can frequently reduce that cost by avoiding hotels, motels, and other lodging establishments close to major tourist attractions and centrally located in cities. These places nearly always cost more than those farther away. Before you decide you need to be five minutes from your final destination, check out the prices of places 5, 10, even 20 miles away. You may have to get up a little earlier to start your day, but when you see the savings, you might not mind so much.

DOLLAR STRETCHER

Don't Rent and Wreck

The cost of insurance can nearly double the daily rate for a rental car, sometimes needlessly. You may already have automatic coverage through your credit card company. Before taking a trip on which you'll be renting a car, call your credit card company. Ask if the company provides automatic coverage and find out: (1) Exactly what is covered. Some cards cover collision but not liability or medical. (2) What the deductible is. (3) If, in the case of an accident that's your fault, you need to pay up front and then get reimbursed by the insurance company, which could mean an enormous outlay of money for you.

Who Ordered the Peanut Butter and Jelly?

❏ When you add up what you spend on taxes, tips, and markup, eating out every night can bloat your vacation budget. Keep those expenses down by scouting around for inexpensive cottages, inns, motels, or hotels that offer units with kitchenettes in which you can prepare your own meals. Then take turns preparing the meals. Remember, it's Mom's vacation, too.

Eating Out Is Cheaper Than Eating Out

❏ You can't stop eating while you're on a trip, but you can stop the costs from skyrocketing. One way to cut your vacation food budget is to eat out. Outside, that is. Make one meal each day a picnic. A loaf of bread from a local bakery, cheese or luncheon meats from a grocery store, and some fruit make a delightful lunch spread out in a park or even at a highway rest area. Best of all, a picnic will cost a fraction of what you'd pay at a restaurant.

Do-It-Yourself Room Service

❏ Save on breakfast costs when you're traveling by picking up juice and a muffin or cereal in the evening and bringing it back to your hotel room. Put the juice in the room's ice bucket, and in the morning you can eat an inexpensive breakfast before you even dress to go out.

Fair-Priced Fare

❏ If you're looking to save money on food when you're on vacation, steer clear of diners and restaurants that are located near large tourist attractions. Whenever possible, get a few blocks or miles away. Or consider bringing a lunch along with you.

Did Someone Mention a Free Trip to Honolulu?

❏ Who wouldn't like to find a way to cut the cost of plane travel? Here's one possibility. Airline reservationists routinely overbook flights by as many as ten seats because on every flight there are usually a number of no-shows. If your plane has been overbooked, you may be asked to switch to the next available flight. If your schedule is flexible, take advantage of the offer, because airlines always offer passengers something in exchange for being bumped. Often this means a free round-trip ticket to anywhere the carrier flies.

DOLLAR STRETCHER

Bigger *Is* Better

Ounce for ounce, travel- and sample-size containers of shampoo, baby powder, shaving cream, and lotion cost a lot more than the economy sizes. You'll spend less if you buy the larger sizes and repackage them in small, airtight plastic containers from outdoor-equipment stores or drugstores.

If I Don't Write It Down, It's Like I Didn't Spend It . . .

❏ Trying to keep track of how much you spend on vacation can be, well, trying. Stay organized by logging your expenditures in a pocket-size ledger from an office supply store or a blank check register, which you should be able to get gratis from your bank.

❏ Another good way to keep track of your travel expenses—and reduce the amount of cash you carry—is to charge as many of your purchases as possible on a credit card. You'll get a detailed record of what you spent and where you spent it, and, if you pay off the entire amount when the bill comes due, you'll have given yourself a free short-term loan.

HEALTH AND COMFORT ON THE ROAD

Cover Me!

❏ Getting caught in a medical emergency on the road can be a nightmare in itself, but it's worse if you then find out that your health insurance won't protect you away from home. If you're worried that this could happen to you, call your insurer before you leave and find out whether you're covered when you travel. If you're not, invest in an extra policy that will cover you. Your own provider may sell separate policies, or the company should be able to point you toward other providers that sell travel medical insurance.

A Gut Feeling

❏ There's nothing funny about traveler's diarrhea when you're the one who's suffering. The best treatment for simple diarrhea is a diet of bland foods such as clear broths and plain white rice, along with lots of fluids. Sports drinks such as Gatorade are effective treatments because they contain electrolytes (salts and potassium) that your body needs.

Regular as Clockwork

❏ OK, nobody likes to talk about it, but many folks get a little off schedule in their bathroom habits when they travel. Here's how to get and keep regular. Eat at scheduled times if at all possible, drink lots of fluids, and increase the bulk and fiber in your diet by eating fresh fruits and vegetables. And don't forget to exercise! Add a morning or evening walk to your day.

If Your Stomach's Not Feeling So Good

❏ Nothing can spoil a day of travel like a good dose of motion sickness. If you have a history of this kind of thing, take a motion sickness medication such as Dramamine one-half to one hour *before* you get into a car or board a bus. Such treatments are of no use once the motion has started.

❏ If you're driving, or if you simply want to avoid the drowsiness that's often a side effect of motion sickness medications, ask your pharmacist if a medicine such as Bonine would be appropriate for you. Such a product should settle your stomach without making you sleep through the fun.

❏ You can also steer clear of motion sickness by avoiding caffeine and heavy meals before you leave. If you get hungry en route, snack on something bland, such as saltines.

The Right Place at the Right Time

❏ If you're traveling in a car when you start to feel queasy, you can sometimes conquer the problem by moving to the front seat. In a bus, sit as close to the front as you can. In a train, sit so that you're facing forward. And if your stomach's uneasy, never try to read in a moving vehicle.

Baby, It's Hot Inside

❏ Stuck in a car without any air-conditioning on the hottest day of the summer? You can make yourself a little more comfortable if you've planned ahead. The night before your trip, fill a liter-size soda bottle three-quarters full of water and freeze it. The next morning, add some more water and pack the bottle in an accessible spot in the car. By the time the heat becomes unbearable, the water will be ready to drink.

❏ Another survival technique for long, hot car trips is to stock your picnic cooler with more than just cold

---

Doctor, Doctor

I f you or a family member becomes seriously hurt or ill while you're on vacation, you should go to a phone and dial 911 or head to the nearest emergency room. But where can you turn for a minor sore throat, a sprained wrist, or an itchy rash?

If you do come down with some minor ailment and are staying in or near a large hotel, ask the concierge to recommend a doctor—many hotels keep lists of on-call physicians. If you're not near a hotel, go to the nearest drugstore and speak to the pharmacist, who will be able to recommend a local doctor.

---

drinks. Dampen a washcloth, put it in a plastic sandwich bag, and keep it in the cooler. Or toss in a handful of prepackaged moist towelettes. Whenever you feel hot and dry, pull out a cool, refreshing cloth.

A Cooler Idea

❏ On a hot day, the ice in your cooler may melt as fast as you can buy it. To keep your cooler cool longer, always buy block ice instead of cubes and take the cooler out of the car or put it in the trunk when you're away from the car.

Who Needs Popsicles?

❏ Looking for something other than junk food as a snack for a long car trip? Here's a nutritious and cool alternative. You'll need a small cooler, some ripe bananas, berries (blueberries and strawberries work well), and perhaps even sliced fresh mango. Peel the bananas and wash and hull the berries. Let the berries air-dry. Place all the fruit in sealable plastic bags and put the bags in the freezer. The next morning, place the fruit in your cooler. You may need to throw in an extra cold pack to keep everything frozen. The fruit will make a refreshing and healthful snack.

Seat Yourself

❏ Airplane seats become about as comfortable as bus seats after several hours, but you can make yourself more comfortable if you book early and request a bulkhead seat. There'll be no seat in front of you, and you'll have a lot more legroom. If the bulkhead seats are all taken,

---

✔ **PROBLEM PREVENTED**

Wave Good-bye to the Trip—But Not to Your Money

What happens if you become ill in the middle of your vacation and need to go home? Or what if your traveling companion suddenly cancels at the last minute, leaving you to pay the difference between single and double occupancy? Unless you've made prior arrangements, you'll probably lose all the nonrefundable money you invested in your trip (airfare, hotel deposits, tickets to sporting or cultural events). For about 7 percent of the total cost of your trip, however, you can purchase trip cancellation insurance, which covers your costs (above the deductible) if you have to cancel at the last minute or even cut short your vacation. To find a company that offers this type of insurance, call any travel agent or check the Yellow Pages under Insurance.

next best is an emergency exit seat, where, again, you'll have a little more legroom. Finally, barring these options, request an aisle seat. You'll have easy access to the aisle and a little more breathing room.

SAFETY AND SECURITY

Mug Me

❑ Muggers and purse snatchers target tourists because they're easy to spot (expensive cameras, funny trousers, disoriented looks) and are usually gawking at the sights the natives are ignoring (tall buildings, street performers). To look less like a stranger, read your map and guidebook in your room (not on the street corner) and walk purposefully, as though you know where you're going.

Don't Talk to Strangers

❑ You don't want to invite a thief—or worse—into your hotel room, but how can you tell the good guys from the bad? If someone knocks on your door claiming to work for the hotel, don't open the door, even to ask for identification. Call the front desk immediately to find out whether someone was sent up.

EMERGENCY REPAIRS

Four out of Five Dentists . . .

❑ To temporarily repair a broken strap or torn seam on a piece of hand luggage, thread some dental floss—which is very strong—into a large sewing needle and make the repair yourself. Waxed dental floss glides through heavy fabric, leather, and nylon more easily than does unwaxed floss. If the white floss shows on the outside of your bag, color it with a marker or a dab of shoe polish.

All Steamed Up

❑ You don't want to look a mess when you're traveling, but not every piece of your clothing is wrinkle-free. A quick and easy way to smooth wrinkled clothing is to hang it in the bathroom while you shower; the steam will relax the wrinkles. Leave more stubbornly wrinkled clothes hanging in the bathroom with the door closed for a few minutes after you get out of the shower.

You Can Iron It Out

❏ If you're staying in a hotel room and need to press clothing but didn't pack an iron, call the front desk and ask whether you can borrow one. Many hotels make irons available to guests, but you have to ask for them.

❏ If the hotel where you're staying doesn't have irons available for guests, you can smooth out a wrinkled garment by laying the item under the mattress overnight. If you feel squeamish about putting your clothes under a

---

Handy Travel Substitutions

It's a given that you can't pack for every contingency when you travel—and why would you want to, when you can so easily make do with something else? For instance:

ITEM	CAN SUBSTITUTE FOR
Baby powder	Deodorant
	Foot powder
	Shampoo (brush the powder through your hair, and it will absorb some of the dirt and oil; cornstarch baby powder works best)
Beach wrap/sarong	Skirt Beach towel Picnic blanket
Nail brush	Laundry brush
Shampoo	Laundry detergent for hand washing
Silk scarf	Belt for skirt or pants Head covering on a sunny day
T-shirt	Pillowcase at a summer house or cottage
Toothpaste	Shoe polish; use with a little water

Loose Socks Sink Trips

We've all made the mistake of dismissing a tender heel or toe at the start of a day of walking, thinking that "it only hurts a little." After a while, it hurts a lot. A blister has formed, and then your choices are to stay off your feet for a day or two—missing out on sight-seeing—or begging a three-day supply of Band-Aids from someone who had the foresight to pack them.

Blisters are usually caused by ill-fitting shoes or loose socks. There are two ways to prevent them. First, if your trip includes a lot of walking, wear shoes that are already broken in and socks that fit. Leave your new leather boots and high heels at home; bring your most comfortable sneakers or shoes. Second, the minute you feel your shoes rubbing, break out the moleskin—soft pads with adhesive backing that you can place directly on your skin. You can find moleskin in the foot care section of any drugstore.

If you do end up with a blister, don't break it, or you'll expose the tender skin underneath. The best first aid for a blister is to keep it clean, dry, and protected with a Band-Aid.

strange mattress, sandwich the clothing between towels, then request more towels from the maid.

Run Away!

❏ What with travel-worn luggage, awkward packages, and crowded seating, sometimes it seems impossible to travel any distance without ruining at least one pair of nylons. But you *can* minimize the damage. To stop a run in your stockings from progressing any further, dab the edges of the run with a little clear nail polish. When the polish dries, it will act like glue, fusing the fraying thread together.

Screw Glue

❏ If the screws in your glasses or sunglasses keep coming loose while you're on the road, place a drop of clear nail polish on the head of the screw after you tighten it.

Jewelry Repairs: Help for the String Section

❑ You reach down to pick up your suitcase and snag your favorite necklace when you stand up. The next thing you know, beads are rolling all over the floor. Assuming that you can find all the pieces, you'll need a good way to hold them together so the same thing doesn't happen again. Pull out the dental floss! Thread the floss into an ordinary sewing needle (one with a fairly large eye) and use it to restring the beads. Nobody will see what you've done because the beads will cover it up—and the floss is strong enough that the necklace won't break again.

FAMILY TRAVEL

OK, Who Wrote Down Bungee Jumping?

❑ Family vacations aren't much fun when they're filled with one complaint after another from the backseat. Minimize the moaning and groaning by involving every member of the family in planning the vacation. Especially for longer trips, give each person a chance to choose one thing (within reason, of course) that he particularly wants to do. This can encourage the younger set to bone up on the areas you're planning to visit and will ensure that everyone gets at least one special treat.

Johnny, Put Down That Ming Vase!

❑ When planning vacations that involve children or grandchildren, it's not always easy to keep the whole family happy. Make things easier and more enjoyable for everyone by choosing informal activities, such as camping or a visit to the beach. Keep your schedule flexible and spontaneous, and steer clear of places such as antiques shops and museums, where small hands can get into mischief and adult nerves will be on edge.

Stop That Car!

❑ A long, hot car trip may make adults irritable, but it can turn otherwise domesticated children into wild animals. When you plan a trip that involves long stretches of driving, schedule frequent breaks. Some rest stops even have small playgrounds. Little ones will be a lot happier (and so will you) if they can get out of the backseat and stretch their legs once in a while.

Are We There Yet?

❏ As any parent knows, bored children are the bane of long-distance travel. One way to cheer them up is to bring along a bag of small, wrapped surprises. Travel games, crossword puzzles, comic books, and other activities are all appropriate. Label each package with the mileage point at which it's to be opened (50 miles from home, 100 miles, and so on). This will keep the youngsters interested and the grownups less frustrated.

 Items for the Kiddie Glad Bag

Keep little ones happy on long road trips with a customized goody bag for each child. They'll thank you by giving you hours of stress-free travel. Here's what to include.

1. Lap trays. Good for eating and coloring. You can buy them at department and discount stores.

2. Coloring books and crayons. Brand-new ones are always more fun.

3. A personal cassette player with headphones. Ideally, bring one for each child to prevent arguments about what to listen to next.

4. Children's music and/or story cassettes. For the car stereo or the personal tape player. (If you rent a car, reserve one with a cassette player.)

5. Favorite books. If there are two adults, one can drive while the other reads aloud.

6. Pillows, blankets, and stuffed animals. With any luck, they'll fall asleep.

7. Snacks and juice. Healthful snacks such as fruit are ideal, but candy works, too.

8. Tissues or moist towelettes. For cleanup after snacks and runny noses.

9. Batteries. You're in for trouble if the Game Boy runs out of power two hours into a six-hour trip.

Things to Do on a Rainy Day

Who says a rainy day has to spoil a vacation? It may just require a change in plans. Consider any of these possibilities.

1. Take in a movie.
2. Explore a museum.
3. Visit the local library. Many offer lectures, slide shows, and other programs.
4. Write postcards.
5. Update your journal.
6. Go to a matinee theater performance.
7. Have afternoon tea.
8. Go shopping. It can still be fun—if you're dressed for the weather. Afterward, plan a warming treat, such as a hot shower or a special snack.

TRAVELING WITH PETS

Dog Days

❏ Trying to decide whether to bring your pet along on a vacation? One factor to consider is the length of the trip. If you will be away for just a couple of days, it will probably cause your pet less stress to stay behind. If, however, your trip will last for two weeks or more and won't involve driving for more than a day or so, consider bringing your pet along.

Travel with Pets: Sleep Easy

❏ Traveling with a pet can be difficult, in part because many motels don't allow pets to stay in the rooms. One way to locate motels that permit pets is to join the American Automobile Association (AAA), which lists pet-friendly hostelries in its publications.

❏ Alternatively, before bringing a pet along on vacation, be sure to call ahead to the places you plan to stay and ask whether they allow pets in the rooms.

Fur of Flying

❏ Air travel can be a particularly stressful experience for a pet. You want Rover to relax, but an owner or vet can cause more problems than are necessary by over-tranquilizing the animal. (The American Society for the Prevention of Cruelty to Animals [ASPCA] advises against tranquilizing animals for air travel.) Here's how you can reduce the stress for your pet without resorting to drugs. For at least two weeks before your trip, practice leading your pet into the crate the animal will be traveling in. At first, leave your pet in the crate for just a few minutes, then gradually increase the amount of time the animal spends in the crate. If your pet is especially nervous, you may have to start this routine more than two weeks before the trip.

❏ If your pet and pet carrier are small enough to fit under the seat in front of you during a flight, you can put the animal more at ease if you bring along just a little food for nibbling. Avoid feeding your pet when the rest of the passengers are having their meals, however, as some folks might be put off by the smell of pet food while they're eating. Although you probably won't have to take your animal out of the crate for feeding, it's a good idea to tell the passenger next to you that you've brought a friend along.

Be Cagey

❏ If you can't decide which travel carrier to buy for your pet, here are some guidelines. Metal cages are fine for car travel because they are airy and you can keep a close watch on the cage and your pet. But because they can collapse, they're not appropriate for air travel. If your pet will be flying, select a sturdy airline-approved travel carrier with no protrusions or sharp corners. You can find these at any good pet store or get one from your veterinarian.

Pup-sicles

❏ Pets, like people, can get dehydrated when traveling. To make sure your pet gets enough water during a plane trip, fill both the water and food dishes that come with a travel crate with water and freeze them the night before the trip. Return the cups to the crate just before your animal goes in. By the time the plane takes off, the ice will be melting, and your pet will have fresh, cold water for the entire trip.

Tag—You're It!

❏ It's hard enough keeping track of luggage when you're traveling, but at least your baggage isn't likely to run away on its own. The same can't always be said of pets. To keep track of your pet en route, make sure the tag the animal's wearing includes the address and phone number *where you'll be vacationing* (in addition to your home address and phone number). That way, if your pet wanders off, any Good Samaritan who finds the animal will be able to contact you where you are (not where you aren't). If you can't be contacted while on the road, list the address and phone number of a friend or relative who will be home and who knows about any health problems your pet may have.

Crating Problems

❏ It's not unusual for luggage handlers to try to pet animals, and if your pet bites, you may be liable. To save yourself potential problems, try writing, in large block letters with a permanent marker, "I BITE" directly on your pet's traveling crate.

TRAVEL DISORIENTATION

Scoping Out a New Town or Area

❏ Arriving in a city for the first time can be disorienting. To start figuring out what's what and what's where, make your first stop the tourist information booth. Airports and train stations in popular tourist areas nearly always have such facilities, and small towns often have roadside booths to point motorists in the right direction. Clerks there can provide maps and answer questions about sites and transportation. Some will even book you a room and—if you've arrived in town via train, plane, or bus—arrange for transportation to your lodging.

❏ Unfortunately, a tourist stepping into some city taxis might as well be wearing a sign that says, "Please take the most indirect route to my destination." You can avoid getting hornswoggled by asking someone—your innkeeper, a hotel concierge, or the cab dispatcher—how much the ride should be and what the most direct route is. Once you know, make sure the cabbie knows you know: "I'm going to the airport. That's about $10, right?"

Get Lost!

❏ When you visit a new city or town, it's all too easy to get hopelessly lost. Here are three things you can do to set yourself straight. First, keep the name, address, and phone number of your lodging with you at all times so that you can jump in a cab if you get turned around (you'd be surprised how easy it is to forget where you're staying). Second, carry a map. Get one from your bed-and-breakfast, inn, motel, or hotel or from a tourist information booth, guidebook, or bookstore in the city you're visiting. Third, pick a landmark, usually a distinctive building, to which you can orient yourself when you're wandering around.

> ### ☑ PROBLEM PREVENTED
>
> ## What Do You Mean My Bags Are in Budapest?
>
> You can minimize the frustration of lost luggage by carrying with you a list of the contents of your bags and an estimate of their worth. Just don't make the mistake of packing the list in your checked luggage!

RECEIVING AND SENDING MAIL

Hold It

❏ Piles of letters and catalogs around your mailbox are a surefire indication to burglars that your home and belongings are unattended. When you're planning to be away from home, stop the pileup by requesting that the post office hold your mail, which it will do for up to 30 days. If you'll be away for more than a month, ask the post office to forward your mail to you at your vacation destination. You can get a form for either option at your local post office.

Label Yourself Prepared

❑ You want to keep in touch while you're away, but who has room for a bulky address book? Save space in your luggage and make writing home easier by taking along labels on which you've written your friends' and family's addresses. When you have your postcards written, just peel off the labels and stick them on the cards.

Don't Forget to Write!

❑ Living away from home for an extended period—whether for business or pleasure—can be exciting, but it can be tedious and lonely, too. One way to ensure that your friends and family will write to you is to supply them with preaddressed labels or even preaddressed stamped envelopes.

BUSINESS TRAVEL

Iron Out Furniture Problems

❑ If you find yourself in a hotel room that doesn't have a desk, call the front desk and ask if there's a library nearby. If there is and it's open, head there to do your work.

❑ If your hotel room doesn't have a desk and there's no library handy, request an ironing board from housekeeping. Most are adjustable, so you should be able to make the top low enough to use with a chair.

Let Your Legs Do the Walking . . . To a Different Phone

❑ Reaching out to touch someone from your hotel room phone can be an expensive proposition. Some places charge as much as a dollar or more for calling card calls! A better idea is to find another phone—try the hotel lobby or the local library—whenever possible.

Seasonal Problems

The site I chose for my current home is partway up a steep hill—and in northern New England, a location like that is always a problem. I knew that getting up that hill in the snow and ice of winter might be hard, so when I designed the driveway, I didn't run it straight up to the house site. Instead, my son and I dug it into the side of the hill, with a switchback to get it up to the house. That increased the length of the driveway, so it took longer to build, but it kept the pitch of the driveway at a minimum.

But that's not all it did. I'm no more fond of removing snow than anyone else, so I designed the driveway to let

nature take care of that as much as possible. When the sun comes up in the morning, it melts the snow on the very top part of the driveway. As the sun comes around to the south during the day, it warms the switchback, then hits the lower section of the driveway as it moves into the west. The snowmelt from the upper driveway helps wash away snow lower down. This system removes most of the snow and ice from the steep section of the driveway, allowing me to get to and from my house safely. A little thoughtful planning and extra effort at the start of that job saved me a lot more work later on.

I've lived in New England for more than 84 years now, and in that time I've had more than my share of run-ins with muddy roads, frozen pipes, and dead car batteries. We Yankees pretty much have to become experts on such things, which is why this section is packed with practical ideas for getting rid of (and getting out of) the mud, drying out flooded basements, safely thawing frozen pipes, and warming up chilled hands and feet. You'll find better, faster ways to clear the snow and ice off your vehicle, great ideas for saving money on fuel, even tips on how to survive a blizzard. And there's room for seasonal fun here, too. Look in these pages for some great ways to save money on your vacation and eliminate hassles at your summer cabin.

SPRING AND SUMMER
When Living Should Be Easy

MUD SEASON

Who Left That Trail of Dirty Footprints?

❏ The bane of the mud season homeowner is mud tracked into the house. A simple, time-honored method of reducing tracked-in mud is to lay down a temporary "boardwalk" made from two-by-eight-inch or two-by-ten-inch boards. Lay the boards end to end along muddy paths, across the lawn, from the garage to the front door, or in any other area where mud would otherwise be picked up and tracked into the house. When the ground finally dries out, allow the boards to dry, then sweep the dirt off and store them for next mud season. Even without pressure treating or painting, boards used this way will stand up to years of mud and abuse.

Mud Mats

❏ Doormats, especially stiff-bristle mats, are a simple solution to the problem of tracked-in mud. Place them outside the entrance during dry weather, just inside when it's raining. If you're lucky enough to have a porch or covered entry, leave the mat outside all the time. Some households keep a mat on each side of the door.

❏ Consider using a different type of doormat during mud season—one with a grate or grill design. Typically made of wood or iron, these grates let you stomp, scrape, and kick mud off your shoes. The debris then

Mud Season

falls down through the slats rather than building up between the bristles or fibers of more traditional mats.

A Grate Idea

❏ Anxious to find a way to ditch the mud before it gets
into the house? Some people go to the extra effort of
installing iron grates—flush with the ground or deck—
in a permanent spot in front of the door. You can sometimes find such grates for a cheap price (or free) at
salvage yards or in the scrap metal pile at the local
landfill.

Scrape It Off—Scrape It All Off

❏ At many an old house entrance, a solution to the
problem of tracked-in mud is the traditional iron boot
scraper, often anchored to the old granite step. Since
mud stubbornly collects in the angle formed by the
sole and the heel of a boot, these scrapers often work
better than mats or grates. You can find old scrapers
at auctions and antiques stores; modern versions are
available at many home supply stores and from mail-
order catalogs.

Kickoff Time!

❏ If you're concerned about heavy loads of mud being
tracked into your house, consider installing a metal
kick plate (available at hardware and home supply
stores) below your door's threshold. A good swift kick
can help dislodge mud from boots and shoes—and the
kick plate will prevent that kick from dislodging any
of your house's siding.

What Is It about Dogs and Mud Puddles?

❏ Dogs tracking in mud can create more of a mess than
humans. Here are some options. Keep the dog in the
mudroom until the mud dries. Train your dog to sit or
wait by the door until the animal's paws dry. Or close
off rooms of the house that have fine wood floors or
carpeting.

Come Clean

❏ What's the best way to clean mud from floors, carpets, and other surfaces? Let the mud dry, then brush or sweep up the dirt.

A Newspaper Campaign against Mudslingers

❏ Tired of those piles of mud building up on the floor of your car or truck? To protect your vehicle's carpet from muddy boots, lay newspaper on the floor. Be sure to change the paper regularly to prevent it from soaking through.

Send Driveway Muck Down the Drain

❏ If your driveway seems to be an endless source of springtime mud, consider improving its drainage. Sometimes this is a simple matter of ditching or light grading—far less expensive than changing the surface. A well-drained driveway is graded slightly so that surface water runs off; it takes on little or no runoff from the land around it (ditches or swales help here); and it has porous, well-drained soil (meaning high sand or gravel content). A local sand and gravel company can help you to evaluate your driveway, often free of charge. (The company will get its money if you have problems.)

DOLLAR STRETCHER

Say Sayonara to Mud

The easiest, cleanest solution to mud in the house is to insist that people remove their shoes when entering. Place a rubber or plastic mat inside, next to the door, for muddy shoes. Keep some slippers or moccasins on hand for your visitors, or have them pad around on your wood floors in their stocking feet (that will help clean and shine your floorboards).

Ditch the Dirt

❏ A more permanent—and sometimes more expensive—solution to tracked-in mud is to cover up the driveway and walkway dirt that creates it. Pavement and pea stone are likely choices as replacements for dirt driveways. Pea stone can inhibit winter plowing, but because it's an aesthetically pleasing choice that's cheaper than pavement, it's appropriate for areas that don't get a lot of snow and for properties that don't have to be plowed out a lot (such as vacation homes).

❏ If you can afford the materials, consider surfacing your dirt walkways with pea stone, gravel, flagstone, or brick. Less expensive alternatives are bark chips and wood chips. The latter two materials produce less mud than does dirt, but they still have a tendency to be dirty—and to get tracked indoors—when wet. You can obtain wood and bark chips at a nursery or garden supply store. For sand and gravel, look in the Yellow Pages under (appropriately enough) Sand or Gravel.

Don't Be a Stick-in-the-Mud

❏ Dirt roads don't fall in as much as they did years ago, but they can still get soft enough to cause a car to get

stuck. If you find your tires spinning uselessly in the muck, one way to get out is to lay logs or branches side by side, corduroy fashion, tight against the spinning tire(s). Say, for example, you have one spinning tire. Jam a branch perpendicular to it, as far under the tread as you can push it. Then lay, say, five or six more branches up against each other in the same way, each one tight against the next. (Picture logs tied together in a raft or your fingers extended and close together.) Sometimes, you'll have to do this for more than one tire. Ease the car slowly onto the branches and keep driving. (Don't worry about leaving the branches in the road—the next driver to come along probably won't mind!)

Branch out from that mud hole! Grab any loose branches you can find and jam them in front of the stuck wheel for traction. Ease onto them carefully—and keep going!

SPRING WEATHER

Visibility? What Visibility?

❏ As the temperatures change with the season, fog and rain become a problem for drivers, especially at night. In addition to slowing down and increasing the distance between your car and the one in front of you, you can reduce the danger by using your fog lights or the low-beam setting of your headlights. They'll light the road rather than reflecting glare from the fog or rain back at you.

High Tide in Your Basement

❏ Melting snow, warm rain, and high water tables mean water in the basements of many homes every spring. If water is coming into your cellar through the sides or stones of the foundation, you may want to hire a contractor to improve the drainage around the outside of the foundation. (Ideally, the grade should slope away from the house on all sides.)

❏ Installing gutters also can help reduce the amount of water coming into the basement. And pointing (cementing the cracks of) an old stone foundation may help to limit the water that gets in.

High and Dry

❏ Boxes of papers and other valuables stored in the basement are always in danger of water damage. To protect such items from being ruined by leaks or flooding, store them on high shelves or on platforms made from two-by-fours set on bricks or concrete blocks.

SUMMER HEAT AND HUMIDITY

Go with the (air) Flow

❏ Does your home feel like an oven during the dog days of summer? Sometimes all a hot, stuffy house needs is a little ventilation. On breezy days, open windows on opposite sides of the house to create a cross breeze. Install a screen door and leave the solid doors open. Make sure fireplace dampers are open: Hot air rising will help circulation.

❏ On still, hot days, you may be better off keeping the windows closed and drawing the shades. Open the windows at night to let cooler air into the house. When using an electric fan, face it out an open window on the

8 Ways to Beat the Damp Basement Blues

In humid climates, summer often brings with it perpetual moisture in the basement—which can rot wood, peel paint, and cause rust and mildew. Here are eight steps you can take to reduce the dampness.

1. Improve the ventilation by installing screens and keeping foundation windows open.

2. Keep doors open.

3. Make sure your clothes dryer is vented to the outdoors.

4. Run an electric fan to help improve air movement. (Be sure to turn it off when you leave for an extended period of time.)

5. Install window exhaust fans.

6. Wrap all cold-water pipes (which have a tendency to sweat) with fiberglass insulation or foam sleeves.

7. Bring stored boxes outside to dry in the sunshine.

8. Fill a couple of cloth bags (roughly the size of a grocery bag) with calcium chloride and hang them from the ceiling to absorb moisture.

Note: Fiberglass insulation, foam sleeves, and calcium chloride are all available at home supply, building supply, and most good hardware stores.

hot side of the house, then open a window on the opposite (cooler) side of the house to allow cooler air to be drawn inside.

Heat Relief

❏ When the summer sun bears down, keep in mind a simple principle: Light colors reflect; dark colors absorb. Choose white or light-colored clothing during the most intense heat. When roofing or painting your house, consider using light colors to keep it from absorbing the heat. (This is a trade-off, however, if you live in a cold-winter climate.)

VACATION OPTIONS

Sharing Is Good

❏ Many people shy away from owning vacation property because they think it is too expensive. If this is the case with you, consider owning the property with one or more other families. After divvying up the cost, you would then divvy up the time spent there and the upkeep. Or if the property is large enough, you could all vacation there at the same time and also work on the place together. You also might consider buying the property, then renting it out during periods when you aren't staying there. (Be sure to consult an accountant before doing this. Such an arrangement could have tax implications.) Local real estate agencies often arrange and manage such rentals for people who live at a distance.

ONE PERSON'S SOLUTION

Hanging In There

I have a summer camp with a small porch and very little open space around it. For quite a while, I was resigned to going without a hammock because I couldn't find any combination of trees and porch posts the right distance apart for hanging one. But I was thinking too narrowly. Recently, from a couple of sturdy eyebolts screwed into the rafters holding up the porch ceiling, I was able to hang two pieces of rope just the right distance apart for my hammock. It's a good (and comfortable) solution for locating a hammock where you don't have properly spaced trees, posts, or walls.

—JIM COLLINS
Hillsborough, New Hampshire

Rent, Don't Buy

❑ How can you have the continuity and security of returning to the same summer place year after year if you can't afford to own it? Consider renting the same vacation cabin or cottage every summer. Most businesses accept reservations a year in advance, and it's typical to see the same families return again and again. By renting the same place at the same time each year, you can gain some of the best advantages of vacation property—happy memories, local knowledge, familiarity, treasured seasonal friendships—without the high cost of buying, maintaining, and paying taxes on property you own.

Low-Rent Districts

❑ How do you find a rental you can afford? Think about what makes a particular area popular at a certain time of year—then point your search in the *opposite* direction. If peace and quiet are the most important features of your summer vacation, look at rentals around ski areas. Consider a summer stay in a college town, where landlords have to cope with empty apartments and a reduced student population. If you like cross-country skiing, consider lakefront—not mountain—properties in the winter. If you're traveling without kids, avoid the busy weeks of summer and school vacations.

Time Your Stay

❑ Some of the most desirable vacation areas are prohibitively expensive during the height of the summer season. Before you write them off, check with businesses and chambers of commerce to see when and where seasonal rates are in effect. Often prices are high between Memorial Day and Labor Day (roughly coin-

DOLLAR STRETCHER

How to Finagle a Cheap (but memorable) Vacation

One inexpensive way to get away for a weekend or longer is to swap something other than your property. If you have skills such as painting, cooking, or carpentry, offer them in return for a stay at an inn or bed-and-breakfast. Or offer baby-sitting services in exchange for accompanying a family to their summer cottage. Be creative. Other people out there are just as interested in saving money as you are.

ciding with the school year). If you can plan your vacation for just before or just after the high season, you could save hundreds of dollars.

Don't Rent or Buy—Swap!

❑ An extended summer vacation is an appealing idea, but it can be prohibitively expensive if you're thinking in terms of renting or owning vacation property. Instead, consider a cheap, creative alternative: swapping houses with someone from a different part of the country or another country. Obviously, not everyone's location offers something as desirable as water frontage or mountain views, but all new locations offer a chance for people to explore and take a break from their normal routines. To arrange a swap, try sending an advertisement to a local paper in an area where you'd like to find a good trade. Or raise the idea to relatives or friends living in other parts of the country or world.

ONE PERSON'S SOLUTION

Mice in the Summer Camp

After years of opening up my summer camp to find myself cohabiting with a family of mice, I decided to try a new approach. My camp isn't too far from my home, so a couple of days before I plan to open it up for the season, I drop my cat off there. I make sure to leave enough water and food for the days I'm gone—but not enough to discourage the cat from doing a little hunting. By the time I'm ready to move in, the mice are tenant history.

—JIM COLLINS
Hillsborough, New Hampshire

SUMMER CAMPS

Sometimes It's Good to Be in Hot Water

❏ When opening up a camp, there's always a chance that you'll damage the hot-water heater or tank when you're getting things going again. If you're concerned about this possibility, be sure to fill the tank before turning on the heater at the fuse box or circuit breaker. Then check the tank by turning on a hot-water faucet. If water comes out, the tank is full, and you can turn on the heater. If water doesn't come out, the tank isn't full; give it a little more time. If water still doesn't come out after a long wait (say, an hour or more), call a plumber.

When Your Camp Becomes a Sand Castle

❏ A perpetual problem at summer camps is sand tracked in by wet feet. A plastic tub of water sitting next to the door is an easy solution. Make it a rule that all bare feet must be rinsed off before coming in.

❏ An outside shower or hose, while a bit more cumbersome, serves a similar purpose.

❏ Another way to reduce the amount of sand coming into the camp is to keep spare sandals or flip-flops

23 Things No Summer Camp Should Be Without

You came prepared for fun in the sun. Now the monsoons have started, and you realize you forgot the books and the board games. Don't feel bad. Nobody can remember everything—unless he's armed with this last-minute checklist.

Binoculars	Extra candles	Life jackets
Board games	Extra matches	Local bird and plant
Books	Extra rainwear	guides
Clothesline	Extra towels	Magazines
Clothespins	Fire extinguisher	Playing cards
Duct tape	First aid kit	Smoke detectors
Extra batteries	Flashlight	Sunglasses
Extra blankets	Insect repellent	Sunscreen

around for swimmers. Have your visitors step out of the sandals before coming in. (Flip-flops also are great for protecting feet on rocky or shale beaches.)

I Never Knew I Had So Many Friends!

❏ Owners of summer camps and vacation properties often get an unexpected bonus—a never-ending supply of people hoping to visit and enjoy the property, too. If you find yourself in that situation, consider looking at your vacation and weekend calendar and clearly setting aside time for family and time for being social. Schedule your visitors only during the days you've set aside for them. Establish a pattern—such as no visitors before the Fourth of July—and stick to it. Over time, your friends and relatives will learn when to ask and when not to.

❏ If adequate space or food is a problem at your cottage, recommend places for your guests to stay and eat during their visit, making it clear that you won't be providing those things.

How to Get Invited Back

❏ What if you are the one hoping to do the summer visiting, and you want to make sure your visit isn't a burden or an imposition? Limit your stay. Offer to bring along supplies or hard-to-find items or delicacies. Think of standard items that all camps can use: extra ice, beer and soda, snacks, charcoal, trash bags, paper plates and napkins. Volunteer to help do chores to earn your keep. Offer to carry away trash.

Don't Forget a Map to the Town Dump

If you arrange a house swap for your vacation, you can almost count on things coming up unexpectedly while you're away. Never leave anyone at your home or summer cottage without also leaving three lists prominently displayed for their benefit.

The first should be a list of important telephone numbers, including neighbors, police and fire departments, hospital emergency room or clinic, plumber, electrician, and veterinarian. The second should be a list of "how and where" for the house, including everything from how to separate recyclables to where to find the fire extinguisher. Finally, your guests will appreciate a list of hours for and directions to the dump and local businesses such as the nearest supermarket, gas station, and pizza parlor. Over time, you'll think of more information to add to the lists, and they'll prove invaluable to your visitors.

FALL AND WINTER
Surviving the Big Chill

PREPARING FOR WINTER

Rake Your Garden Clean

❏ Garden debris will harbor fungi and pests if you let it lie on the ground all winter. What to do? When the harvest is finished, rake the garden thoroughly to remove any stalks, fallen leaves, and mulch. Burn this debris or put it in a compost pile well away from the garden.

Leave 'Em

❏ Raking and bagging leaves is a seemingly endless chore in the fall. If you're tired of picking up after your trees (and your neighbors'), eliminate some of the bagging. Instead, rake leaves into a six-inch layer of winter mulch around shrubs. The mulch will keep the ground temperature even throughout the winter. This is a particularly good approach if you're dealing mostly with curly leaves, such as oak; they make looser, more aerated mulch than flat leaves, such as maple. Remove the leaves in the spring to let the soil warm up. Don't use leaves as mulch for perennial beds. They'll mat down and hold too much moisture for such plants.

Bough Down

❏ Snow makes a good insulator for perennial beds, rock gardens, and berry patches, but in many areas of the country, it melts or blows away as fast as it falls. To hold snow in place, try trimming branches from Christmas trees or wreaths after the holidays and using the boughs as mulch. Just place them loosely over the area you want to protect, then remove them in the spring.

Don't Let Your Hose Run

❏ Outside water spigots are always vulnerable to damage from freezing. So before the first hard freeze, remove any hoses from spigots, drain the hoses, and store them in loose coils. Shut off the flow to outside faucets, then drain each spigot and cover it with newspaper. Wrap the newspaper in a plastic bag and secure the plastic with rubber bands or tape. The newspaper will be an effective insulator, and the plastic will keep the newspaper dry.

Desalinization

❏ Spreading a layer of rock salt on exterior steps and sidewalks is a good way to melt the ice, but salt can damage nearby plants when it washes into the soil. How can you keep your traction without losing your garden? Ditch the salt and spread sand, cinders, or kitty litter over the ice instead.

CLOSING THE SUMMER CAMP

The Cupboard Should Be Bare

❏ Mice, squirrels, and other pests can make a mess in a closed summer camp. To keep their damage to a minimum, store dry foods in tightly closed glass or metal containers. (Mice can easily chew through things such as cereal boxes, plastic bags, and the plastic lids on hot chocolate containers.)

☑ PROBLEM PREVENTED

A Prewinter Checkup for Your Car

A leaky exhaust system can be especially dangerous to winter drivers. When you run the heater while your car is stopped in traffic, that faulty exhaust can funnel carbon monoxide right into the passenger compartment. Make a complete examination of the exhaust system part of an annual prewinter auto checkup—and ask your mechanic to check a few more things while he's at it. For instance:
- Antifreeze/coolant
- Battery
- Drive belts and hoses
- Heater core
- Lights
- Radiator (should be cleaned every year or two)
- Thermostat
- Tires
- Wipers

Checklist for Closing Up Camp

The bathing suits are packed away, the barbecue has been cleaned for the last time, and the boat's out of the water. What have you forgotten? To prevent problems when you open up next spring, this is the time to be sure you have taken care of the following tasks.

- Drained water completely
- Turned off propane at tanks
- Turned off circuit breakers
- Closed fireplace and wood-stove dampers
- Cleaned out and defrosted refrigerator, leaving the door open
- Disconnected appliances
- Closed and locked windows
- Cleaned gutters
- Checked for and removed any tree limbs overhanging the roof
- Removed or hidden valuables
- Pulled dock and raft on shore
- Removed all cans and bottles that could freeze and explode
- Spread mothballs or cedar chips on stored linen and bedding to deter mice

Keep Out Jack Frost

❑ If you've had problems in the past with damage from frost inside your cabin, make sure to leave all room and closet doors partway open when you close up for the season. If you close off each room, those on the sunny side of the house will be much warmer than those on the shady side. And that means frost is likely to form on the outside walls of those closed rooms.

Theft Guards

❑ Off-season security has become an increasing problem among summer camp owners. To ward off winter burglars, take a few extra precautions when you close up your camp. Put your television set in a cabinet; put your VCR or stereo under a bed; hide guns and other valuables in drawers or closets. Leave the curtains and shades up so that anyone can see there is nothing to steal and passersby can see anybody who enters.

❑ To make sliding glass doors extra secure, cut a piece of broomstick to fit snugly in the track behind the door that opens. Tuck the broomstick into place before you leave, and any would-be intruders will have a hard time forcing the door open.

Put a Ban on Midwinter Snacks

❑ Porcupines have been known to chew wooden boats and paddles (especially the handles, which hold salts where you've gripped them).

To keep the winter nibblers at bay, store your boats and paddles out of reach—from the rafters or on racks high up off the floor.

❏ Similarly, hang up life jackets to keep them away from mice.

INSIDE THE WINTER HOME

How Dry I Am

❏ In winter, your house can get as dry as the Sahara, especially if you heat with wood. The resulting dry air is uncomfortable for humans and unhealthy for woodwork and furniture, but you can augment household humidity without augmenting your budget. Just put a little extra water in the teakettle when you boil water, then leave the kettle on the burner as it cools. It will continue to steam for 10 to 15 minutes.

Don't Pay the Piper

❏ Severe cold spells can freeze pipes near exterior walls or vents, in basements or crawl spaces, and under porches. Besides cutting off the water supply, frozen pipes are a serious threat because they can burst under the pressure of expanding ice, then flood unchecked when they thaw. To protect vulnerable pipes when a hard freeze is predicted, wrap them in fiberglass insulation, foam sleeves, or newspaper and cover the insulating material with plastic to keep everything dry. Attach the insulation with duct tape, string, or wire.

❏ Protect especially vulnerable pipes and those that have frozen before with electric-powered heat tape (available at hardware stores and plumbing supply stores). Attached along the length of the pipe, this tape generates a steady supply of warmth when it is plugged in, keeping pipes from freezing.

❏ Insulation protects pipes from freezing, and so does heat tape. So combining the two should be a really good idea, right? Wrong. Never place insulation on top of heat tape. Doing so could cause a fire.

Keep Your Powder Dry and Your Water Flowing

❑ Moving water is slow to freeze. To keep water flowing inside vulnerable pipes, open a nearby faucet and let cold water drip from it very slowly. Leave the appropriate cabinet and closet doors open to allow warm air to reach the pipes. And if you're going away during a cold snap, set the thermostat a bit higher than you otherwise would.

Yikes! Frozen Pipes!

❑ If a water pipe freezes, the ice inside may expand enough to burst the pipe unless it is thawed promptly—and bursting can mean you end up with broken pipes *and* a flood on your hands. But the wrong approach to

Simple Ways to Cut the Cost of Cold Snaps

In many areas, a disproportionate chunk of the annual heating bill is generated during winter's few periods of deep cold. No matter what heat source you use—oil, gas, electricity, or wood—you can cut heating bills by adopting temporary measures to keep the thermostat turned down.

1. Temporarily close off heat to some rooms by shutting doors. (This requires a heating system that can be controlled room by room.) Shut the doors to unheated closets, the pantry, and the basement and attic.

2. Hang blankets over the windows at night. Tape or thumbtack the sides and bottom of the blankets to the walls or windowsills to maximize the insulation value. (Press the tacks or tape under the bottom of the sill and over the top of the frame to hide any damage to the finish.) Remove the coverings on the south side of the house during the day.

3. Cover cracks around doors and windowsills with rugs, newspaper, towels, or other insulation.

4. Use electric space heaters in living or work areas. These are more efficient than the furnace for localized heating, and they will allow you to set the thermostat lower for the whole house.

5. Put on a sweater.

6. Cook a hot meal.

thawing pipes can result in another set of problems—even explosions and fires. What to do? First, determine as closely as possible which area is frozen. Usually several feet or more will freeze. This will always be in a place most exposed to the cold and along a pipe leading to faucets or appliances where water is not running. The process of elimination will lead you close to the trouble spot. Open the nearest faucet so you'll be able to tell when the water starts running again (and to eliminate any possibility of steam buildup). Wrap the affected area of the pipe in rags, place a pot underneath the pipe, and then pour boiling water over the rags. (The rags help to hold the heat on the frozen spot.) Repeat until the water starts flowing through the pipe.

❑ An alternative approach is to apply heat from a handheld hair dryer or heat lamp. If you do this, work from the open faucet toward the frozen area, to allow any steam that is created to escape. Never use a propane torch or heat the pipe hotter than you can touch. And always be extremely careful to keep any electrical cords away from water.

Flood Control

❑ When a pipe bursts, it doesn't take long for major flood damage to occur in your house. To protect your home, teach everyone in the household how to shut off the main water valve. You'll often hear a loud bang when a pipe breaks, and you should race to turn off that valve to reduce flood damage. If you have an electric hot-water heater, turn it off at the circuit breaker at the same time. Once you've located the leak, find the valve controlling the water supply to that area and close it; then you can turn on the water to the rest of the house.

Quick Fixes for Leaking Pipes

❑ When frozen pipes burst, they usually burst all over town, and you may have to wait a while for a plumber to make repairs. How can you make a temporary fix in the meantime? If you're dealing with pinpoint holes or small cracks, wind waterproof tape, such as

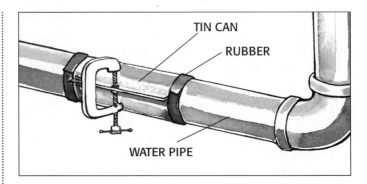

electrical tape, tightly around the problem areas. Larger breaks require a rubber pad and pipe clamp (available at hardware stores). Wrap the pad around the pipe, then screw the clamp around the pad to hold it tight. In a pinch, cut a tin can into a flat sheet and hold it onto the rubber pad and the pipe with a C-clamp. Don't forget that these are just short-term solutions; you'll still need to hire a plumber to make permanent repairs.

Bread upon the Water(s)

❏ When you're repairing a leak in a copper water pipe or doing any soldering on existing copper plumbing, you have to be sure the pipes you're working on are completely clear of water. Even a dribble left in the line will keep the copper pipe from reaching sweating (soldering) temperature and make it impossible to melt solder and make connections. No matter what you do to drain the line, however, sometimes a little water creeps down the pipe to upset the work. What to do? An old plumber's trick to keep a pipe dry is to plug it carefully—a foot or so back from the problem area—with a wad of bread. The bread keeps the drip at bay while you work, but it will dissolve once the repairs are complete and the full force and flow of the water are restored.

Dammed Ice

❏ Excess heat loss from a home can cause ice dams on the roof. These small glaciers in the eaves and valleys of roofs form when the roof's surface heats above freezing but the outside temperature is still cold. Dams can cause water to back under shingles, shakes, or tiles and leak into the house, damaging insulation, paint, and structural members. If you've been plagued by ice dams in the past, here's how you can stop them from recurring. Keep warm air away from the roof by sealing nearby openings around light fixtures, bathroom fans, plumbing vents, electrical outlets, chimneys, attic hatches, and the like, using caulk or weather strip, as appropriate.

❏ If ice dams continue to be a problem, have a builder or handyman examine the attic insulation to make sure it is stopping the heat from getting into the attic and warming the roof. Have this person check the attic vents as well. Inlet vents along the eaves and outlet vents in the peak are designed to funnel cold outside

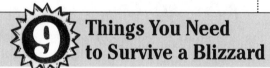

9 Things You Need to Survive a Blizzard

When a winter storm strikes, the power to your house may go out for hours or days. It may be impossible to travel to stores—which likely will be closed anyway. Stock up before the emergency with the following supplies, store them where you can find them quickly (even in the dark), and you'll be prepared to weather any storm.

1. Flashlights and extra batteries. Battery-powered camping lanterns and hands-free headlamps are very helpful. Use candles for light only if no other option is available. Burning candles create a fire hazard at a time when fire fighting would be extremely difficult.

2. Portable, battery-operated radio and extra batteries to keep up with emergency bulletins—and to keep your spirits up.

3. First aid kit.

4. One week's supply of food that does not require refrigeration or cooking, such as canned goods and sandwich fixings.

5. Manual can opener.

6. One week's supply of essential prescription medications. (Be sure you don't allow these to go out-of-date.)

7. Extra blankets and sleeping bags.

8. Fire extinguisher.

9. Bottled water. Lay in a week's worth at two quarts per person per day.

air under the roof, above the insulation. These vents may need to be enlarged if damming is a problem, especially on a roof with a shallow pitch.

High-Level Snow Shoveling

❏ One cause of ice dams is snow piled on the roof, blocking roof vents. To keep dams from re-forming, shovel or rake the snow off the roof if it blocks the vent pipes. (You also should start shoveling if the snow piles up two feet or more, at which point its weight may threaten the structure.) Be extremely careful when shoveling snow from a roof. You may damage the shingles with your shovel blade, and you may damage yourself if you fall off!

HEATING WITH WOOD

Wait Until the Smoke Clears

❏ A smoky fireplace or woodstove not only smells up the house and soils walls, ceilings, and furniture, but it also builds up creosote deposits on the stovepipe and chimney, which can lead to a dangerous chimney fire. If your fire is smoky, you may be able to correct the problem by changing the firewood you burn. Avoid

Fireplace Accessories You Can't Do Without

When you start working with a fireplace or woodstove for the first time, the following tools (available from fireplace supply stores and hardware stores) will make the job easier and neater. Be sure the wood carrier is heavy enough to support several sticks of firewood and the gloves are both insulated and fireproof. As for the metal tools, such as pokers and tongs, look for wrought iron. It hides dirt well and doesn't transmit heat to your hands as much as other metals.

1. Canvas wood carrier for carrying logs without messing up your clothes
2. Gloves
3. Long-handled brush
4. Metal ash bucket
5. Poker
6. Shovel
7. Tongs

softwoods such as pine and hemlock, which contain a lot of smoke-producing resins, and stick to hardwoods such as oak, ash, maple, and beech.

❏ Another way to eliminate smoky fires is to make sure the wood you burn is well seasoned—that is, with minimum moisture content. Typically, this means letting cut-and-split firewood dry outdoors under cover for close to a year before using it.

❏ If you've lost track of how long your firewood has been drying (or if you didn't cut it yourself and don't know how well seasoned it is), you can monitor its moisture content. Every two weeks or so, weigh the same log. Once the weight stops dropping, the wood is about as dry as it will get.

Other Smoke Signals

❏ If your stove or fireplace tends to be smoky when you first start a fire, then burns normally, it may be the cold pipe or chimney that's keeping it from drawing. To help your flue get started, try this trick. Build your fire, then place a couple of pages of crumpled newspaper on top of it. Light the newspaper and let it burn out before you ignite your real fire. The newspaper will generate some warmth to get the air moving up the chimney without producing a lot of smoke.

Fat(wood) Lights Your Fire

❏ If you're frustrated with your efforts to light a fire in a fireplace or woodstove, inadequate starting materials may be the problem. Crumpled newspaper is the least expensive material to use as a base layer, but chemically impregnated fire-starter sticks burn hotter and longer. Slivers of very dry wood work well for kindling, but many people prefer fatwood, a highly flam-

DOLLAR STRETCHER

Double Coverage for Your Woodpile

If you cover a woodpile with a plastic tarp, you may end up replacing the tarp every year, after it shreds and disintegrates from the effects of wind and ultraviolet rays. To get more life out of a new tarp, cover it with the old one, which may no longer be waterproof but will act as a shield against the sun's harmful rays.

Heating with Wood

mable, resin-filled kindling made from southern pine. Most fireplace suppliers sell fire starters and fatwood.

HEALTH AND SAFETY

Warm Hands in Hup, Two, Three

❏ Cold hands are the bane of many winter travelers and outdoors people. The U.S. Army has developed a long-term method for training the blood vessels of your hands to stay open even when the body is cold, keeping the hands warmer. This method also helps warm some people's feet.

To begin this treatment, you should be dressed lightly in indoor clothing. Fill a container with hot tap water (104° to 108°F). Prewarm your hands under warm water for a couple of minutes, then dry your hands and cover them with mittens or gloves. Carry the hot water to an unheated area—a porch, unheated garage, or front yard—then remove the mittens and plunge both hands into the hot water for ten minutes. Your body should feel uncomfortably cool, but don't let yourself get severely chilled. Now cover your hands, return inside for five minutes, and reheat the water in the container. Warm and dry your hands again, cover them for the trip outside, and repeat the ten-minute soak. Repeat the entire process a third time.

Army research says you must follow this method every other day for six weeks—a total of 18 days, with 3 ten-minute sessions each day. That's a lot of effort, but many people report dramatic improvement in their circulation as a result. This conditioning may last as long as several years, although some people have to retrain their blood vessels every year.

Put a Lid on It

❏ If your hands (or feet) are cold, put a hat on. This old skier's lore is based on physiology. Your head is laced with blood vessels close to the surface (which is why scalp wounds bleed so profusely), and your body automatically sends blood to the scalp to warm the brain. Covering the head will keep these blood vessels warm, allowing more blood to flow to your extremities.

Help for Hypothermia Victims

❏ Prolonged exposure to cold, wet conditions can lead to a dangerous lowering of the body temperature, called hypothermia. Symptoms include uncontrollable shivering, slurred speech, stumbling, and drowsiness. To treat hypothermia, get the victim into dry clothes and warm her slowly, starting with her trunk. Use your own body heat to help, perhaps by getting in a sleeping bag with the victim. Warm the arms and legs last to avoid driving cold blood toward the heart and risking heart failure. Seek medical help immediately.

❏ Never give a hypothermia or frostbite victim caffeinated drinks, hot chocolate, or alcohol. Stimulants or depressants can hasten the ill effects of cold. Instead, serve warm soup or energy drinks such as Gatorade, or just plain warm water.

Reach Out and Call Someone

❏ If a major snowstorm hits while you're at work and your children are at school, your family may be separated. How can you make sure you're able to find each other at such a time? Develop a plan for communicating and getting back together in an emergency. Ask an out-of-state relative or friend to be the family contact. (In a severe snowstorm, long-distance calls often are more reliable than local calls.) Adults should call the contact immediately and develop a plan that can be relayed as other calls come in. Make sure all members of the household carry the name and phone number of the contact person with them at all times.

DRIVING

Forestall the Ice Age

❏ Did you make it safely to your destination during the snowstorm, only to find that when you returned to your car, a polar ice cap had formed on your windshield? It may be that your defroster is actually causing the problem. This time, you'll just have to scrape, but you may be able to avoid a repeat performance. When you run your car's defroster during a snowstorm, the snow that accumulates after you park outdoors is likely to melt and then freeze on your windshield. Next time you're driving through a snowstorm, try turning off the defroster at least ten minutes before you park. This will give the windshield time to cool down. If you park indoors, brush the windshield before you leave the car to remove accumulated snow that may freeze. You'll be glad you did when you return.

When the Car Turns Into an Ice Sculpture

❏ If ice from a winter storm forms a stubborn sheet on your car's windshield overnight, start the car and get the defroster going. Then fill a pan with hot (not boiling) water. Pour the water slowly over the windshield. The heat will melt the ice, and the defroster will keep it from refreezing. Once you're driving, keep the defroster on to keep the windshield clear.

Break the Ice

❏ In really miserable winter weather, such as freezing rain, the doors on your car may freeze shut. If this happens, try smacking the side of the door, near the edge where it opens, with the palm of your gloved hand or even your foot. Doing so may break the icy bonds. If this fails, try one of the deicing sprays sold at auto

---

💲 DOLLAR STRETCHER

Let Everyone Think You Just Drove In from Miami

Want to improve your fuel economy in winter? Get all that snow off your car. The weight of the snow and the increased wind resistance it causes dramatically increase fuel consumption. Scraping or brushing the snow off the roof, trunk, and hood of your car will result in better mileage.

---

parts stores and many gas stations. Sprayed around the edges of the doors, these chemicals may melt enough of the ice to let you in. (Be sure to keep such sprays in the house or garage—not inside the car—so they're available when you need them.)

❏ If the keyhole is filled with ice or frozen snow, spray it with deicer. (Some discount stores sell deicers in containers small enough to be carried routinely in a purse or jacket pocket.) Or heat your key with a cigarette lighter or match and quickly insert it into the lock; the warm metal may melt the ice. If this doesn't work, try heating the head of the key while it's in the lock. Wear gloves when you touch the hot key!

❏ Once you've broken through the ice shield and into your car, how can you avoid a recurrence of the problem? Spray a light coat of silicone or WD-40 on the rubber gaskets inside the door. This will sometimes prevent ice from sticking and jamming the door.

On the Skids

❏ Stopping a car that's skidding on ice has always been scary. Now it's confusing, too, because to control a skid properly, you have to remember what kind of brakes your car has. With old-fashioned brakes, the best way to control a skid is to pump the brake pedal about once a second; the gaps between applications of brake pressure allow the wheels to turn and the car to be steered. (Locked-up wheels don't steer properly.) With an antilock braking sys-

A Winter Emergency Kit for Your Car

I f you travel frequently in winter, you may be trapped at one time or another by severe snow. Keep the following items in your car all winter, and you'll be ready to brave the blizzard.

- Flashlight with extra batteries
- First aid kit with pocketknife
- Supply of essential prescription medications (be sure you don't allow these to go out-of-date)
- Several blankets or sleeping bags
- Plastic bags (for sanitation)
- Matches or lighter
- Extra set of mittens, socks, and wool cap
- Small sack of sand for generating traction under wheels
- Small shovel
- Booster cables
- Set of tire chains or traction mats
- Cards, games, and puzzles
- Brightly colored cloth to use as a flag
- Canned fruit and nuts; energy bars
- Manual can opener
- Chemical hand warmers (available at many outdoor-equipment stores)

tem (ABS), the correct procedure is to step hard on the brake pedal and keep your foot down. The ABS automatically pumps the brakes many times faster than you could, and you can continue to steer the car normally. If you're not sure whether your car has an ABS, consult your owner's manual.

Shovel Off in Buffalo

❏ A snow shovel is a useful thing to carry in the car to remove major accumulations, dig yourself out of drifts, or spread sand for traction. Unfortunately, most shovels are too unwieldy to carry in the trunk. A good portable option is an avalanche shovel, carried by backcountry skiers. These one- or two-piece, broad-scoop shovels are less than three feet long when assembled and weigh about a pound. They are available at ski and mountaineering shops. Or pack a child's

Traction and Humility

Four-wheel-drive vehicles are great for winter travel, but they aren't foolproof. Those fools who assume that four-wheel drive will pull them through any snowdrift frequently get stuck. I learned this one January when I was trying to find the start of a cross-country ski trail in the Colorado Rockies. The snow seemed awfully deep on the road to the trail, but it was packed, so I assumed other vehicles had made it, and I just kept going. After all, I was in four-wheel drive. Near the top of a large hill, the snow was nearly a foot deep. Suddenly, I drifted off the shoulder of the road and lodged firmly against a row of small trees.

I tried all the usual tricks for getting out—rocking the truck, digging snow from under the body, shoveling sand and gravel under the wheels—but the truck only ground in deeper. Spotting smoke up the hill, I hiked to a house to seek help and discovered what had made the tracks on the road: an old snow groomer from a ski area.

In the end, I had to call a tow truck from the nearest big town, an hour away. The truck was able to pull me out—to the tune of $200. And the ski trail? Turns out I had already driven a mile up it. That's what the four-wheeling mentality will do for you.

—Dougald MacDonald
Denver, Colorado

shovel. Save these short-handled shovels for emergencies, and don't pile them too heavily with snow. They're murder on the back.

A Portable Beach

❑ Rear-wheel-drive cars are disappearing in snow country because their traction is so poor. But rear-wheel-drive pickups, vans, and station wagons are still around—and still getting stuck on snow-covered hills every winter. If you drive such a vehicle in snow country, you'll need a way to improve its traction. A classic—and effective—approach is to carry 40 or 50 pounds of sand, packed in burlap or nylon bags, in the bed of your truck or rear end of your van or station wagon. (These bags are available at hardware, garden supply, and building supply stores.) The extra weight will put more of a load on your rear wheels, and the sand can be spread on the ground for additional traction if you get stuck.

Rock and Roll

❑ When you get stuck in snow or mud, gunning the engine will only dig your wheels in deeper. Try easing forward or backward gently—sometimes you can just slip out of the jam. If that doesn't work, "rock" the car. Drive forward as far as you can, quickly put the car in reverse and go back as far as you can, then quickly go forward again, and repeat. Often the car's momentum will clear a track and allow you to break free. This method is hard on the transmission, so if a couple of rock and roll sessions fail to free your car, call a tow truck.

Reach for the Tank Top

❑ If your car performs poorly on cold mornings, water vapor in the air inside your fuel tank may be condensing and getting into the fuel. To minimize this effect, make it a point to keep the gas tank at least half full in winter.

✔ **PROBLEM PREVENTED**

The No-Salt Spray

The radiator in the front of your car is especially vulnerable to corrosion from road salt. When you wash the car, make sure to spray through the front grille to clean the accumulated salt off the radiator and fend off rust.

Stranded!

❏ If you drive enough in snow country, blizzard conditions may someday trap you in your car. What should you do? The first rule in such an emergency is to stay in the car, or you may get lost in the blowing snow. Leave the car to find help only if you can see your destination within 100 yards. Let passersby or rescuers know you're in trouble by displaying a sign, hanging a brightly colored rag from the radio antenna, and raising the hood if the wind isn't too strong.

❏ To keep warm when a blizzard leaves you stranded in your car, run the engine for about ten minutes each hour. Turn the heater on full blast during that time. Make sure the exhaust pipe is clear of snow, and crack a downwind window for ventilation while the engine is running. The rest of the time, do some exercises, such as clapping or "running" in place, to keep your blood circulating. For the same reason, don't sit in one position for too long. If there is more than one person in the vehicle, huddle together for warmth and take turns sleeping. Use whatever insulation you can find, including newspapers, maps, or floor mats, to cover your torso.

✔ **PROBLEM PREVENTED**

Sweep Away the Snow

To be prepared for snowstorms that strike when you're away from home, cut off half the handle of a standard broom, then leave the broom in your car trunk. The sawed-off broom will be much stronger than the brush on a standard snow scraper, and you'll be able to clear the car in half the time.

The Stages of Life

After working on other people's houses for years and building two of my own, I knew what I wanted when it came time to build my current home. The first decision I had to make, and maybe the most important one, was where to put it. I knew that a south-facing slope was the best place for a house in New England, so I got topographical maps for the towns I thought I might want to live in and colored in with crayon every accessible south-facing slope I could find. On the weekends, my wife, son, and I drove around to look at the sites I had marked. Some weren't right for us, and others weren't for sale. One farmer refused to sell to me, thinking I

was just like all the other "city folk" and would complain about his cows after I bought the land. I finally found the right piece of property on the south face of a steep, rocky hill. The slope kept the trees from interfering with the view and allowed the sun to hit the site all day long, while the top of the hill to the north blocked the cold winter wind. It was useless to the farmer who owned it, and he sold me 40 acres for a good price. By taking my time and doing my homework, I found a site I knew I would never regret choosing, and I got it at a good price.

I might not have been so smart—or so patient—when I was younger, but I've learned a thing or two over the years. And not just about buying land either. I know more about raising a family now than I did when I started out, and I'm getting this "senior citizen" thing figured out, too. (If folks are willing to charge me less because I'm over 50, that's fine by me.) That's why I know the tips in this section are good ones.

"The Family" offers some bright ideas for coping with homework, keeping the lines of communication open, and helping teenagers to find jobs (and money). "On the Move" suggests ingenious ways for selling your old house and checking out a new one, provides a step-by-step time line for moving, offers lifesaving last-minute packing tips, and tells how to find your way around that new city you've moved to. And "Getting Older" tells you how to cope with everything from loneliness to absentmindedness to chronic health problems—and explains where you can get those valuable senior discounts.

THE FAMILY
Oh, Those Growing Pains!

YOUNG CHILDREN

Mommy, I'm Bored

❑ Sometimes a boxcar full of toys isn't enough to interest a young child with a short attention span. To get more play value out of the toys he already has, try the old hideaway trick: When he's not looking, pilfer a couple of toys and stash them away in a closet. Later on, when your child complains about being bored, bring out one of the toys that's been in hiding. Because it's been out of sight, it will seem almost new again, and he'll take some time getting reacquainted with it. It's a little sneaky—but effective.

Give a Gold Star

❑ If you're looking for a way to get a small child involved in housework, make up a chart listing all the chores he has to do before the end of the day, then ask him to draw a picture of each chore. Make sure he knows that after all his chores are done, you'll reward him with a gold star or sticker on his chart, and perhaps a special treat.

Toys for Grown-Ups

❑ Looking for a good home for those stuffed animals and action figures that your youngster loved but outgrew all too soon? When a child no longer uses a toy that's still in good condition, pass it on to an older adult who occasionally plays host to grandchildren or other young relatives or friends. It will provide the older person with something "new" for young visitors to play with. Many nonparents and older folks aren't up on what's hot with today's kids. Giving them toys that your child has enjoyed could make them a big hit with the children in their lives. (It can save them money, too.)

EDUCATION

A Desk of One's Own?

❏ A desk dedicated to homework and studying may be ideal but is not always possible due to space or budget limitations. Plus, some kids feel isolated sitting alone in their rooms and actually work better where they can interact with family members. How can you set up an efficient work space for your child? Identify a spot with enough room to spread papers out, good light, and the necessary writing and art supplies. Your child will be

Planned Party-hood

Does it seem that kids' birthday parties become more elaborate—and expensive —every year? Before you stress out playing Can You Top This, consider the alternatives. Here are a few possibilities.

• If your young child loves fire trucks, ask your local fire department if you can hold a party at the station house or bring the kids in for a close-up look at the trucks.

• Let your child invite a few friends out to a roller rink, amusement park, or video game arcade. After the activity, take everyone out for ice cream sundaes.

• If you live in a small town, invite your child to attend a special event in the city—a basketball game, an ice or gymnastics show, or a theatrical performance. Make it something exciting and special that he's always wanted to do. If the budget allows, let him bring a best friend along.

• Plan a treasure hunt. Plant clues around the house, in a playground, or in a limited area within a park. Award small prizes and provide goody bags for all the guests to take home.

• Have a baking party. Make cookies or cupcakes and set out sprinkles, raisins, nuts, candies, and other items for the kids to decorate them with. Have a contest to see who can make the most beautiful (or craziest or funniest) cupcake.

most productive wherever she feels most comfortable—whether it's a coffee table in the living room or a card table on the porch. Sitting on the bed is OK, too. Get a lightweight portable drawing board (available at art supply stores) for her to lean on. For the desk-less student, simplify setup time by keeping school supplies in a portable carrier that packs up easily—a tool kit, lunch box, basket, or discarded suitcase or briefcase.

Study Guides

❏ All kids struggle with homework from time to time, but if yours is having serious, ongoing difficulty, talk to his teacher. Find out whether other students are having similar problems or whether your child is falling behind the rest. Discuss the problem and how the three of you can work together to solve it. The teacher may recommend special tutoring or screening for learning disabilities.

❏ If you need to hire a tutor, your child's school is a good place to start. Teachers often work as tutors on the side after school. Your child's current teacher also may know of a retired teacher who's interested in tutoring. Or check with a local college for information on students who tutor to earn extra money.

Testing, Testing

❏ Does your child study hard the night before a test—and then forget everything by the next day? Studying out loud with a tape recorder is a great technique for self-testing and aiding memory. Hearing the subject explained in her own voice will help her remember better because her aural sense will reinforce what her eyes have read. If her schoolbook includes quiz questions, she can tape a "test rehearsal" to reveal how well she knows and understands the material in the first place. But if she's really stumbling over difficult concepts or a lot of hard-to-remember facts, just reading aloud and playing the tape back can help.

Much Ado about Literature

❏ Let's face it, classic literature such as Shakespeare's plays can be rough going even for the best of students.

A recording of the work can be a helpful solution; check your local library for a copy. Suggest that your child read along as the actors speak their lines. Their vocal inflections and phrasing will help bring the words to life and shed light on the meaning and characters.

KIDS AND COMPUTERS

The PC Alarm Clock

❏ You might think your kids should use the home computer as much as they can because of its educational benefits, but the bills can mount up fast if they log on to certain on-line services. If you're concerned about the expense, set a maximum daily allowance of time on such services. Teach your kids to set the alarm on the computer before logging on so that they won't lose track of time. Or simply put a kitchen timer by the computer and make it a rule that they set the clock before dialing up.

Kid-Proof the Hard Drive

❏ Children are natural explorers, and the computer opens up a vast terrain. But if the whole family is sharing a computer, how can you make sure your child doesn't accidentally rewrite that business presentation you've been working on for the past month? Invest in one of the computer programs that allows children access only to their own files. One example is KidDesk Family Edition, made by Edmark Corporation, and available for less than $45 from most software suppliers.

❏ An alternative is to create a computer folder of documents and programs for each child and strictly enforce the embargo (or put passwords on sensitive files). Just to be safe, though, back up all your vital documents frequently.

Grandma On-Line

❏ If grandparents are far away and feeling out of touch, set up an on-line connection that allows them to communicate with family members on a casual, routine basis. Sending E-mail is an especially good way to cross generational lines. Kids who balk at writing letters or talking on the phone often become great communicators when a computer is involved. (They'll probably enjoy showing off their superior technical skills to the older folks, too.) And introducing an older person to the Internet can open up a whole new world, providing access to information about travel, hobbies, senior groups, health issues, and much more.

❏ If you need buying advice or help setting up the equipment, you can hire a computer consultant, usually for an hourly fee (check the Yellow Pages under Computers—Service & Repair). Or call your local high school and ask the computer teacher to recommend a computer-savvy high school student who can help you get up and running. After that, it's easy to master the basics.

❏ If the older generation in your family seems interested but hasn't yet moved into the electronic age, consider whether a computer and modem for the grandparents would make a good Christmas gift. See if other relatives would be willing to share the cost. If possible, visit for the holidays and set up the computer as part of the gift.

THE FAMILY UNIT

Prevent Video Vegetation

❏ Have potatoes begun to sprout on your couch where the kids used to be? To prevent video vegging (whether it's TV or mindless computer games), set up a system that requires your kids to *earn* screen

TIME SAVER

Don't Think— Just Chop

Want your kids (or spouse) to help out with dinner but find it's easier to do it yourself? Don't give up trying to share the workload with family members, but to get good results from inefficient helpers, do the organizing and thinking for them. Instead of issuing a general request, such as "Please make a salad," assign a very specific task: "Please chop all these vegetables with this knife and put them in that salad bowl."

Although this requires some planning and setup on your part, it streamlines the job for your helper and eliminates wasted time spent looking for things and deciding which ingredients to use. Just think of yourself as the brains of the operation, with an extra pair of hands at your disposal. Of course, you should always encourage initiative in the kitchen, but in its absence, at least you'll get those vegetables chopped.

time. The parameters and the rate of exchange are up to you. For instance, if they're allowed to watch TV or play on the computer an hour a day for "free," insist that they earn anything extra by spending comparable time engaged in some other activity. It doesn't have to be chores or homework—just something you want them to do more of, such as reading, playing outside, or spending time with a younger brother or sister.

❏ To bring excessive TV watching under control, set limits. But don't go overboard—severely restricting TV time will only make it more attractive. Let kids know you expect them to be selective TV consumers. Have them plan in advance what they want to watch and budget the time for it (after their homework is done). No channel surfing themselves into a stupor is allowed.

TIME SAVER

Can a Billion Chinese Be Wrong?

Putting dinner on the table night after night is an ongoing challenge for most busy families. One smart strategy for weeknights is to build meals around the world's favorite grain: rice. It's cheap, nutritious, and filling, and because of its mild taste, it can serve as the foundation for a wide range of meals. Keep a large supply on hand, along with frozen vegetables or salad ingredients, and you'll always have the basis for a healthful, homemade dinner. Round it out with an easy entrée—take-out roast chicken, frozen burritos—and voilà! Dinner is served.

To make preparing this simple food even simpler, invest in a rice cooker or an automatic steamer (available at kitchen supply stores). These turn off automatically when the rice is done or the preset timer rings, so you can set up the rice and walk away. Make a large quantity and save what's left over. The next day, you can reheat it fast in the microwave.

Since rice takes on the flavor of whatever it's mixed with, let kids experiment with their favorite condiments and toppings. Ketchup, soy sauce, salad dressing, salsa, hoisin sauce, and cheese sauce are all valid options.

Meet Them Halfway

❏ Do your kids love getting together with their out-of-town cousins, but you balk at the thought of hosting a houseful of company? To make get-togethers easier for everyone, meet friends or relatives halfway and spend the day doing something you all enjoy. It's especially easy when the weather's warm, and this gives you a chance to establish a fun midyear family tradition. Pick a central location such as a state park, lake, or beach. The best sites are places where you can relax, set up a picnic or cookout, and engage in some other activity—go for a hike, pick blueberries, swim, or play volleyball. Split up the job of bringing food and supplies. Since nobody has to play host, this approach avoids the problem of having to clean up the house before and after the party!

Matchmaker, Matchmaker

❏ Let's say your dad is newly retired and feeling a little lost and your ten-year-old could use more supervision after school. Is there a practical solution here? If you'd like to encourage a closer relationship between your child and an older relative or friend, try a little behind-the-scenes matchmaking. Does Grandpa have a hobby or interest your son or daughter might enjoy? Suggest they go golfing together, to a sports event, or swimming at the local gym. If he's a coin collector, buy your child a starter set as a gift, then recommend Grandpa for expert advice. Sharing a mutual interest can strengthen the bonds of a relationship without forcing the issue.

COMMUNICATION

Long-Distance Dads

❏ It can be tough for a divorced parent to maintain a close relationship with the kids when they're no longer living in the same house. An increasingly popular approach is to buy a pair of fax machines—one for the absent parent and one for the kids. Volunteer to cover the long-distance charges and encourage the kids to fax you their latest drawings, stories, riddles, and so on. It's not as good as being there, but it's a step in the right direction.

Car Talk

❑ Having trouble getting your teenager to talk about what's going on in her life? Communication is key dur-

---

ONE PERSON'S SOLUTION

The Clean Team

When my husband and I decided to leave our corporate jobs and set up a home-based consulting business, we knew we'd have to reduce expenses for a while. But since we had more time to spend with our daughters (ages 11, 13, and 15), we figured it was worth it.

One of the first things to go was the housekeeper who came every two weeks to clean, costing us about $120 a month. In light of our new lifestyle (and lower income), the expense no longer made sense. However, with five active people and a start-up business operating under the same roof, the house would have gone to wrack and ruin if we hadn't set up a system to keep things under control.

I devised a job chart listing a number of household chores to be done every week,

ing the adolescent years, but it's often hard to get kids to share information. If your teen seems evasive or uncommunicative, try waiting until you're alone in the car to get her to open up. Whether you want to address a serious issue or just get closer through conversation, she'll feel less pinned down because you'll be driving and not making eye contact. And there's one other practical advantage: She can't escape.

such as dusting, vacuuming, washing the floors, and cleaning the bathrooms. Each girl could sign up for one or more jobs of her choice and earn $5 for every one she completed (subject to the management's approval, of course). It was my job to spell out exactly what was required for each job and to maintain quality control.

So how's the system working? Beautifully—and in my view, it offers many benefits besides just a clean house. The girls are learning good household skills (and rest assured, if we had boys, they'd be doing housework, too). It reinforces the idea that taking care of our home is everybody's job. Since we all contribute to messing it up, we share the job of cleaning it. (The girls have always been responsible for personal things such as their rooms and laundry.) It also encourages a good work ethic. There's a clear connection between the effort the girls make and the amount of money they earn. If one of them wants extra cash for something special, she works extra hard to get it.

Since we started the weekly job chart, our house is staying reasonably clean, and we're still spending less than we would on a housekeeper. But the way we see it, by giving our girls a chance to earn money, we're not really spending it—just recycling!

—DEBBY CARROLL
Elkins Park, Pennsylvania

Yup, Nope, and Other College-Level Conversations

❏ Do you get frustrated when you try to carry on a phone conversation with a child who's away at college and get nothing but one-word responses? Try giving him some control over the situation. Tell him you'll pay for collect calls from his dorm room. That way, he can call you when he's feeling sociable and roommates aren't around to listen in.

MONEY AND WORK

A Can-Do Kid

❏ You know that it's important to encourage your child's sense of responsibility from an early age, but you're not quite sure how to start. Try putting her in charge of the household's returnable bottles and cans. Assign her the job of collecting and rinsing them, then helping you return them to the store. In exchange, let her keep the deposit money from each returned can. She might even expand the business at some point by picking up returnables from a neighbor who usually tosses them out. Besides establishing good recycling habits, it's a great way for her to learn about earning and saving money. If you'd like to help her nest egg grow, offer an incentive: For instance, you can contribute $5 for every $10 she saves.

All That Allowance Allows

❏ A weekly allowance can be an important tool in teaching financial responsibility. But at what age should kids get one, and how much should it be? As soon as your child is old enough to understand the concept of budgeting, an allowance makes sense. The amount should depend on his age and maturity and how much you feel he can handle at one time. Amounts will vary from family to family, but the important thing is that you both agree beforehand on which expenses the allowance will cover. Come up with an amount you can agree on by working out an estimated weekly budget covering any fixed and daily expenses (transportation, lunch) plus miscellaneous expenses you define together (books, magazines, movies, CDs, tapes, school supplies). If he has a hard time making the money last through the week, you might need to reevaluate the budget to see if it's realistic. But if he's blowing it all at once, talk to him about how he can better live within his means.

Have Rake, Will Travel

❏ Do local kids—including yours—need more opportunities for earning money? One solution is to help set up a job directory through the school. Kids sign up and list their names, phone numbers, and the services they offer, such as baby-sitting, housework or yard work, tutoring or teaching computer skills, walking dogs, or doing errands for homebound people. Copies of the job directory are distributed to parents and other people in the community. You might want to give a copy to your minister and the local senior center, where people in need of such services are likely to turn for help. If your school is too big or difficult to work with, try this on a smaller scale in your neighborhood or through the YMCA or another organization.

Career-Hopping

❏ College selection committees are placing more and more emphasis on nonacademic factors such as meaningful work and volunteer experience. But good opportunities aren't always easy to find. If you're concerned about this, encourage your school to organize a summer apprenticeship program to help students learn more about a field in which they're interested. The program would match up students with adults who work in a particular area and are willing to share advice and information about their field. The student would visit the work site and get hands-on experience (paid or unpaid). The main purpose is to gain valuable experience and insight for the future. Start by talking to your child's guidance counselor; you may find that a similar program is already in operation.

ON THE MOVE
Buying and Selling,
Relocating and Settling In

SHOPPING FOR A HOME

Readin', Writin', and Resale Value

❑ One concern you may have when shopping for a house is finding one that will have a high resale value. Even (or maybe especially) if you plan to stay there for a long time, you want to do all you can to ensure that when you or your heirs eventually resell the property, you'll recoup your costs and maybe even come out ahead on the deal. How can you increase the odds that the house will still be valuable when it's time to resell it? One way is to choose a home near schools, even if you have no children and don't plan to have any. Homes close to schools consistently fetch higher prices.

Climate Control: Is This Really a Hot Deal?

❑ The agent says the home has central air-conditioning. How can you be sure of the condition of the unit? Turn it on to make sure it works. Then ask the owner or agent to let you see the filters. Take a look at them and ask when the owner last cleaned them (during the cooling season, this should have been done within the past month or two). The condition of the air-conditioning is an indication of how well the previous owner cared for the unit and how well she cared for the entire home.

❑ Likewise, ask to see the furnace. Find out how old it is and when it was last serviced. (Read the service stickers on the furnace to confirm the answer to the second question.) It should have been checked at least once during the past year. Beware of any furnace that's more than 10 to 15 years old. Either move on to the next place or deduct the cost of a new furnace from your offer.

Face It! The Sun, That Is

❏ Are you shopping for a home in a cold region and wondering how to keep your heating costs as low as possible? One answer is to put southern exposure on the list of important features you want in your new house. A western exposure is second best for taking advantage of the sun's rays. A southern or western

12 Things to Consider When Choosing a New Town

Don't sign anything until you get answers to these 12 questions. A good real estate agent should be able to handle them all.

1. How good are the schools? (This is important whether you have children or not if you ever want to resell the house.)

2. How easy is it to get in and out of town? Are there direct routes to the interstate?

3. What are the tax rates? Are there city or state income taxes? A state sales tax?

4. How close is the nearest "good" grocery store?

5. Is the area safe? Can you walk around alone at night?

6. How long will your commute to work be? Is public transportation available between this town and the one where you'll be working? How frequently do the trains/buses/subways run?

7. Are services that are important to you available? How's the local library? When is it open? Where is the nearest mall? Does the town have a running track that's open to the public? Public tennis courts or a golf course?

8. Does the town have its own museum? Orchestra? Theater? YMCA?

9. How close is the nearest hospital?

10. How is trash handled? Are you likely to get curbside pickup, or will you be expected to visit the recycling center yourself? What hours is it open?

11. What kinds of emergency services are available?

12. If you have a pet, is there a vet in town? How about a kennel?

A Moving Time Line
Part I

So little time, so much to do. Here's a little help to keep you organized.

3 to 4 Months Before the Move

• Contact several moving companies for written estimates.

12 Weeks Before the Move

• Hire a mover. (This may seem awfully far in advance, but if you're planning to move during the summer, it's a good idea to book well ahead.)

6 Weeks Before the Move

• Go through your belongings and decide what to take with you and what to discard. Hold a yard sale or moving sale.

• Gather together all your family's important personal documents, including medical and dental records, car registration, and birth certificates. (Those will go with you on the plane or in the car.)

4 to 6 Weeks Before the Move

• Visit the post office and fill out change-of-address forms for your doctor, dentist, and lawyer; magazine and newspaper subscriptions; on-line computer services; utilities (gas, telephone, electricity, water); trash removal; insurance (life, medical, automobile, homeowner's); credit cards; Social Security office; pension; bank; employer (for your W-2 forms); department of motor vehicles; and any other miscellaneous accounts you may have.

• Start using up the food in your refrigerator and cabinets. The goal is to avoid carrying any unnecessary food with you on the move. Donate extra canned goods to a local food bank.

• Have your child's school send transcripts and records to the new school.

exposure also is vital if you plan a garden or even intend to keep lots of houseplants.

Don't Be Punished for Prepaying

❏ Mortgage contracts can be confusing, and if you don't read them carefully, you may end up spending more money than you have to. How can you keep your costs to a minimum? For one thing, watch out for a prepayment penalty in any mortgage contract. You probably know that there are enormous financial benefits associated with paying a little early on your mortgage. Although nearly all the payments you make for the first several years of your mortgage go toward interest, extra payments go directly toward the principal. So by making just one extra payment each year, you'll save money and pay off the loan more quickly. But some companies charge a penalty for paying off the loan early. Find out before you apply if the company charges a penalty. If it does, try to have the contract changed. Or if you have the option, take your business elsewhere.

A Moving Time Line Part II

The big day's getting closer, and you have crossed off several items on your list. Now it's time for a new list.

3 to 4 Weeks Before the Move

• Update your personal address book—you want to be able to keep in touch!

• Send notes, postcards, or change-of-address forms from the post office to friends and relatives, notifying them of your new address.

• Arrange for nonessential services such as cable TV and on-line computer services to be shut off. Some of those services won't prorate your bill, so if you shut off cable service on May 5, you'll have to pay the charge for all of May.

• Start collecting boxes and items you'll need for packing (a large magic marker, packing tape and a tape gun, scissors).

2 Weeks Before the Move

• Arrange to have the billing changed and the service turned off for utilities (water, electricity, telephone, gas) in your old home after you move and turned on in your new home or apartment before you arrive. Be sure the electricity and phone will still be in service at the old residence on moving day. The moving company (and probably you) will need these services.

1 Week Before the Move

• Return library books and rented videotapes.

• Finish packing.

• Visit your new home, if possible, to make sure it's cleaned to your standards.

• Pick a closet or bathroom in your old home in which to store any items you're taking in the car or on the plane with you. Post a sign on the door saying, "These items do not go."

Moving Day

• Take one final walk through the house to make sure you have everything.

• Turn off the lights and take your phone. Lock all the doors and windows.

HOME INSPECTIONS

Inspect the Inspector

❏ You've selected a house you like, and now it's time for an inspection. But how do you find a reliable inspector? To be on the safe side and avoid a possible conflict of interest, don't ask the real estate agent (who ultimately works for the seller). Instead, contact the American Society of Home Inspectors (ASHI), which certifies house inspectors. The organization certifies only those inspectors who have passed rigorous professional tests. To get a list of inspectors in your area, check out the ASHI's certified membership list on the organization's Web site.

They Don't Do Windows

❏ It can be confusing figuring out exactly what is and what isn't involved in a home inspection. How do you know exactly what to expect when you hire an inspector? Generally speaking, a standard home inspection

A Head Start on House Inspections

You're not a house inspector yourself, and you've never been particularly good at fixing things around your apartment. That doesn't mean you can't be a wise shopper when it comes to buying a home. Here are some warning signs—visible to anyone—that the house has bigger problems than the owner may be letting on.

1. Danger above. While you're walking through the house, check out the ceilings. Are there water stains or spots? That could mean roof problems or leaky water pipes.

2. That sinking feeling. Check the fixtures on sinks and baths and look at the bowls. Are there yellow stains? Those may mean that the pipes are old and rusty.

3. Trouble on tap. Turn on the water. Does it run clear or brown and cloudy? Unless the water department is working on the water main, discolored water is a problem. And how's the water pressure?

4. Power matters. If appliances are part of the deal, turn them all on. And that means turning on all the burners on the stove.

is a visual check of the readily accessible areas of the major systems (heating and cooling, for instance) and components of the building (such as the foundation and roof). Inspectors aren't necessarily qualified to check for radon, they don't check the insides of chimneys, and they don't check for termites as part of the standard inspection (although they can recommend professionals for those jobs and may be licensed to perform such tasks themselves for a separate fee). To find out more specifically what you'll get, ask for a sample of a final report and use that as a starting point for questioning the inspector. Don't stop asking questions until you know exactly what you're getting for your money.

SELLING A HOUSE

A Seller's Market (analysis)

❑ If you're concerned about whether the amount you're asking for your home is appropriate, conduct your own informal market analysis. Get hold of local real estate booklets (they're free, and you can usually find them near the checkout at the grocery store) and the real estate section of the local newspaper. Read over the ads for homes that are comparable to yours. (Comparable means a similar location and the same number of bathrooms and bedrooms.) If the houses for sale are in the same price range, you'll know the price you've set is in the ballpark.

❑ An even more realistic snapshot of the market is based on the prices for which comparable homes have already been sold. To get this information, visit any real estate agent and ask for a market analysis, which will include a listing of the prices of homes comparable to yours that were sold in the past six months.

First Impressions Count

❑ If your home's not in perfect condition, it can be troublesome deciding just how much to fix it up before

On the Move

you put it on the market. What's a worthwhile investment in the sale of your house, and what's money down
the drain? It's generally best to take care of major problems such as a leaky roof (or simply tell the potential
buyer about the problem), but you probably shouldn't
undertake major renovations. (A kitchen renovation
that suits you to a tee may not appeal to prospective
buyers.) Outside, concentrate on the overall appearance of your home's exterior. Mow the lawn and plant
some flowers. Trim those hedges and wash the windows. Make your home look clean, neat, and inviting
to folks driving by.

❏ Should you redecorate before you try to sell your
house? That depends. Focus on making your home
look clean and pretty. If that means a new coat of paint
(of a neutral color), fine. But steer clear of drastic redecorating measures and wacky wallpaper or wild
color combinations.

❏ What else can you do to gussy up the inside of your
house without spending everything you'll make on the
sale? Clean and perhaps replace switch plates, door-

3 Steps to Finding the Right Mover

Whether you're moving around the block or across the country, you need to hire a mover you can trust. Here's a quick checklist to help.

1. Listen for the right question. When you phone the moving company, the salesperson should offer to send someone to your home to calculate an estimate. If she doesn't, move on to the next listing in the phone book.

2. Get it in writing. Never settle for a verbal estimate, which isn't binding. Get a written esti-mate—a binding estimate, if possible, but nothing less than a non-binding estimate. Nonbinding estimates contain clauses that protect you as well as the moving company.

3. Check up. Ask for recent references and call them. Also, call the local Better Business Bureau (you can find it listed in the White Pages) and ask for a reliability report on the movers you're considering. That will tell you whether any complaints have been lodged against the company.

knobs, and cabinet knobs. Polish the kick plate on the door. A few touch-ups here and there can go a long way toward making your place more appealing.

The Oddball Gets the Second Look

❏ When a lot of properties in one area are up for sale, it can be a challenge to make your home stand out from the rest. One way to do that—at no expense—is to list your home at an odd price. For instance, if you hope to sell for $125,000, list it for $125,603.95. That'll get folks at least to stop at the real estate agent's office or keep reading your ad.

What Do You Mean It's a Steal?

❏ One of the most worrisome parts of selling your house is having a constant parade of strangers tromping through it. Sometimes you can't tell whether they're more interested in buying your home or seeing what's inside so that they can come back later and clean out the contents when you're not around. The best way to ensure that only serious prospects see your home is to request that your agent show the property only to folks who have prequalified with a mortgage broker or bank. A prequalified shopper will have met with a lender, given his financial information, and obtained an OK (in writing) for a loan of a certain amount. It's a good way to keep your home safe.

> # Gun Owners, Take Note
>
> If you're a gun owner, you need to ask your mover what the company's policy is regarding the transportation of firearms. Most movers prefer not to take them, but some will, depending on the make, model, and serial number. Moving companies do not, under any circumstances, take ammunition.

Home Is Where the Bread Is

❏ Looking for a way to make prospective buyers picture themselves at home in your house? There's plenty of truth to the theory that the way to a home buyer's heart is through his nostrils. Pop a loaf of yeast bread in the oven shortly before the visitors walk through the door; the smell makes any house more inviting. And

5 Items a Pro Won't Move Across State Lines

The movers can't take them, so don't even ask.

1. Plants. In the back of a truck, your plants will either freeze or burn—either way, they won't survive the trip. (And you can't bring plants into some states unless they've been approved by a state agricultural inspector.) If you can't bear to leave your favorite ivy behind, take cuttings instead. Wrap them in a very damp paper towel until you arrive at your destination, then place the cuttings in a glass of water. After they sprout roots, simply replant them.

2. Alcohol. It seems pretty harmless (if you're over 21, that is), but it's illegal to transport alcohol over state lines. So how do the authorities know if your movers (or you) are transporting alcohol? Well, they don't, unless they pull your movers (or you) over. But as they say, better safe than sorry.

3. Flammable items. Paint, paint thinner, aerosol cans, and tanks for gas grills. Temperatures inside moving vans can reach 150° to 200°F and ignite those items.

4. Stamp and coin collections. Movers won't take any collectible of great value.

5. Pets. Sparky has to ride with you in your car. If it's a long-distance move, Sparky should take a plane.

since it's the smell that's important rather than the taste, shortcuts are fine. If you're not a bread baker, use the packaged bread dough in the refrigerator section of the grocery store or whip up some brownies. (Chocolate is just as persuasive as yeast.)

PACKING UP

Look for Handy Wraps

❑ To avoid the hassle of washing newspaper-wrapped dishes after you unpack, look in your kitchen drawers and cupboards for alternatives. You're packing those dish towels anyway. Why not wrap them around a few plates? You might even want to use some of your bathroom towels this way. It's a lot easier to toss them in the washing machine as you unpack than to scrub all those dishes by hand.

Hold It!

❏ In your search for free boxes, concentrate on stores that buy in bulk but sell items individually. Following that logic, you may want to try local discount drugstores and department stores.

❏ Alternatively, check your own office or a local office supply store for boxes (those stores may give them away, too). Copy paper boxes are perfect; they can hold a lot of weight and usually have lids.

Dumbbells Go in a Shoe Box

❏ Trying to figure out how heavy is too heavy for boxes? The experts recommend that you pack boxes so that they weigh no more than 50 pounds, but 30 to 40 pounds is better. The best way to stay within those guidelines is to pack heavy items, such as books, in the smallest boxes available.

 TIME SAVER

The Most Important Box of All

It may not matter if you can't find the cheese grater right away or if you don't unearth the old photo albums for six months after you move, but there are some necessities of life that you absolutely must be able to locate the minute you set foot in your new digs. (Anyone who doubts this has never arrived at a new home at midnight and been unable to find the box with the toilet paper.) When you pack for any move—no matter how short the distance between old home and new—set aside one box that's clearly labeled and contains the following essentials.

- All-purpose cleaner
- Bucket
- Eating utensils for one meal
- Flashlight
- Food for one meal
- Light bulbs
- Litter box
- Paper towels
- Pet food
- Prescription medications
- Radio
- Soap, towels, washcloths
- Swiss Army knife (a basic model with a can opener, screwdriver, corkscrew, and scissors)
- Telephone
- Toilet paper
- Toiletries

I Know I Put It in a Brown Box . . .

❑ How can you make sure you'll be able to find specific belongings after you settle in? Label each box as you pack it. Here's one method. On each of the four sides of the box, write, with a dark-colored marker, which room the box will go in (kitchen, for instance). That saves you from having to rotate every box three times before you can tell where it goes. On the top of the box, make a list of what's inside (utensils, dish towels, corkscrew).

❑ Alternatively, keep track of what goes into each box on a master list that you keep with you at all times. Assign each room a letter (kitchen = K, bathroom = B, living room = L), then label each box with a letter and a number. If, for example, you have three boxes that belong in the bathroom, your list would read, "Bathroom: 3 boxes: B1—towels; B2—shower curtain; B3—shampoo and soap."

 DOLLAR STRETCHER

Cheap Labor

Why is it that when you tell your friends that you're moving, they're suddenly going out of town on the very same weekend? It's because nobody wants to spend an entire day hauling your heavy stuff out of one house or apartment and into another. What you really need is some cheap labor, and the local college is a good place to find it.

Don't be discouraged if you're moving during the summer; depending on the size of the town, there may be many students who are sticking around and are in the market for a job. To find and hire these students, call local universities or colleges and ask for the career planning and placement office. Tell them you're looking for students to help you move. Many times the office can give you the names of students; other times you'll be asked to send in a job description. Since fair prices vary so much from town to town, it's best to ask a staff member in the office what she feels is a fair price. (And don't plan to get started at 7:00 A.M.; students are notoriously late sleepers.)

❏ No matter how you label the boxes, make sure to use clear packing tape so you don't obliterate your lists!

Are All These T-Shirts Really Going?

❏ You've run out of boxes. Now what? One option is to place clothes and other soft goods in your luggage, tote bags, and sturdy paper shopping bags (with handles). (This works best if you're transporting things yourself. Professional movers may not take kindly to items that are likely to spill out of their containers.)

❏ Alternatively, put lightweight items in large trash bags. To keep from confusing your clothes with the trash, use transparent bags.

Moving Day Triage

❏ If you can see early on that you're not going to have enough boxes to pack everything, perform a little triage on the items you still have left to pack. Separate (1) those items that absolutely have to be packed in sturdy boxes, (2) things that need to be contained but perhaps not covered, and (3) pieces that really don't have to be contained at all. For example, the contents of the medicine cabinet probably should be carefully boxed. Linens, which aren't particularly heavy, might go in sturdy paper grocery bags. And books (assuming they're not precious collectibles) may be fine if you just tie batches of them up with string. This is particularly true if you're moving a relatively small number of items a short distance by car—as opposed to transporting the contents of a large house across the country in a rented truck.

You're moving that throw pillow anyway—tape it to the front of the TV screen to prevent breakage in transit.

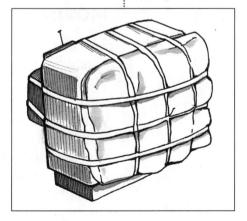

You'll Both Rest Easier

❏ If you didn't save the carton your TV came in and don't want the picture tube to get damaged in the move, tape a throw pillow to the screen. Use the quick-release variety of masking tape that painters use;

you'll find it at hardware and paint stores. It will come off easily and won't leave a residue.

❏ If you don't have a throw pillow handy, pack the TV so that the screen is facing a mattress.

Look Inside Before You Plug It In

❏ When you're packing up everything in your home, it seems as if your belongings expand to take up twice the normal amount of space. To solve this problem, take advantage of the empty spaces in and around your belongings. For instance, tuck items such as blankets, pillows, and towels into your washer or dryer and use masking tape to seal the doors closed. Use the quick-release variety of tape that painters use; you'll find it at hardware and paint stores. It will come off easily and won't leave a residue.

❏ If you have trouble getting the tape to stick to your washer, it's probably because there's some soap residue on the machine. Wipe the washer down with glass cleaner and dry it with a paper towel before you tape it up.

If It's Empty, Use It!

❏ If you're moving your household goods yourself and run out of boxes, pack odds and ends in other containers: dishpans, wastebaskets, laundry baskets. If it will hold something, fill it up!

MOVING

Like, in January

❏ If you're handling a move yourself (as opposed to hiring professional movers) but the costs are still mounting, save money by moving during the slow season. Rental rates on trucks and vans increase dramatically during the summer (if you live in a college town, that includes September). You may be able to save as much as 30 percent if you time your move for other months.

Loading a Truck: A Weighty Issue

❏ If you've never loaded a truck before, you may be wondering how to start. The most important safety rule to follow is that weight must be evenly distributed in the truck. That means you shouldn't put all the weight up front, on either side, or toward the back of the truck. One good way to start is to load the heaviest items, such as furniture, first, along the inside perimeter of the truck. Then work your way toward the center.

❏ As a secondary factor, keep convenience in mind. The last thing you load will be the first thing you unload, so choose wisely. For example, pack rugs right near the door so you can lay them down before unloading furniture.

A Tip about Tipping

❏ Wondering if you need to tip your movers? Although it is certainly not mandatory (don't let anyone tell you it is), it is usual for customers to give the crew a tip and perhaps lunch (pizza is a favorite) if they are especially pleased with the service. If you do decide to tip, be aware that there is no industry standard. Some folks give each crew member $10, others more.

UNPACKING AND GETTING SETTLED

Clean Your Room!

❏ Trying to keep kids out of the way may be a concern when you get to where you're going. One good way to keep them occupied is to unleash them on their own rooms right away. Pack up the kids' rooms last so that their stuff

---

✔ PROBLEM PREVENTED

Oops! There Goes the China Cabinet

The basic insurance coverage most professional movers offer is 60 cents per pound per item. That means that if they drop your $5,000, 20-pound Ming dynasty vase, you'll get back only $12—and you'll need a receipt proving the worth of the item. Since there are additional charges for additional coverage, your best bet for more realistic coverage may be your homeowner's or renter's insurance. If you don't have such insurance, this is the perfect time to get it. The best way to find an agent is to have friends or colleagues recommend one. Barring that, check the Yellow Pages under Insurance.

---

will come off the truck first. That should keep them occupied and out of the way.

Map Out the Situation

❏ Getting settled once you've moved to a new home in a new town takes time. If you're looking for ways to speed up that process, try getting the whole family involved. Stop by the local library, chamber of commerce, or city hall and get a map of your new town. Hang it in the kitchen, pinpointing your home with pushpins or a magic marker. Draw up a list of businesses, services, and government offices you need to locate: library, department of motor vehicles, post office, grocery store, Laundromat, schools, YMCA, hospitals, church, bus stops or train station, anything you can think of. Leave an empty column next to the place names. Hang the list beside the map. If the kids are old enough, ask them to make phone calls to find out

---

ONE PERSON'S SOLUTION

Hello, Dolly!

We didn't want to spend the money on professionals, so we moved ourselves into our new apartment. By the end of the day, we were bushed but still had boxes and furniture to move around the apartment. And since we'd already returned the truck (and the dolly), our backs were aching after about an hour. As it turned out, the hardware store down the block rented tools. I called, and, sure enough, it also rented dollies—for $3 a day. It turned out to be the best $3 we spent that weekend.

—JIM DEACUTIS
Mount Vernon, New York

---

the addresses and opening hours of each place and write them next to the name on the list. If your kids are smaller, help them push the pins into the map (or let them make dots with a magic marker) to indicate the location of each place you want to find. Soon you'll have your own annotated map of town. Once it's finished, replace any pushpins with magic marker dots, then take the map along on a walking or driving tour so that you can connect the information you have to the real places.

Get Some Street Smarts

❏ Does the thought of finding your way around a new city by car give you nightmares of honking horns, one-way streets that all seem to go the wrong way, and traffic circles from which there's no escape? No problem. Before you brave the traffic at rush hour or when you're late for an important meeting, go for a Sunday drive. (Before setting out, check the calendar listings in the local paper to make sure a major event isn't taking place in town that day.) Generally speaking, the streets will be far less crowded than on a weekday, and the drivers (including you) will be considerably less frantic while you're finding your way around. Then, when the pressure is on, you'll have all the shortcuts figured out.

The New Kid in Town

❏ You've moved to a new town, and suddenly you're the new kid on the block. How do you start meeting people, especially if you're shy? Become a regular at various places around town. Buy your newspaper from the same vendor every day. Stop by the same hardware store for your new home needs once a week for several weeks. Have your morning coffee at the same diner on your way to work. It's a sure way to get noticed by the locals, many of whom are likely to start conversations with you.

GETTING OLDER
You Got It All Together—
Now Where Did You Put It?

LONELINESS AND ISOLATION

Are You Lonesome Tonight?

❏ If you miss being around young people and are looking for a way to fill some lonely hours, volunteer to teach a scout troop some skill—perhaps how to make Christmas decorations, how to bone a chicken, or how to identify edible greens and mushrooms. If you don't know a scout, contact a grade school teacher or Sunday school teacher and ask him to help you find one. Or call your local elementary school to see if any youngsters could benefit from a little extra help and attention.

❏ If you prefer people your own age or older, visit a shut-in, either in person or by phone, once a week. Or read to a blind person or volunteer to deliver meals-on-wheels. A local nursing home or senior center can help put you in touch with these opportunities.

Look for a Study Buddy

❏ If you'd like to expand your horizons and meet new people at the same time, take a course at a local community college or at the YMCA. Choose something that will give you a new interest or a new source of pleasure. Learn something new about music, art, or computers. If you don't want to (or can't) drive yourself to school, ask the school for a list of other students and see if you can work out a ride.

Feed Me, and I'll Be Your Friend for Life . . .

❏ If you find yourself becoming lonely when you spend time alone, consider adopting a pet. People with pets live longer and happier lives than people without them. Think about how much work the pet will require before you choose it, but remember that some animals, such as cats and fish, take very little work.

Set Up a Neighborhood Watch

❏ If you live alone and are concerned that no one would know if something happened to you, develop a buddy system with a neighbor. Share your plans with each other and watch to see if the lights in each other's houses go on and off at the appropriate times. Or ask someone who drives by your house on the way to and from work to keep an eye out for your signal (a particular light turned on or a shade raised, for example). Make sure your buddy has a list of numbers to call if things don't look right.

❏ Another way to make sure someone is keeping an eye out for you is to speak with your neighbor on the phone once or twice a day—just to assure each other that you are both all right.

THE GRANDCHILDREN

Reach Out and Touch a Grandchild

❏ Grandchildren can be one of the greatest joys of getting older. But if they don't live nearby, staying a part of their lives can require some extra effort. One way to keep in touch with a young grandchild is to buy a favorite book and tape-record yourself reading it. Then send the book and

Before You Move In with a Grown Child

Are you about to move in with your son or daughter? Here are three ways to help make it work.

1. Be sure you like each other (that's not the same as loving each other).

2. Be sure you both understand what you expect from each other. Talk about it and, at the slightest hint of misunderstanding, keep talking—and listening.

3. Try to keep in mind that your child isn't a child anymore. Don't treat him like a ten-year-old, even if he acts like one.

the tape to the youngster. It's the next best thing to being there to read the child a story.

Grandma, You Have to Be Neater!

❏ Another way to keep up communication with the grandchildren is to encourage joint activities. Send a picture frame and ask the grandchild to draw a picture to put in it and send it back to you. Or get a coloring book and color it together by sending it back and forth. Self-addressed stamped envelopes will help ensure that you get a response.

BUSINESS AND FINANCE

Get Yourself a Deputy

❏ Looking for a way to make sure your bills get paid in the event that you are temporarily (or permanently) unable to do it yourself? Appoint a friend or relative as your attorney-in-fact. You can do this by filling out a durable power of attorney form (available at stationery stores), signing it, and getting it notarized. (To find someone who can notarize the document for you, look in the Yellow Pages under Notaries Public.) Then, if you can't cope with your affairs, somebody else can.

3 Mistakes You're Most Likely to Make with Money

I t ain't the things you don't know, what gets you into trouble," someone once said. "It's the things you know for sure what ain't so." Never do any of the following:

1. Never assume that if investments are sold by banks, they are insured by the Federal Deposit Insurance Corporation (FDIC). Read the fine print or ask. The FDIC doesn't insure investments.

2. Never keep all your money in bonds or savings accounts. If you do, you may run out of money before you run out of time.

3. Never move to a new town or state without really understanding the tax situation where you're going. The fact that there isn't an income tax doesn't necessarily mean that it's a better place (financially) to live. What other kinds of taxes are there?

Life-and-Death Decisions: What Do You Want?

❑ Concerned about what medical decisions might be made on your behalf if you are too sick to make them yourself? If you want to stay in control of the medical care you receive, establish a living will, which will set out your wishes. (A living will states your preferences as to whether, for example, you want to be put on life-support systems.) You also should give somebody a health care proxy to act on your behalf in making health care decisions—and make sure you explain to that person exactly what lifesaving measures are acceptable to you. The social service department of your local hospital can probably give you forms for both a living will and a health care proxy, or you can get more information by calling your state bar association, located in your state capital. (For the number, call information by dialing the area code plus 555-1212.) Once you've filled out the forms, make sure family and friends know where to find them if they're needed.

Combat the High Cost of Leaving

❑ You know that funerals are among the most expensive purchases a family makes—almost as much as a new car. You want to have a little input into what happens after your death, but you're not sure where to start. One of the best approaches is to discuss what you want with your family, your pastor, and the local funeral director. Tell them whether you prefer cremation or burial. If you want a casket, what kind? Decide what you want the funeral home to provide and whether the service should be at the funeral home or

DOLLAR STRETCHER

Cash In on Your Years

Everyone is giving senior discounts these days. Here are just a few of the things you should expect to get for less.

- Tickets on buses, trains, and planes
- Merchandise in many stores (sometimes only on specific days of the week)
- Car insurance
- Prescription drugs
- Admission to national parks
- Movie tickets
- Meals in restaurants (sometimes only during specified hours)

Eligibility for some of the discounts starts as early as age 50, but to take advantage of the reduced prices, you have to ask. You'll get paid to do it, so do it.

in a church. If you prefer to be remembered through memorial contributions to a favorite charity in lieu of flowers, make sure your family knows that—as well as any other preferences you may have. It's a good idea to put your wishes in writing and make sure family members know where to find the list.

❑ Another way to combat the high cost of funerals is to consult a memorial society—a nonprofit organization that advises consumers on funeral arrangements. Not only do such groups provide information, but some actually arrange funerals, and because they arrange so many, they can get you a volume discount. Your pastor can help you find one of these societies.

DOLLAR STRETCHER

Where There's a Will . . .

You know that if you don't have a will when you die, the law is going to dictate who gets your property. You'd rather make the decisions yourself, but you're concerned about the expense of having a will written. Relax. It doesn't need to be an expensive process, and you can minimize the costs by making sure you're prepared before you visit the lawyer. Write down all the pertinent information— the names and addresses of your relatives, as well as a list of what you own and what you would like to do with it. That will save time—and, therefore, money—when you meet with the lawyer.

FORGETFULNESS

Is the Smoke Alarm Your Dinner Bell?

❑ If you know dinner is ready because the smoke alarm goes off, maybe you need a timer that hangs on a cord around your neck. These are available at hardware stores and through catalogs. The gadget will remind you that something is finished cooking even if you doze off or get distracted.

That Reminds Me . . .

❑ If you can't remember what you were going to do, go back to the place where you decided to do it. It may jog your memory.

❑ Has the title of a book or movie somebody told you about slipped your mind? Try to imagine the person who told you telling you again. Sometimes that will help.

FATIGUE

My Get-Up-and-Go Just Got Up and Went

❏ Do you feel tired all the time? Take a tip from athletes: Eat high-energy foods—carbohydrates, such as pasta and whole grain bread, and lots of vegetables and fruits. Cut back on refined sugar, fat, and alcohol.

❏ Maybe the reason you have no energy is that you aren't eating regularly. If you can arrange it, get together with friends every day to play cards, chat, knit, or watch TV. Make a brown-bag lunch a part of your plan. Or if you all like to cook, rotate preparation of a lunch. You'll all feel better for having had a meal and some company.

6 Ways to Train Your Spouse in the Family Finances

Your spouse has always hated dealing with money. You're good at it, and you've handled the family finances for years. But what would happen if you got seriously sick? Your spouse would be completely confused, overwhelmed, and frustrated, that's what—just when she's already got her hands full caring for you. You can keep that from happening if you take preventive measures now. For example:

1. Keep good records. A set of binders devoted to bank accounts, insurance, and taxes will help a lot.

2. Put it in writing. Compose a memo about what you have, where it is, and why. Make sure your spouse knows where to find that note.

3. Keep it simple. Use one bank (unless your deposits are more than $100,000, in which case you'll have to spread it around to stay insured) and one insurance agent.

4. Get the other person involved. (True, this is easier said than done!)

5. Get the other person educated. Be sure your spouse understands how to write a check, what the insurance covers, where the records are kept, and so on.

6. Bring in an expert. Introduce your spouse to the accountant, lawyer, or bank officer you rely on for help and advice.

He's Ready to Retire; You're Not

You spent many years raising your family, and as important as those years were, you're now finding new excitement in a job outside the home. The problem is, just as you're getting *into* that other world, your husband wants to get *out*. He's ready to retire—and he wants you to join him. What can you do? Here are some options.

1. Explore the possibility of working part-time.

2. Consider taking a seasonal job so that you can take extended trips with your spouse without giving up your work entirely.

3. Put a time limit on your work commitment. Agree that you'll work for two more years, for example, and then retire.

4. Discuss what he might do with his time while you're working. Is a part-time job a good idea for him? How about taking up a new activity such as wood carving or golf?

5. Suggest that he look into volunteer opportunities by calling the local chapter of the Retired Senior Volunteer Program. (Check the White Pages of the phone book for the number.) Perhaps when he sees how much other people can benefit from his help, he won't need you at his side all the time.

❏ Another way to fight chronic fatigue is to exercise regularly. Contrary to popular opinion, exercise gives you energy; it doesn't make you tired.

Get an Expert Opinion

❏ If straightening out your diet and exercise routines doesn't take care of ongoing tiredness, it may be time to have a talk with your doctor to see if you have a physical problem. Consider the possibility that you may be depressed. And don't forget that depression is a treatable ailment.

ARTHRITIS

Be a Cutup

❏ If you can't manage to cut your food with a regular knife and fork because arthritis has left you with only one functioning hand, perhaps a one-handed knife would help. With this handy utensil, also known as an Alaskan ulu knife or a rocker knife, you cut your food by rocking the knife back and forth instead of anchoring the food with your fork. It really works! Look for ulu knives in mail-order catalogs.

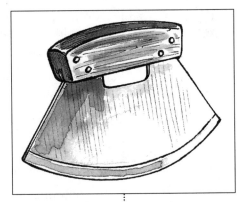

KP Duty Never Was Any Fun

❏ If peeling potatoes gives you grief, look in a kitchen supply store for a potato peeler that has a fat rubber handle. You may find it easier to hold than your old one.

This simple knife lets you cut food with ease—and without having to anchor vegetables with your other (arthritic) hand.

❏ Another approach is to cook the potato first, then let it cool slightly. When it's cool enough to touch, run warm water on it, and the skin will slip right off. (If you have arthritis, the warm water will make your hands feel better, too.)

❏ Alternatively, try using an old-fashioned apple peeler. These are available from mail-order catalogs and kitchen supply stores.

Apple peelers aren't just for apples. Use one of these old-fashioned gizmos to get the skins off potatoes, too.

Stay out of Hot Water

❏ Boiling water can be hazardous to your health! If you have trouble picking up a pot full of water, try using an electric coffee urn instead of a kettle to boil water.

Arthritis

(Coffee urns are available anywhere small appliances are sold. Get one just for this purpose, or everything will taste like coffee.) Then you can pour the boiling water out of the spigot instead of lifting a heavy pot.

❏ If you're cooking something you would normally put into a pot of boiling water, put a frying basket or metal strainer into the pot before adding the food. When the food is cooked, lift out the basket. Let the water cool before you empty the pot.

❏ Sometimes the boiling liquid in that pot isn't water. Instead of trying to lift a pot to pour a hot liquid such as soup, use a ladle to remove the liquid from the pot.

Coffee Filters: We Have Liftoff!

❏ If you're ready to give up making perked coffee because you're having so much trouble getting the paper filter off the pile, try using little tongs with rubber tips. These are easy to manipulate with arthritis-ridden hands, and they'll take off one filter at a time. You can find these tongs in catalogs or where coffee filters or coffeepots are sold.

Coffee filters can be hard to separate, but the solution is at the tip of your tongs.

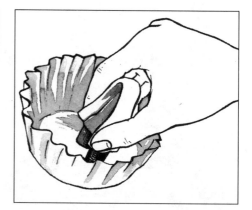

Open-Door Policies

❏ If you have trouble opening doors, visit a hardware store and pick up a set of doorknob turners. They slip over knobs and faucet handles and give you a better grip.

❏ Alternatively, get some lever adapters (available at hardware stores). They clamp onto round doorknobs to convert them into lever handles that you just have to push down—with your arm or elbow, if that's easier.

❏ If you have difficulty grasping the refrigerator door handle, tie a loop of rope through the handle. Put your arm through the loop and pull.

Let There Be Light

❏ If the little knobs on lamps are difficult for you to turn, invest in a gadget that allows you to turn on a metal lamp by simply touching the base. These are available at hardware stores and are easy to install.

HEARING LOSS

Say It Again, Sam

❏ Looking for ways to deal with a loss of hearing? Try taking advantage of technology. This means more than just asking your doctor about getting a hearing aid. Try picking up an amplifier for your telephone at a discount store or hardware store. Look in mail-order catalogs for an alarm clock that flashes lights instead of buzzing, or one that attaches to the base of your pillow and vibrates to wake you at the appointed time.

❏ If you have trouble hearing conversation, try reading lips. Ask friends and family to speak slowly and enunciate clearly rather than shouting.

Man's Best Ears

❏ If your hearing loss is severe, you might want to think about getting a hearing aid dog. Such a pet will alert you when the doorbell or telephone rings, when the alarm clock goes off, when somebody calls your name,

Gadgets to Go

Looking for gadgets to make your life easier as you confront arthritis, hearing loss, or decreased mobility? Whether you're in the market for an ulu knife or a vibrating alarm clock, one of the following specialty mail-order suppliers is likely to carry it. Just call toll-free directory service at (800) 555-1212 to get the listings for Enrichments, adaptAbility, and Hear-More. They'll be glad to take your order or send you a catalog.

when a car horn honks, or when a siren or smoke detector sounds. The animal also will become your best friend. For help in finding and training a hearing aid dog, contact the National Education for Assistance Dog Services (NEADS), P.O. Box 213, West Boylston, MA 01583 or the Delta Society, 289 Perimeter Road East, Renton, WA 98057.

Don't Settle for Silent Films

❏ You used to enjoy going to the movies, but you stopped going when you could no longer hear what the actors were saying. It's time for a return engagement! But this time, ask at the movie theater for amplification equipment. The Americans with Disabilities Act requires theaters to make such equipment available.

LIMITED MOBILITY

Fear of Falling

❏ If you're afraid of falling (and you should be!), you need to make things in your home more secure. Start

---

✔ PROBLEM PREVENTED

6 Warning Signs That It May Be Time to Move

You don't want to move, but you are beginning to think maybe you should. Do any of these problems sound familiar?

1. You go for days at a time without seeing another person.

2. You frequently have weeks when you don't go outdoors or get any exercise.

3. You have fallen or become ill and have been unable to get help.

4. You are scared and lonely a lot of the time.

5. You aren't eating properly—because it's difficult for you to shop, cook, or both.

6. You've been camping out in the living room because you can no longer get upstairs to your bedroom.

If any of these sentences describes you, it's probably time to start looking for a new place to live. Do it now, while you can still decide what's best for you. Don't wait until somebody else makes the decision for you.

---

by making sure your throw rugs don't throw you. Tack them down, place rug pads underneath them, or sew rubber jar seals (the kind used to top Mason jars for home canning) to the base of the rugs to keep them in place. Look for the jar seals in kitchen supply stores.

❏ To guard against falls outdoors, always wear proper footgear, especially if it's slippery outside. Boots with good traction or cleats that strap onto your shoes (available from mail-order catalogs) are a must.

Walk More, Fall Less

❏ If you're feeling insecure, use a cane. It's better than a wheelchair!

❏ One of the best ways to protect yourself against dangerous falls is to exercise. People with weak muscles fall a great deal more often than people with strong ones.

No More Hairy Carries

❏ If you can get around with help but need a way to carry things, think about getting a sturdy, collapsible wheeled cart from a mail-order catalog. It will give you something to lean on and a place to put packages. For places you can't take the cart (such as the movies), get a walker or a wheelchair.

❏ You can get around pretty well with your walker, but you need both hands to maneuver it—and that makes it difficult to carry anything. Consider attaching a basket or carrying pouch to the walker. You can find one of these contraptions at most medical supply stores or in mail-order catalogs.

Don't Get Around Much Anymore?

❏ If you're relying on a wheelchair and are looking for ways to increase your independence, consider getting

Kangaroos aren't the only ones who find pouches useful. Attach one to the front of a walker, and you can keep yourself and your belongings moving.

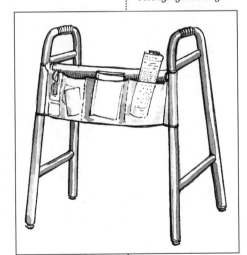

a service dog. These animals turn on the lights, carry parcels, and pick things up when you drop them. To find out how you can adopt and train such a pet, contact the National Education for Assistance Dog Services (NEADS), P.O. Box 213, West Boylston, MA 01583 or the Delta Society, 289 Perimeter Road East, Renton, WA 98057.

It's the Law

❑ If you want to visit a restaurant or movie theater but aren't sure you'll be able to operate your wheelchair or walker there, call ahead to make arrangements. The Americans with Disabilities Act requires public and commercial establishments to make provisions for people who can't get around very well.

To Market, to Market

❑ If getting your marketing done is a problem because you don't drive anymore, try buying staples only every two months. Keep a record of how much you use in two months and then go to the market and buy that amount—even if you have to do it by taxi or ask a friend to drive you. The list should include everything from cleaning supplies and paper goods to food. If you have the freezer space, it could include butter, bread, meat, and fish as well.

❑ If you don't have enough storage space to accommodate two months' worth of supplies but can't get to the market frequently, call around to stores near you to see which ones deliver. Track your use of each staple item over a shorter period of time, then call in your order and ask the store to bring it to you.

OTHER PHYSICAL CHALLENGES

Start a Cookie Contest

❑ Anyone who has to get blood drawn all the time knows how frustrating (not to say painful) this can be. You probably can't control the frequency with which the blood has to be drawn, but you *can* control what the procedure does to you. Start taking a prize cookie with you on each visit. If the nurse gets the needle into your vein on the first try, she wins the prize. Otherwise, you get the cookie.

❑ You can also have a cookie contest with your doctor or with a technician who is following some medical condition. If the news is good, they get rewarded with the cookie. If it isn't, you get to eat it.

ONE PERSON'S SOLUTION

The Right Place at the Right Time

Like many people, I lived for a long time on two floors. I loved my home, but every time I flew down the stairs to answer the doorbell, I wondered how long it would be before I landed in a heap at the bottom. Finally, I decided to take my own advice and get rid of the stairs before they clipped my wings.

Moving, I discovered, isn't all bad. You can get rid of tons of stuff you've been keeping for decades. (I felt as though I had lost 50 pounds!) You get to build a new nest that will fit better than the one you outgrew long ago and shed all the hazards you've secretly worried about for years.

You can live in a bright, clean, cheerful space and in a way that has much more to do with how you live now instead of how you lived 30 years ago. Try it; you might like it. I did.

—JOAN CLEVELAND
New York, New York

Other Physical Challenges

Oh, My Aching Back

❑ You enjoy traveling but get discouraged by the aches and pains you sometimes encounter en route. How can you minimize the discomfort? Remember that it's not the weather that brings on aches and pains—it's the *change* in the weather. However damp and cold it may be where you live, once you're used to it, you'll have less pain than if you go to another climate—even a nicer one. So whenever schedule and finances permit, try to plan one long trip to another climate rather than several shorter ones. That will give your body a chance to get accustomed to the weather.

Let's See . . .

❑ If you're having trouble seeing, focus first on improving the lighting. Invest in a good reading lamp. Look for a flashlight that hangs from a cord around your neck so that you can put the light on the book in your lap. Carry with you, in your pocket or purse, a small flashlight on a key chain. All of these are available at good hardware stores.

❑ If you're having vision problems, keep magnifying eyeglasses in as many strategic locations as possible. You'll need one pair on a stand near your favorite reading chair and a few more to keep in your pocket, on your bedside table, and in the kitchen (so you can read labels and directions).

Silent Cal's First Editorial Comment

President Calvin Coolidge finished his second term of office and left the White House in 1929, less than a year before the stock market crash that would signal the start of the Great Depression. Shortly after his retirement, he filled out a form to become a member of the National Press Club. In the space that asked him to state his occupation, he wrote, "Retired." The space next to it asked for comments. There he wrote, "Glad of it."

Social Issues

Once a man who had just moved into a new house asked me to build a wooden mantel for his fireplace. When I came to work, he had peanuts on the counter and a refrigerator stocked with beer. He told me to feel free to help myself while I worked. Then, on his way out the door, he mentioned that the fireplace wasn't drawing air very well and wondered if I could figure out what the problem was. I left the peanuts and beer alone while I went to work on the mantel, but I didn't forget his question. By the time he got home that evening, I had the answer. I told him that his chimney wasn't drawing because the damper was covered with bottles. He couldn't

figure out how I knew that because I wasn't dirty enough to have been mucking around in the chimney. What he didn't know was that I had worked before with the mason who had built that fireplace, and I knew he liked to drink beer while he was working. When he was done with a bottle, he'd just leave it in the unfinished chimney. Clearing off the damper wasn't hard—and neither was figuring out the problem. Sometimes it doesn't take a lot of technical expertise to fix something—just a little "people sense."

Those are the kinds of problems that are covered in this section. To solve them, you don't have to know carpentry or plumbing, but you do have to know people. Here you'll find ideas on how to please even the most difficult-to-buy-for person on your holiday gift list ("Gift Giving"), what to do about dinner guests who offer more help than you want ("Entertaining") or visitors who arrive unexpectedly ("Sticky Social Situations"), and how to handle folks who are always late ("Pet Peeves"). You'll also find gift ideas for new parents, new homeowners, every member of the family, friends in nursing homes, and the kids' teachers—plus great ideas for wrapping and a wonderful way to get your packages delivered on Christmas Day. You'll learn how to save precious time when preparing for dinner parties, how to make houseguests feel welcome without a lot of extra trouble or expense, and five ways to create inexpensive but elegant centerpieces. You'll discover tactful ideas for deflecting personal questions you don't want to answer, tips for making conversation with strangers, and thoughtful suggestions for comforting grief-stricken friends and acquaintances. Then keep on reading to find out how to put an end to annoying telemarketing calls—and even how to make a busy doctor listen to you!

GIFT GIVING
All I Want for Christmas Is a New Credit Card

SHOWER AND BRIDAL GIFTS

A Gift of a Certain Age

❏ When two 18-year-olds get married, the list of possible gifts is endless—they need everything from linens to kitchen appliances. But when two adults (say, over the age of 35 or so) marry, the list shortens considerably, since most people that age have all the basic household goods they need. What *they* need are gifts such as lawn mowers, barbecue grills, and lawn furniture. But those are big purchases for one person. One solution is to split the cost of a large item with several of the couple's friends and present it as a group gift.

Now You're Cooking!

❏ Need a good gift for a bridal shower? Kitchenware is nearly always a hit, but without recipes, how useful is it? Next time you give a cooking-related gift, try this presentation: Purchase a pie plate—a fancy ceramic one, one made of glass, or even a tin one—and line it with a pretty fabric or paper napkin or a dish towel. Then fill it with the (dry) ingredients for your favorite pie recipe: a small bag of flour, tins of cinnamon and nutmeg, some fresh apples, and, of course, the recipe. To keep everything in place, wrap the pie plate in some tulle (a netlike fabric available at fabric stores) and tie it at the top with a pretty ribbon.

❏ Alternatively, choose any other recipe—a casserole, cake, pizza—and present the recipe and ingredients in the appropriate baking dish or pan.

Try Self-Publishing

❏ Looking for a meaningful and functional bridal (or housewarming) gift on a limited budget? Copy some of your favorite recipes onto recipe cards, writing on the fronts only; if you need more room, continue the recipe on another card. Then purchase a photo album, the kind with plastic-coated pages. If you have just a few recipes, buy a small one; if you have a bunch, choose a larger album. Place the recipe cards in the album, under the plastic, and you have an instant cookbook! The plastic protects the cards and is easily wiped clean.

HOUSEWARMING GIFTS

Time for an Upgrade

❏ When you're trying to choose a gift for someone who's just built or purchased a new home, consider giving a gift certificate to a home decorating store. That will allow your friend to purchase those extras that make a house feel more like a home. Building a house is an extraordinarily expensive proposition, and to save money, many folks cut costs on the extras—light fixtures, switch plates, floor coverings—making do with the most basic rather than the most attractive. Whether your friend has planned the construction himself or has recently bought a house from someone else, he's sure to appreciate a chance to add those finishing touches.

Country Mouse in a City House

❏ It's hard moving from the country or the suburbs to the city. There's a lot more to see and do, but it's often not as pretty. If you know someone who's just moved to the city and is finding her new location awfully sterile, bring back the green with a gift of a windowsill garden. You can get the materials for such a gift at any garden center. Purchase a window box—they come in all sizes and materials, from plastic to terracotta to wood—then tuck a small bag of potting soil, some herb seeds (basil is very easy to grow outdoors), and perhaps a small watering can in the box. Tie the whole thing up with a big ribbon.

❑ A less expensive option is to present your friend with a single terra-cotta pot into which you've slipped a packet of seeds.

FOR NEW PARENTS AND BABIES

A Gift Faux Baby

❑ Looking for an innovative way to present a baby gift? You need a baby outfit, six or seven cloth diapers, a baby blanket, and, if you like, a couple of small toys. Ball up one of the diapers, making it as round and as smooth as possible, and wrap another diaper around it. Fill out the rest of the outfit with more cloth diapers—like a tiny scarecrow—then tuck the "head" into the neck of the baby outfit. Swaddle the whole thing in the baby blanket, tucking the toys inside.

To dress up a baby gift, ball up a cloth diaper and wrap a second diaper around it to form a "head" (A). Stuff more diapers into a baby outfit (B). Add a bonnet and tuck the end of the "head" into the outfit (C). Wrap the whole thing in a baby blanket (D) and add a few small toys if you wish.

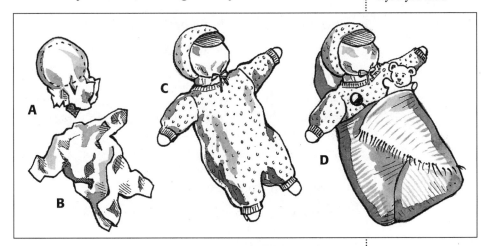

With Six You Get . . . Housecleaning!

❑ After someone has had a second (or third or fourth) child, it can be challenging coming up with good gift ideas, since there are probably lots of hand-me-down clothes and toys around for the new baby. A gift that will surely be appreciated is an offer of a day (or more) of housecleaning. A nice way to present the gift is on a homemade certificate: "This card entitles the bearers to one (1) day of housecleaning."

❑ If you don't have the time to spend cleaning some-one else's house or feel that having you do the house-work would embarrass your friends, pitch in with some friends and buy a day of housecleaning for the new parents. To find a service, check the Yellow Pages under House Cleaning.

Break the Fast-Food Fast

❑ Looking for a gift idea for new parents? Once every-one arrives home, there's so much to do that many fam-ilies end up living on fast food. If you like to cook, consider preparing a meal for the family, or make up some entrées that they can freeze and then pop in the oven or microwave. Soups, stews, and casseroles are good choices (they travel well, too). Include a list of in-gredients and reheating instructions. It's a good idea to find out if there's anything family members don't eat before you head into the kitchen.

Thanks, We Needed That

❑ They don't need diapers, they have plenty of clothes, and if someone buys them another rattle, they'll scream. So what do these new parents *really* need? How about an evening alone together, compli-ments of you? Offer the new parents a night (or week-end) of free baby-sitting—at your home. Present the couple with a note card with this message: "This card entitles the bearers to one (1) night of baby-sitting, at their convenience, at my home."

❑ Make your offer even more romantic by accompa-nying it with a picnic basket into which you've tucked a bottle of wine, some cheese, candles, and a cassette tape or compact disc of romantic music.

FOR FAMILY AND LOVED ONES

Massage Message

❑ Stumped for a gift for your sweetheart? If you're able to spend some money, consider treating him to a mas-sage (especially if he has a high-stress or very physical job). Massages are wonderful for relieving tension and muscle soreness, but they're an indulgence that folks rarely think of giving themselves. Depending on where you live, you may be able to get a massage for between $30 and $80 an hour. To find a masseur or masseuse, check the Yellow Pages under Massage and Massage—Therapeutic.

ONE PERSON'S SOLUTION

If the Tissue Fits . . .

My boyfriend and I had just moved to a new apartment, and everything was still packed away in boxes. When I decided to buy Tom a little gift one day, I suddenly realized I had no idea where the wrapping paper was. It was around 9:00 P.M. (he would get home at around 9:15), and I had neither the time nor the inclination to start looking.

   I stood in the living room for a minute, trying to think of a solution, when I saw the red shoe box from Tom's new running shoes peeking out from under the sofa. That's what gave me the idea. It's a good thing we never put anything away, because that shoe box was the answer to my problem. I opened the box, and, sure enough, there was enough tissue paper inside to wrap the gift. I crumpled it up to make it look fancy, wrapped the box, and tied it up with a ribbon I had left over from Christmas.

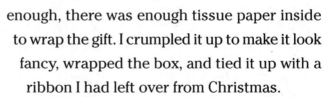

   Ever since then, I've been saving the tissue paper from shoe boxes—just in case I need to wrap a present.

—Lori Baird
Astoria, New York

A Picture-Perfect Gift

❑ Your kids want to give Grandma a nice gift, but they just can't seem to scrape up the airfare to Paris. What to do? Purchase some plain, inexpensive picture frames from a discount store and help the kids decorate them. Buy fancy yarn or twine (gold and silver are especially pretty) from a crafts store, or use any scraps you have on hand. Using a clear-drying craft glue (such as Elmer's) or an acrylic medium (a combination adhesive and varnish available at art supply stores), adhere the decorations to the frame. Finish by inserting a photo of the family.

6 Better Wraps for Your Gifts

Have you seen the price of good wrapping paper? Why bother—especially when there's so much of it just lying around! For example:

1. Last year's wrapping paper. If you remove it carefully, you can reuse it next year.

2. Wallpaper scraps or samples. Visit a local wallpaper store, which you can find by checking the Yellow Pages under Wallpapers & Wallcoverings—Retail. When a particular wallpaper pattern or line is discontinued, stores no longer need the sample books and may give them away. The samples make beautiful—and sturdy—gift wrap for small packages.

3. Maps. Old road maps, maps of the world, and topographical maps make interesting and educational wrapping paper. Choose a map of your home state, a state or country that the recipient of the gift particularly likes, or any old map you have around.

4. Magazine covers. Especially during the holidays, most magazines come out with special covers. If a gift is small enough, the cover makes lovely wrapping paper.

5. Fabric. Use what you have around or make a trip to the fabric store. Many stores sell pretty print cottons with cute designs— Santas, candy canes, birthday hats—for as little as 99 cents a yard. Rather than wasting time trying to hem it, cut the fabric with pinking shears. That gives the material a decorative border and prevents it from raveling.

6. The Sunday comics. They're colorful, convenient, and cheap!

You Gotta Hand It to Them

❏ Can't decide what to give Grandma for Mother's Day? Here's an idea that's especially appealing if the kids are small. Purchase some fabric paints from a local crafts store and a T-shirt or sweatshirt (in Grandma's size) from a discount store. Prepare a work area—this could get messy—and lay out some newspaper. Pour a little paint onto a paper plate, dip your child's hand into the paint, and make handprints on the shirt. Let the paint dry before you wrap the shirt, then read the instructions on the paint container for fabric care. Include those instructions with the gift.

❏ If a shirt isn't Grandma's bag, purchase a plain canvas tote bag from a discount store and decorate it with handprints.

FOR STUDENTS

The Little Chill

❏ Is your daughter (or son or niece or nephew . . .) off to college? And you want to help her get off to the right start? You could buy her a T-shirt that says "Mommy's Little Girl," or you could help her out with something really useful. Most colleges have a service from which students can rent small dorm refrigerators, which can come in handy for storing sodas and snacks. Offer to pick up the (usually very modest) rental fee for a month (or a semester).

Phone Home

❏ Student life can be lonely, especially for freshmen, many of whom have never been away from home before. If you're looking for a gift to help a student cope with loneliness, help him keep in touch with the folks back home by offering to pay for a dorm phone installation (most dorm rooms do not come with a phone). If you're braver (and have deeper pockets), pick up the tab on a day's worth of long-distance service.

❏ Alternatively, give your student friend a long-distance phone card. Many convenience stores sell phone debit cards that come in set denominations—$5, $10, $20. They're good for either long-distance or local calls. To use the card, the student dials an 800 number and then is prompted to enter the phone number she wants to call, followed by a secret code (printed under a scratch-off patch on the back of the card). When the money on the card runs out, she just throws the card away.

BY AND FOR KIDS

Keep Them Occupied

❏ Need a quick gift for a child? Here's one that costs just a little—and you can probably find all the supplies you need at a discount drugstore or even a grocery store. Start with an empty shoe box. Cover the lid and box separately with plain paper (use brown paper bags if you don't have any other paper) and write the child's name on the top in big letters. In the box, place a small box of crayons, a pair of rounded craft scissors, a few sheets of construction paper, and a small bottle of clear-drying craft glue such as Elmer's (or whatever crafty items you can find). To get the child started, challenge him to decorate his new crafts box.

Multiple Choices

❏ If you want to give small remembrances to a number of children (say, all the youngsters in the neighborhood) at Christmas, it can be a challenge to find something they'll like that won't break the bank. A couple of possibilities are a special Christmas ornament for each child or an oversize gingerbread man (with the child's name on it) for each youngster.

FOR TEACHER

Make a Note of This

❏ Coming up with gift ideas for your child's favorite teacher can be a real chore. You want to give something that is special but doesn't smack of bribery. Note cards are a functional and thoughtful gift that kids of almost any age can make themselves. Visit your local art supply store and buy some heavy white or light-colored paper and some 4⅜- by 5¾-inch envelopes. Cut the paper into 5½- by 8¼-inch rectangles, then fold each in half so that the short sides meet. Now you have note cards with blank insides. Help your child decorate the fronts of the cards with markers or crayons. If you want to get fancy (or if you have an older child), attach some flower petals, leaves, or glitter to the front of each card, using a clear-drying craft glue (such as Elmer's) or acrylic medium (a combination adhesive and varnish available at art supply stores). On the back of the card, make your child's "seal," the way commercial card companies do: "Cards by Tommy," for instance. For

DOLLAR STRETCHER

3 Inexpensive but Beautiful Trim Ideas

Store-bought ribbons? They're expensive and look, well, store-bought. If saving money and sprucing up your gifts sounds like a good idea, try some of these beautiful handmade trims.

1. Scan your backyard for some pretty leaves—if there's snow on the ground, snip a couple from your favorite houseplants (ferns are especially lovely). Fresh or dried flower petals work well, too. Roll out a piece of waxed paper, waxed side up, on your ironing board. Lay the leaves and petals close together on the paper, then place another sheet of waxed paper, waxed side down, on top of the decorations. Turn off the steam button on your iron (this requires dry heat) and press the paper very briefly on low, just until the two pieces of waxed paper stick together. Let cool, then cut the paper into pretty shapes, leaving a border around the leaves or petals. You can glue or tie these shapes to your gifts.

2. Pinecones. If you can't find them in your yard or a park, try a crafts store. Pinecones are beautiful on their own, but if you like, dab them with a little white acrylic paint to give them a snow-dappled effect.

3. Last year's Christmas (or birthday or Mother's Day . . .) cards. If you received any particularly pretty cards last year, use them as decorative gift tags this year. Remove the front of each card. Then, on the back of the image, cover any writing by gluing on a piece of clean paper. When it dries, cut out the image, write a new message on the back, and attach it to a gift.

each teacher gift, stack together five cards and five envelopes and tie them with a pretty ribbon.

Chalk It Up to Experience

❏ What if your child isn't very artistically inclined, but she still wants to give her teacher something she's made herself? She can easily manage a homemade paper clip or chalk holder. To make this, she'll need some clay from a hobby shop. Make sure to get the kind that doesn't need to be fired (baked) to harden. Have your child shape some clay into a bowl shape—about 3 inches in diameter for paper clips or 4½ inches in diameter for chalk. Remember, it doesn't have to be perfect! Let the clay dry, then have the youngster paint it with acrylic paints. If she likes, she can finish the bowl by coating it with a layer of acrylic medium (a combination adhesive and varnish available at art supply stores).

A Recipe for Straight A's

❏ If your child doesn't enjoy crafts but wants to remember a teacher at Christmas or the end of the school year, consider giving a simple gift of food that the child has made himself. A basket of homemade cookies or a loaf of quick bread doesn't take a lot of time (or cost a lot), and it's a gift any teacher will appreciate.

FOR YOUR MAIL CARRIER

Neither Snow, nor Rain, nor . . . Tired Feet?

❏ Money is the standard gift for letter carriers and paper deliverers,

---

TIME SAVER

A Handmade Gift Even You Can Make

Even if you're truly crafts challenged, a jar garden makes a great gift—and it's hard to mess it up! The basic idea is to transform a large Mason jar (or any clear glass container with a lid) into a terrarium. In addition to the jar, you need charcoal pellets (from a pet store that sells fish), potting soil, and a small, humidity-loving plant such as an African violet.

Pour about half an inch of charcoal pellets on the bottom of the jar. Follow that with about two to three inches of potting soil. Make a little well in the soil, insert your plant, and pack the soil lightly around the roots. To make the terrarium more decorative, cover the soil with small marbles or pebbles. Water the plant, then replace the lid. Since moisture is trapped in the jar, the plant needs watering only once every four to five months. Instruct the recipient to keep the jar in a semi-sunny location.

and it's much appreciated. But if you prefer a more sub-tle present, how about a treat for her tired feet? A pair of fuzzy slippers, some woolly socks, or even some soft, squishy innersoles would be received with pleasure.

A Toast to the Letter Carrier

❏ If you don't have money for a gift for your letter car-rier and you're usually home when your carrier drops by, here's an idea. Present him with a homemade cer-tificate for a "complimentary hot drink" when he stops at your home during the cold season (or, if you prefer, complimentary cold drinks during the summer).

FOR SOMEONE IN THE HOSPITAL OR NURSING HOME

Pass the Remote

❏ There are few things worse than being cooped up in the hospital. If you know someone who will be there for more than just an overnight stay, you can be sure that he will have a fair amount of boredom to contend with. If you want to bypass the usual gift of magazines, think about picking up the tab for his television rental. It doesn't do much for the intellect, but it sure helps pass the time after visiting hours are over.

Nail the Perfect Gift

❏ Even if someone is in the hospital for only a minor illness, she can start to feel pretty blah after a couple of days. If you're looking for an appealing gift for some-one who's under the weather, consider treating her to a manicure. Some hospitals offer a manicure service; to find out if yours does, call the hospital's main num-ber and ask for patient services. If the hospital itself doesn't have such a service, check with a local beauty salon (look in the Yellow Pages under Beauty Salons). Many will send a manicurist to the hospital.

He'll Take Comfort in This

❏ Choosing a gift for someone in a nursing home can be challenging. You'd like to get something practical but comforting—and maybe entertaining, too. And you know it can't take up too much space. Here's an idea. Purchase an inexpensive basket from a crafts or discount store and line it with some attractive paper or a pretty washcloth. Then fill it with some photographs of home and family members, a pair of warm slippers, maybe a book—whatever you know will appeal to your friend's or relative's interests and emotions.

Forbidden Pleasures

❏ What's the ideal gift for someone in a nursing home? Perhaps one of the hardest things about living in such a facility is that things you could get at home with no problem are suddenly scarce—or even verboten. As long as you know that your friend's or relative's health permits it, a real treat could be a little something he can't get easily—perhaps a bottle of wine or a favorite food. Keep the portions small so you don't overwhelm him, and he's sure to be delighted.

❏ If your friend in a nursing home has problems remembering things, it may not be wise to leave a gift of food in her room. (The whole box of chocolates could be gone in half an hour because she won't remember that she's already sampled them.) How can you make sure she gets your gift without overdosing on it? Ask at the nurses' desk if you can leave your gift there and if the nurses would be willing to dole out the pieces gradually.

FOR JUST ABOUT ANYONE

Try a Little Show-and-Tell

❏ Looking for a gift that costs a little but means a lot? If you're proficient at a craft or sport—knitting, cooking, skiing, golf, ceramics, woodworking—that a friend or loved one wants to learn, give the gift of your time and spend the day with him teaching that skill.

Far Better Than Fruitcake

❏ Lots of people—particularly those who have recently lost a loved one—tend to get a bit down over the holidays. If you have a friend who needs cheering up by the middle of December, try this variation on the "Twelve Days of Christmas." At a discount or crafts store, pick up a small, inexpensive Christmas stocking. On the night of December 13, place a small gift in the stocking and, when your friend isn't looking, hang it from her doorknob with a note. The note should instruct her to leave the stocking on the door each night

DOLLAR STRETCHER

Gift Wrap: Go the Extra Yard

There's nothing more maddening than trying to wrap a large gift and realizing you don't have enough paper. Most store-bought rolls don't have enough paper for very large gifts, and combining several rolls would be expensive. One solution is to make your own wrapping paper. You need a large roll of brown or white craft paper (available at office supply stores), some colorful acrylic paints, cookie cutters (optional), and several household sponges.

First, decide on a simple design—Christmas trees, dinosaurs, mittens, dogs—then trace or draw the shapes on the sponges and cut out the shapes with scissors or a sharp knife. (If you have trouble cutting standard household sponges, purchase some pop-up sponges—the kind that you buy in flat rectangles and that expand when moistened. You can find them at kitchen supply stores and some grocery and hardware

stores. Draw your design on the dry sponge with a pencil, then cut it out with scissors.)

Second, clear a work space, either on the floor or on a big table, and lay out some newspaper. Roll out as much craft paper as you can comfortably work on and cut it from the roll. Pour your paints onto paper plates, moisten the sponges with a little water, dip them in paint, and start sponging your shapes on the paper. Use bright colors, especially if you choose brown paper, and sponge the shapes close together—it'll look better when you wrap a small package. Let the paint dry, then either store the paper rolled up or use it right away.

If you're in a hurry, an alternative is to wrap the gift with the blank paper, then sponge on the paint.

This homemade wrapping paper makes a clever gift in itself. Roll it up, and present it with a pretty ribbon tied around the roll.

until Christmas—and not to peek to see who's filling it. You'll have to return each evening and sneak the next gifts into the stocking. (If returning every day is impossible, try recruiting an accomplice or two.) It's fun to increase the number of gifts each day (5 candy

ONE PERSON'S SOLUTION

Santa Express

For once in my life, I finished all my Christmas shopping weeks before the holiday. On Christmas Eve, however, I opened my closet door to grab a sweater, and to my utter horror, I saw my Christmas gift for my brother—who lives in another state—leaning against the wall. I felt terrible and was sure there was no way to get the gift to him by Christmas. I decided to mail it anyway, hoping he'd at least get it by the 26th.

I was surprised to learn that I could use Express Mail on Christmas Eve and the post office would indeed deliver the gift on Christmas Day. Better yet, the postmaster told me that the letter carrier would deliver the gift dressed as Santa! Apparently, many town post offices provide that service—it's called Express Mail Santa—and, aside from the cost of delivery (around $10), there's no extra charge. Vic got his gift and was thrilled, and my conscience was cleared. (To find out whether the town you're mailing to offers Express Mail Santa, call your local post office.)

—SUE DONNELLY
Flushing, New York

canes, 6 Christmas cookies—all the way up to 12 paper snowflakes) and, if you're feeling inspired, to tuck in a silly rhyme. On Christmas morning, when you finally reveal your identity, you'll find that you've vastly brightened your friend's holidays.

GIFT WRAPPING

The Portable Gift Wrap Station

❏ Having trouble clearing a space for your gift wrapping? Set up your ironing board and do your wrapping there. It's the ideal height, gives you space to work without taking up a lot of room, and is easily set up and taken down as needed.

A Basket Case

❏ Everyone loves getting food treats such as cookies, candies, and fudge, but sometimes you want to present them in a fancier way. Dig out those old berry baskets—the small, plastic baskets berries come in. Cut some fabric into strips (to keep them from raveling, use pinking shears) and weave them in and out of the plastic. Or use heavy yarn. Line the basket with a pretty paper napkin, then arrange your goodies in the basket.

To dress up the goodies you're about to give, thread pieces of scrap fabric or yarn through the plastic of a simple berry basket. Add a bright paper napkin, pop in the food, and you're ready to go.

It's a Wrap!

❏ Sure, you could put your bread, cookies, muffins, and fudge in a plastic bag to give a friend, but that's boring and not very imaginative. Try this instead. Purchase some colorful cellophane (available at grocery stores and crafts stores) and wrap each piece of candy, muffin, or loaf of bread separately. Twist one or both ends, close with a twist tie, and add a ribbon. For a nice finishing touch, place the treats in a basket and tie a ribbon around the handle.

ENTERTAINING
Having Fun without Going Broke

DINNER PARTIES

Guess Who's Coming to Dinner

❏ Sometimes it's hard to come up with just the right guest list, even for a small party. To ensure that everyone will get along and have a good time, invite at least a few people who you know are good guests—folks who can converse easily with others, whether or not they are already acquainted. Then try to make certain that every guest knows at least one other guest so no one feels lost.

Who Invited the Kids?

❏ Some parents assume that an invitation to them is also an invitation to their children. If guests arrive with their children without consulting you in advance, you should welcome the youngsters. If they're very young (and most likely will not be eating the adult menu), tell the parents that they may have juice, milk, or whatever you feel is appropriate from the refrigerator. Offer them the opportunity to make sandwiches (or other snacks) for the kids. Then return to your own food preparations or entertaining duties.

What's for Dinner?

❏ You're tearing your hair out, trying to decide what to serve at your party. Don't. Instead, plan to serve simple, good food, not fancy or fussy dishes. That way, you're more apt to avoid failures, and your guests will feel comfortable and well fed. Pasta with salad and fresh bread is always a good bet; so are one-dish meals, hearty sandwiches with homemade soup, or lasagna. If you have an outdoor grill, you can simplify your entertaining by using the grill for all kinds of meats, including lamb, turkey, and pork.

Sorry, I Gave Up Food for Lent

❏ These days, it's not uncommon for individuals to be on special diets, whether for health or other reasons. How can you be sure that all your guests can eat the food you're preparing? To avoid major menu conflicts, casually ask dinner guests if they have any dietary restrictions when they call to respond to your invitation. If so, try to have at least one substantive thing that the guest can eat. A guest who is allergic to the shrimp in the appetizer you planned can probably still eat vegetables and dip, and a vegetarian will be appreciative if you prepare a small portion of lasagna with his needs in mind.

Your Last (Re)course

❏ You want to serve dessert, but you don't have time to make it, or you just don't like to bake. Buy a fresh pie at a farm stand (during the summer or fall) or a cake or cookies at a good bakery. (Transfer the cake to a nice serving plate, cookies to a basket lined with a colorful cloth napkin.) Before long, you'll develop a couple of favorite sources you know you can count on.

Try a Little Temperance

❏ It's a fact of life that many individuals have drinking problems. How

TIME SAVER

Time's Up!

The guests are knocking at the door, and you're still in your slippers, whipping up a sauce. It's the stuff nightmares are made of, but it won't happen if you do as much as possible ahead of time.

Plan your menu so that you can do most of the preparation the day before the big event. Make appetizers and dessert earlier in the week, then freeze them. (Don't forget to pull them out of the freezer so they have time to thaw!) For your main dish, plan on a casserole that you can assemble ahead of time or something simple that you can throw on the grill as guests arrive (so all you'll be doing right before dinner is buttering bread and tossing a salad). Also, try setting the table early in the day, or even the night before. By preparing ahead, you'll be able to spend time with your guests and maybe even enjoy your own party.

can you entertain such friends safely and graciously? If you are inviting a friend with a drinking problem to dinner, be sure to have plenty of hors d'oeuvres and serve your meal shortly after the person arrives, keeping the cocktail hour short. As the host, be sure to serve all drinks yourself instead of having people get their own; that way, you can monitor the flow of alcohol. Or serve only nonalcoholic beverages. Of course, if necessary, you should quietly offer to drive the guest home at the end of the evening or even offer her the guest room.

Liquor License

❏ These days, many dinner guests prefer drinks that are nonalcoholic. What should you have on hand? Be able to offer them sparkling water, fruit juice, or soda. For instance, if you have cranberry juice and diet cola on hand in addition to sparkling water, guests will have a reasonable choice of beverages.

 DOLLAR STRETCHER

Help! I Need Somebody!

You have only two hands with which to cook, serve, greet guests, clean up, and so forth. Where can you find some help without hiring a professional caterer? Here are a few possible sources.

• Teenage (or college-age) sons or daughters of your guests

• A baby-sitter whom you already know

• Students from a local high school cooking or home economics class (call the school to ask about this)

• Students from a local vocational school that has a restaurant or catering program

• A teenage (or college-age) neighbor

Do expect to pay any of your hires reasonably; don't be a skinflint just because you're working with students. (Your costs will still be considerably lower than if you hired a caterer.) Discuss payment with them in advance, and make it clear ahead of time exactly what you expect them to do (perhaps serve hors d'oeuvres, greet guests and take coats, park cars, or wash dishes).

What Can I Bring?

❑ When guests ask what they can bring to a party, are you at a loss for an answer? Don't panic. Instead, ask them to bring something specific—say, a tossed salad, an appetizer, or a cake. (Don't ask them to bring a main dish, which might require precious oven space and conflict with your menu.) Be sure to keep a list of who's bringing what so that you don't end up with five desserts and no salads.

❑ If you are intent on handling the entire menu yourself, when guests ask what they can contribute, you can ask them to bring a beverage. This satisfies their desire to be helpful and also cuts your entertaining costs.

Keep Your Guests In the Know

❑ If you're having trouble deciding which guests should sit where for a large dinner party, follow this rule of thumb: Make sure each guest knows one other person seated near him at the table. If that is impossible, try to seat people together who have something in common (say, a passion for golf or gardens).

Why, Rover Could Just Jump for Joy!

❑ If your dog or cat gets agitated when there are a lot of guests in the house (or if the animal tends to steal food), consider placing him in a kennel for the night. Your pet will be properly cared for but out of the way, and your peace of mind may be well worth the expense.

The Quick-and-Dirty Approach

❑ You look around your home and worry that you'll never be able to get it clean in time for the party. If you've run out of time and a thorough cleaning is out of the question, your best bet is to concentrate on the

---

✔ PROBLEM PREVENTED

No Thrills, No Spills

To avoid spilling drops of wine when pouring it from a bottle, turn the neck of the bottle slowly in a circular motion after you have filled the glass and before you pull the bottle away from the rim. Have a cloth napkin handy to catch any drops that may escape.

Entertaining

essentials. Straighten up clutter. Make sure the kitchen counters and bathrooms are clean. Put out fresh soap and hand towels for your guests. Check the supply of toilet paper. You'll be less frazzled when the guests arrive, and you can do your thorough cleaning after the party, when your home will really need it.

DOLLAR STRETCHER

7 Favorite Party Favors

Everyone loves party favors. But won't they break your already-bulging budget? Not if you keep them simple and imaginative. Here are a few ideas.

1. Colorful hard candies stuffed in small baskets
2. Inexpensive holiday ornaments
3. Tiny, potted herbs
4. Votive candles (have one lit at each place setting)
5. Homemade chocolates bundled in cellophane
6. Homemade potpourri or sachet
7. Tiny toys (a yo-yo or Matchbox car for each person)

China Patterns: Play with Matches

❑ You've accumulated various patterns and styles of china over the years, and now that you've invited 12 people to dinner, you realize you don't come close to having 12 of everything from one set. Don't worry! Mix and match, blending colors and styles. Use dinner plates from one pattern, dessert plates from another. Give each person a teacup or coffee mug in a different pattern. You can unify the look with matching place mats and napkins or by using one style of drinking glass, and you may be creating a topic of conversation for your guests.

Greetings!

❑ Guests can feel lost if they arrive at the door with no one to greet them, especially at a large party. To make them feel comfortable immediately, be sure that a host or another guest is posted at the door to welcome guests, take their coats, and direct them to where people are gathered.

I Don't Know a Soul!

❑ If you arrive at a party and feel as though you don't know anyone, ask the hostess if you can pitch in and help by passing hors d'oeuvres, taking drink orders, and the like. Chances are, by doing one of these things, you'll meet someone you'd like to come back and talk with later on.

What the Well-Dressed Host Is Wearing

❏ How can you look nice but stay comfortable while entertaining? Dress simply. Don't wear tight clothes or high heels. Don't wear a lot of jewelry or pieces that dangle. Women can wear a skirt or nice slacks and a sweater (elastic waists hidden by a belt are great); men can wear a turtleneck or sweater and slacks. A blazer dresses things up, and you can slip it off while preparing food.

Hold All Calls

❏ What should you do if the phone rings during a party? Don't answer it (unless a guest is concerned that the caller might be a baby-sitter). Turn on the answering machine as the party begins, then return calls after the party or the next day. (If the answering machine is located in the area where you're entertaining, turn the

---

 Inexpensive but Elegant Centerpieces

If you can't afford fresh flowers for your dinner table every time you entertain, here are a few alternatives.

1. Use a healthy potted plant, preferably with blooms, in a nice planter. (Go ahead and buy one; it will last much longer than freshly cut flowers.)

2. Use a small antique or reproduction wooden box with a lid. Put saltshakers and pepper shakers inside it.

3. Arrange a little cluster of framed family photographs in the center of the table. Mix old and new shots. They are bound to spark conversation, especially if this is a family dinner.

4. At holiday time, fill a glass bowl with old Christmas balls.

5. Use food as the centerpiece. If you're serving soup or chili, put it in a large tureen with a serving ladle and place the tureen in the center of the table (on a trivet or hot pad). Or if you have a decorative dessert that doesn't need refrigeration, place that in the center of the table.

Dinner Parties

Entertaining

volume down to avoid distractions as callers leave their messages. Also, adjust the setting, if possible, so the machine will pick up as soon as the phone starts to ring.) Your guests should have your full attention.

Fill Those Awkward Pauses

❏ Silence can be deadly at parties. If you're concerned that a lull in the conversation might kill the atmosphere at your next gathering, put a little background music on the CD or tape player. Generally speaking, jazz or classical music is a good choice; either of these is less distracting than rock. (You can signal a change of atmosphere from cocktails to dinner by changing the

Situation Savers Every Home Should Have

Extra guests, too much food, too little time. What else could possibly go wrong? Here are some lifesavers that should be required equipment in every house.

1. Extra folding chairs. You didn't expect Tom and Sue to bring the kids, but they did. Fortunately, you have something for them to sit on. Store the chairs under the bed, in the back of the closet, or on their sides behind the sofa.

2. Small folding table (aka a card table). This is where you park the kids during Thanksgiving dinner. It also comes in handy as a place to put food if the table is too crowded or you're serving a buffet.

3. Big, white sheet. This can double as a tablecloth in a pinch.

4. Cooler. Just in case your company shows up with food and there's no more room in your refrigerator. Of course, it's terrific for picnics and tailgate parties, too.

5. One pound of pasta, 2 cloves fresh garlic or 1 teaspoon garlic powder, 3 to 4 tablespoons olive oil, 1 or 2 cans (6 ounces each) chopped clams, and 1 pinch dried oregano. Cook the pasta. Meanwhile, sauté the garlic in the olive oil, add the clams and their juice, and mix in the oregano. Pour over the cooked pasta. Dinner for four—in about 15 minutes.

6. Paper plates. These will come in handy when you don't want to wash dishes before dessert, to send home leftovers with your friends, or for days when you just don't feel like cleaning up.

7. Fire extinguisher. Just in case.

style of music—say, from pop to jazz or from jazz to classical.) Don't crank up the volume unless everyone is planning to dance; guests want to be able to talk to and hear each other.

The Food: Go for Global Warming

❏ If you're afraid you can't keep the food warm long enough for everyone to be served once it comes out of the oven, buy one or two warming trays (available at department stores or kitchen supply stores). You just plug one of these in 15 minutes ahead of time, then place a meat platter or casserole dish right on top; the tray will keep your dish warm as long as it's plugged in. (Don't place antique or very fragile pieces on the warming tray. Old paints or glazes could become damaged, and heat could crack particularly fragile china.)

Appoint a Wine Steward

❏ It's hard to serve dinner and wine at the same time, especially if you are hosting a party by yourself. Minimize the confusion by appointing one guest to be the wine steward, asking him to pour the wine for all the guests.

How Can I Help?

❏ Having guests try to help in the kitchen while you are cooking and serving can become a frustrating tangle. So when they ask to be of assistance, give them assignments *outside* the kitchen. Ask them to take drink orders, pass hors d'oeuvres, or pour water in glasses on the dinner table. Certain guests might even enjoy helping by playing with the children.

❏ If a well-meaning guest really wants to help you in the kitchen and you'd prefer to handle the preparations yourself, let him give you a hand with the serving. When you're ready, fill each serving dish you plan to use and ask the guest to carry it to the table or sideboard. Then hand the guest the serving utensils and ask him to place one next to each dish.

The Kids Want to Help

❏ Kids often want to help at parties, but you probably don't want them pouring the wine or preparing the soufflé. To avoid mishaps, give them jobs they can handle. Ask older children to play with younger children. Delegate an older child to pass cold hors d'oeuvres or collect coats. A younger child could accompany an older one who is passing hors d'oeuvres and hand out cocktail napkins. Don't have them carry hot dishes, light the candles, or do anything else that an adult should handle.

Candles, Candles, Burning Bright

❏ Candlelight is lovely, but if you rely on it for your only light at the dinner table, chances are your guests won't be able to see. To deal with this dilemma, augment the candles with a few lamps placed around the room. If you use 40-watt bulbs, the light will be soft and atmospheric, but enough to allow your guests to see what they're eating.

❏ Alternatively, if you love candles but are afraid they're too dim, use at least three or four pairs. Candlesticks don't have to match. To unify the look, use only ivory-colored candles. You can add votives in selected spots around the room.

Ahead by a Lap

❏ "Lap suppers" are great—until guests try balancing dinner plates on their knees while sawing through pieces of meat, or that delicious sauce runs off the plate and onto someone's slacks or dress. What can you serve on such occasions that won't be messy or awkward to eat? Choose foods that are easy to eat without a knife and not too runny. Lasagna or another thick casserole with a tossed salad and garlic bread is a good bet. Baked or broiled fish and meat loaf are safe, too.

Please Be Seated

❏ If you're having a lap supper but don't have enough chairs for all your guests, be creative. The kitchen stool, piano bench, ottoman, garden bench, even patio furniture can work well and add a little flair to the seating plan.

Living Room Drapes

❏ When you serve a lap supper, how can you make sure your guests don't go home with spaghetti sauce on their best skirts and slacks? Select large, buffet-style cloth napkins—the kind that guests can drape across their entire laps to protect their clothes. (You can buy these at most stores that sell cloth napkins—discount stores, department stores, linen stores, kitchen supply stores. Or buy some inexpensive, brightly colored dish towels in a soft, smooth cotton.)

The Procrastinator's Guide to Cleanup

❏ You don't want to stay up until the wee hours cleaning up after your party, but you also don't want to get up to a disaster area in the morning. Here are some suggestions. Rinse dishes and put away leftover food. If you used table linens and cloth napkins, toss them in the washing machine and run them through while you're cleaning up. This will get wine and food stains right out of the fabric before they have time to set. Remove any scraps of food from upholstered furniture so grease doesn't set in. If some of your guests were smokers, brush any cigarette ashes off furniture and carpets. Make sure the oven or grill is turned off and the fire in the fireplace is extinguished. Then go to bed. Everything else can wait until morning.

Warming Up Your New House

Housewarmings are held to welcome friends, family, and new neighbors to your new home. The party can be large or small, but it's usually informal, and you don't serve a meal—just hors d'oeuvres, sandwiches, or dessert (or any combination of these), along with beverages. Housewarmings are generally held during the late afternoon or early evening, much like a cocktail party. Guests aren't meant to stay for more than about two hours. You might invite adults only or entire families. It's customary for guests to bring small gifts for the home, but some might come bearing a bottle of wine or champagne or a contribution of food.

WEDDINGS, SHOWERS, AND ENGAGEMENT PARTIES

The List

❑ If you can't decide whom to invite to the wedding, start with a guest limit (probably based on your budget). Begin your guest list with relatives, close friends, and others whom you *must* invite. Move on from there, until you reach your limit.

Just Mom, Dad, and 400 of Our Closest Friends

❑ If you're afraid the wedding guest list is going to grow beyond your limit, start by keeping the number of people in the wedding party (bridesmaids, groomsmen, ring bearers, and flower girls) small. That way, you can eliminate the number of dates and spouses who must accompany wedding party members, and you send a signal to friends and family that the wedding will be small.

Play Musical Chairs

❑ You're hosting a wedding and can't figure out where to seat everyone. Pick up a large bulletin board or piece

Visual aids are helpful—and give added flexibility—when you're planning seating for a wedding reception.

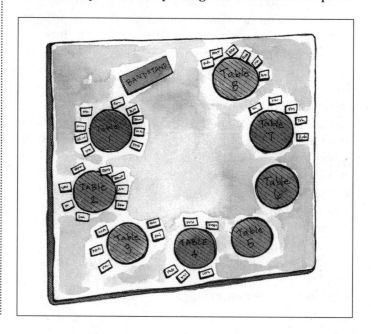

of cardboard at a discount store and cover it with felt (also available at discount stores or fabric stores). Add cutout felt circles or squares to represent the tables at your reception. Then cut out tags from the felt. As invitation responses arrive, use a fine-tip marker to write each attending guest's name on a tag. Decide which groupings of guests would be appropriate (say, seating those with similar jobs or hobbies together), then gather the name tags accordingly and stick each group of tags on an appropriate felt "table." As more responses arrive, you can keep rearranging your seating plan up to the last minute.

❑ If you prefer, tack paper "tables" and name tags directly onto a bulletin board instead of using felt. But don't use Post-it notes; they tend to lose their adhesiveness if they're left up a long time or moved around a lot, and you wouldn't want Great-Aunt Susie to lose her seat.

Should I Come Bearing Gifts?

❑ If you're worried about whether to take a gift to an engagement party, don't. Engagement parties are not showers. Their purpose is to announce the engagement and formally introduce the couple to each other's family and friends. If you don't want to arrive empty-handed, take something small—a gift of food for the party, a bottle of champagne, or a bouquet of flowers.

OUTDOOR PARTIES

Traffic Control

❑ When you host an outdoor party, you want your guests to stay outside as much as possible. How do you keep them out of the kitchen? One way is to set up all beverages outside—canned or bottled beverages in a cooler and glasses, garnishes, and other accoutrements on a table nearby.

Keep Your Cool

❑ You have plenty of room outside for all your guests. What you *don't* have is sufficient cooler space for drinks. Here's a solution. Set an inexpensive child's plastic sled on the lawn under a tree. Fill it with ice, then set canned beverages in the ice. The drinks will stay cold, and the brightly colored sled will add to the party decorations. (This works best on days that are not oppressively hot.)

❏ An alternative is to use a child's metal wagon. Fill the wagon with ice and add bottled and canned beverages. The metal keeps things cold, and because the wagon is on wheels, you can move it around easily (either to keep it out of the sun or to serve guests).

KIDS' PARTIES

Less Is More

❏ Large birthday parties are often stressful for small children and their parents. How can you increase the fun and decrease the stress? Use this rule of thumb: make the number of youngsters on the guest list equal the birthday child's age. (For instance, if your child is turning four, invite four friends.) Be a little flexible about the number, allowing for a sibling or member of a group of friends, so no one feels left out.

Simple Treasures

❏ Too many activities—or games that are too complicated—can be stressful for little ones as well as for the adults in charge of the party. To help youngsters enjoy the occasion, be creative but offer just a few simple things for them to do. Try a treasure hunt outdoors (they can hunt for unshelled peanuts, wrapped candy, or small toys), face painting, a piñata, blowing soap bubbles, Simon says, or a simple craft. Don't forget that most kids just like to play; if they seem happy playing with dolls or in the sandbox, don't force them to take part in organized activities.

HOUSEGUESTS

Say It with Flowers

❏ You want your house to look attractive, but you can't redecorate just because houseguests are coming. How

A Barn Dance to Remember

One Fourth of July, we planned a barbecue and invited all the neighbors. Everyone brought food, as well as extra tables and chairs. We set up the grill, turned on the boom box, and hung the flag from our barn door.

As the party progressed, the sky grew darker and darker. Purple clouds assembled right above us. With a crack of thunder, rain hammered down fast and hard. As we scrambled to cover the food, I had an idea: Move the party into the barn.

Quickly, we shoved aside the lawn mower, snowblower, rakes, and wheelbarrow. We dragged the long picnic table just inside the narrow barn door. Then we ferried food, plates, and utensils inside as well. Drenched and laughing, we all squeezed around the table. Bees followed us, swarming around the one bare lightbulb above the table. Outside, the youngest children ran around in bare feet, soaked and squealing with delight. This wasn't the outdoor party we'd planned, but it is the one we all remember best.

—BOYD ALLEN III
Exeter, New Hampshire

can you spruce things up quickly? Place a few new potted plants (some with blooms, if possible) around the room in which your guests will be sleeping. Or place a small bouquet of fresh flowers (perhaps from your own garden) on the nightstand or bureau. This will brighten up the room and make it appear well cared for.

Welcoming Touches

❏ Wondering how to make your overnight guests feel welcome without going to a lot of extra expense? Take a tip from the better hoteliers and place a little something extra in the bedroom where your guests will be sleeping. A friend who wakes up thirsty in the middle of the night will welcome a small pitcher of water with a drinking glass on a nightstand. A couple of brightly wrapped, good-quality chocolates left on the pillow will be a pleasant surprise for any guest.

Make a Clean Sweep

❏ You have to share a bathroom with your houseguests and are looking for ways to put everyone at ease. First, make sure bathroom fixtures—sink, toilet, and tub or shower—are clean. Second, sweep the bathroom floor. Third, clear a space for guests to put toothbrushes, cosmetic kits, and so forth. You can even make up a little guest basket with trial sizes of toothpaste and shampoo, as well as disposable razors. Finally, set out clean towels—a bath towel, hand towel, and washcloth for each person—where guests can easily reach them. If there is no room for these in the bathroom, you can lay them on the bed. Tell guests to hang them over the shower rod or on a robe

---

Why New Yorkers Have a Ball on New Year's Eve

For at least 200 years, clock-watching has never been more respectable than on New Year's Eve. During the eighteenth century, Americans used to gather outside churches to observe "watch night" services—quiet precursors to today's New Year's Eve parties. At the turn of the twentieth century, people in many parts of the United States shot off cannons and firearms when the clock struck midnight on New Year's Eve. In 1908, the city of New York banned the use of firearms and fireworks above a crowd, so the Artkraft-Strauss Sign Company designed the now-famous illuminated ball that still drops to the center of Times Square every December 31 at midnight.

hook in the bathroom after use. Or if you have time, mount one or two brass clothes hooks on the back of the guest room door. They'll be out of the way and probably get plenty of future use.

Let Them Be Self-Serving

❏ Fixing breakfast for a houseful of guests can be a logistical nightmare if one guest wants to sleep late while another rises early. One solution is to make breakfast a self-service operation. The night before, set out cereal bowls, plates, utensils, glasses, and coffee cups along with cereal, muffins, and so forth. Tell guests that fruit, milk, and juice are in the refrigerator and they may help themselves. Premeasure coffee and water into the coffeemaker so it just needs to be switched on. Your houseguests can help themselves to breakfast when they are ready, and they will feel right at home.

Endless Summer

❏ Have you ever been stuck with houseguests for longer than you wanted to be? If you're searching for a way to limit the length of a visit, try specifying in your invitation (whether in a letter or on the phone) how long you expect the guests to stay. You can do this tactfully by saying something like, "Why don't you spend a night with us during your trip?"

So . . . Will You Still Be Here for Christmas?

❏ Sometimes you don't care how long a friend stays; the problem is that you need to know ahead of time so you can plan meals and other commitments. If you're not sure of an expected houseguest's plans, ask directly (but tactfully), "How long can you stay?" Then you'll know what to expect.

STICKY SOCIAL SITUATIONS
How Nice to See You! Who Are You?

FRIENDS AND ACQUAINTANCES

Expect the Unexpected

❑ If a friend or relative stops by unexpectedly while you're busy, you don't have to cause hurt feelings by shoving her out the door. Instead, offer your visitor a cup of coffee or tea (or some other beverage) and say, "I'm glad to see you! Why don't you chat with me while I fold the laundry (or rake the leaves or unload the dishwasher)? I'd love the company!" You can both enjoy a brief visit without completely disrupting your schedule.

Shaggy Dog Story

❑ If you've invited guests who want to bring their dog and you don't want the dog to visit, say so tactfully. Explain that you don't have enough room in the house or yard to accommodate the dog, that you have a cat, that a neighbor's dog is especially vicious, or that someone in your family is allergic to dogs.

❑ If your guests are insistent (or simply arrive unannounced with the dog), set limits. Offer to have the dog stay in the garage or the basement.

Sorry, I Have to Wash My Hair . . .

❑ A friend or acquaintance calls and asks, "What are you doing Saturday night?" You have no idea whether the person is issuing a social invitation or about to ask you a favor, and you don't want to be trapped either way. So be a little vague. Answer that you aren't sure, you'll have to check your calendar or with your spouse. That way, you can always accept or decline once you find out what the person wants.

I Like Your Outfit— That's Why I Bought It First!

❏ If you have a friend or coworker who tries too hard to emulate everything you do or wear, try to emphasize to the person the traits that make her unique. Praise her technical knowledge or sense of style; ask for her opinion instead of offering your own. This should encourage your friend to feel more confident about her own tastes and less insistent on emulating yours.

Do I Know You?

❏ Not recognizing someone whom you think you should know is embarrassing. If you run into such a person, immediately reintroduce yourself ("Hi, I'm John Smith"). Most people will take the cue (and will be relieved if they have forgotten your name, too) and reintroduce themselves as well.

❏ If someone starts to introduce you to another person and suddenly draws a blank for your name, step in quickly and introduce yourself. Later, you can reassure the introducer that no offense was taken; it happens to everyone.

Who Gets the Friends?

❏ When friends divorce, each may want your loyalty, and you can easily feel torn. If you have been friends with both, try not to take sides. Don't criticize either person. Listen empathetically but refrain from offering advice. Be available to do things with each person. Don't invite both to a party or other gathering without telling both of them. If children are involved, let them know that you are still their friend, too.

SOCIAL ENGAGEMENTS

This Stand-Up Act Isn't Funny

❏ You suddenly realize you've stood someone up—forgotten a date or dinner invitation, even a meeting or dentist's appointment. What should you do? Telephone

---

ONE PERSON'S SOLUTION

Same Time Next Week

Late one Sunday afternoon, I went to a cocktail party. I put on my tweed blazer and khaki slacks. I grabbed a vase filled with flowers for the host and hostess. (I was taking the opportunity to return the vase, which I had borrowed from them.)

I got to my friends' home a little early but rang the doorbell. When they answered, they were wearing casual clothes. *They're casual people anyway,* I thought to myself. They remarked about how dressed up I was. I peered past my friends into the house. No one else was there. Suddenly I realized that I must have the wrong date for the party. Quickly I said, "I'm still wearing my Sunday

clothes, and I'm on my way to do some errands. I wanted to return this vase to you." After a few more pleasantries (including their apology for not inviting me to stay because they had to get dressed to go to another party), I wished them a good afternoon and left. When I got home, I checked my calendar. I'd been a week early for the party.

—RUSSELL C. BUCHANAN
Mendham, New Jersey

the aggrieved party immediately and apologize sincerely. If there's a legitimate reason for the mix-up (say, your spouse forgot to tell you about the appointment), offer the explanation along with your apology. Or go to the person's house or office and apologize in person. Follow up with a note and a small gift, such as flowers or homemade bread.

I'm Late! I'm Late! For a Very Important Date!

❏ En route to an out-of-town meeting or appointment, you realize that you've drastically underestimated your traveling time and you're going to be significantly (more than a few minutes) late. What do you do? Stop and call as soon as you can. Apologize, tell the person when you expect to arrive, and ask if it will still be convenient for her to meet you, or if she'd prefer to reschedule. If you were meeting at a restaurant, call there and ask if you can speak to the person you were meeting or if the hostess will at least give her a message.

After Garlic, What's for Dessert?

❏ If you've just eaten a garlicky meal and you're worried about your breath, try one of these remedies. Chew and swallow any fresh parsley that was served as a garnish to the meal. Or carry with you a tiny plastic bag of fennel or anise seeds and chew them after a particularly strong-tasting meal.

VOLUNTEERING

Just Say No—Graciously

❏ If someone calls asking for your volunteer help and you just don't have the time, thank the person for thinking of you but say that you can't do it right now. Explain that you need to keep prior commitments before taking on anything else. If you think you might be able to help in the future, say so. Don't volunteer someone else's name (unless you've checked with that person first).

Promises, Promises

❏ Ever been part of a community or civic organization where a group member hasn't followed through? Those can be tough situations because it's hard to fault someone who's volunteering his time. If you're in one of those groups, you can use a couple of strategies to help make sure things get done. First, ask someone in the group to take notes and distribute a clear "action list" outlining the tasks agreed on by the group—with the expected dates of completion. Second, designate a person to make follow-up phone calls, checking the status of the tasks (and jogging someone's memory at the same time, perhaps). Third, make it easy for people to follow through by suggesting tasks that would be easy for them to complete. One person might be most comfortable sharing cooking skills, while another has good writing skills or community contacts. Still another might be willing to share a pickup truck, a gas grill, or free time during the week. Make it a point to match your requests for help to the appropriate individuals.

CONVERSATIONAL ISSUES

Green Hair Looks Good on You!

❏ Commenting on someone's new hairstyle or haircut may be embarrassing, especially if you don't like the new look. Don't just say, "You got a haircut!" That leaves the person wondering exactly how odd the hairstyle appears. Instead, make a positive comment such as, "I like your new bangs!" or "I like that length on you!" Singling out one aspect of the new look that truly is appealing can smooth over an awkward moment.

A Weighty Conversation

❏ Acknowledging someone's weight loss can be tricky. Don't ask, "Have you lost weight?" The person might not have lost weight, or might even have gained; answering your question could make your friend feel embarrassed. Instead, just say, "You look terrific!" The person can accept the compliment with or without mentioning weight loss.

Justice Miscarried

❏ When a friend or relative has a miscarriage, it may be hard to know what to say. Don't quip, "Cheer up! You're young; you'll have another." Instead say, "I know this is a tough time for you" or "I'm sorry you've had to go through this." If you know the person well enough, offer to listen if she feels like talking. You can even send or take her a bouquet of fresh flowers.

No Kidding

❏ What do you answer when someone asks, "Why don't you have children?" A brief reply should defuse the situation. Try simply saying, "It wasn't in the cards for us," then change the subject. That way, you have answered the question without being rude but also without revealing any personal details or reasons. The person to whom you are speaking should get the message.

❏ If it's hard to come up with an appropriate reply when someone asks, "When are you going to have another child?" try a little humor. Say, "I don't know; I'll have to ask my spouse." Then laugh and change the subject.

It's All in the Delivery

❏ How do you answer when someone asks, "Was your baby planned?" Just reply, "We've been planning on this for nine whole months!" Then change the subject.

How to Talk Dollars and Sense

❏ If you're uncomfortable when someone asks how much you paid for something, just reply, "Enough" or "More than I wanted to" or "You can get it for a good price at . . ."

❏ If someone asks you how much money you make and you are uncomfortable discussing the matter, just laugh and reply, "Not enough!"

Look, Mommy! That Lady Walks Funny!

❏ What should you say when your young child points out a person's physical handicap? Be concrete and brief. Don't avoid the question, but don't gush to compensate for your own embarrassment. Say, "The stick helps him walk" or "The wheelchair helps her get from one place to another."

PARTIES

What Do You Say After "How Are You?"

❏ If you end up sitting next to a stranger at a party, how can you get beyond the initial awkwardness? Ask the person how she met the host (you might be in for a funny story; it also could reveal other interests you share). Ask the person where she is from. As a last resort, ask the person what she does for a living. You can also try a compliment, if it's not too personal (such as "That's a terrific tie" or "I love that pin"). Compliments help people relax and loosen up—and the tie or pin might have a story behind it.

Simon Says Use the Soup Spoon

❏ If you don't know which utensils to use during a dinner party, take your cue from your host or hostess, or surreptitiously watch another guest who is sitting directly across from you.

Reciprocity Rules

❏ You've been a guest at someone's home on one or more occasions, but you just don't have the time or space to reciprocate in kind. How can you pay back your host? First, always be a good guest. Offer to help in ways that you know your host will appreciate—say, by bringing a special hors d'oeuvre or by greeting other guests. Second, don't forget to thank your host for the invitation. If you feel comfortable doing so, bring a small host(ess) gift or send one when you have returned home. Third, think of other ways you can help this particular friend—perhaps by walking the dog, house-sitting or tending plants while the person is away, or taking the children on an outing.

Bully for You

❑ You're inviting a group of friends to your child's party, but your child wants to leave one member of the group out, claiming that the child is a bully. (Perhaps you agree that the child is disruptive.) If at all possible, invite the youngster but tell the parents that you are asking all parents to stay at the party to watch their own children while you act as party director. That way, the problem child should be under the watchful eye (and discipline) of his own parent, and hurt feelings can be avoided.

WEDDINGS

Always a Bridesmaid

❑ A good friend or family member has asked you to be in her wedding party, but you're uncomfortable

---

✔ PROBLEM PREVENTED

Limousine Logistics

You don't want the mother of the bride stranded without a ride to the wedding reception after the ceremony. You don't want the matron of honor's husband hopping in the limo when there's only room for the bridesmaids.

To avoid these mishaps, decide beforehand—with both families—who will ride in the limousines or other specially rented vehicles. Be specific, stating who will ride with whom, in which car. Note that the groupings will change after the wedding ceremony (for instance, the bride usually rides with the bridesmaids to the ceremony; the bride and groom ride together after the ceremony). Make a written list and give one copy to the limousine driver(s) and another to the best man.

If there are special guests (such as grandparents) for whom you would like to provide transportation, you can rent a luxury sedan with driver (usually from the limousine company) or designate a reliable friend with a nice, clean car to do the honors.

Weddings

355

Whose Wedding Is It, Anyway?

One summer, a wedding invitation appeared in our mailbox. I opened it and read it. I read it again. I had never heard of the bride or groom, but I assumed one of them must be an acquaintance or business associate of my husband's. I tossed the invitation in the pile of mail on the kitchen table.

A few days later, I mentioned it to my husband. "Sure, I saw the invitation," he recalled. "Who are the bride and groom? People you work for? Relatives?"

We called my parents and read them the couple's names. No luck. We called my husband's mother. She'd never heard of them either. We were stumped. By now I was certain the invitation had been mailed to the wrong guests. Friends dared us to go anyway—the reception was being held at an exclusive yacht club right on the bay, and it was bound to be fun. I thought about it. What would I buy for a gift?

Finally, I decided that I just couldn't crash the wedding. So I packed up the invitation and returned it to the mother of the bride with a note explaining that the invitation must have been sent to us in error, but to please give the unknown couple our best wishes anyway. My problem solved, I forgot about it.

A week later, we got a phone call. The groom was actually my husband's cousin's stepson, who lived about 600 miles away (no wonder we'd never heard of him). We were the only relatives of the groom who lived near where the wedding was being held, so we were invited. We went. The bride's mother thought the whole thing was funny. "I know who you are," she said to me in the receiving line, "but you don't know who I am." The reception at the yacht club was a blast.

—Linda Buchanan Allen
Exeter, New Hampshire

accepting (perhaps you can't afford the expense or you feel that you won't fit in with the rest of the party because of age or other reasons). Decline graciously. Thank the person for honoring you with the invitation, then say that you just don't feel you can fulfill the role at this time. (You can even use a little humor, such as "My bridesmaid days are over!") If you feel comfortable doing so, offer to help in another way—say, hiring someone to stay at the house and watch over gifts while everyone is at the wedding (or doing it yourself), picking up the flowers, or driving an elderly or out-of-town guest to the wedding.

Wedding Bell Blues

❏ If your wedding is called off after the invitations have gone out, how do you inform people? Guests should be called as soon as possible. You might want to enlist your parents' help with this, especially in calling their friends and relatives. Call your own friends if you can; otherwise, perhaps your best man or maid of honor will be willing to help by making some of the calls. Think of a standard, brief explanation to give to everyone. (You might say, "We decided it was really necessary to postpone [or cancel] the wedding" or "The bride [or groom] had second thoughts he or she couldn't resolve.") Your close friends will know the truth, and no one else needs details.

What Do You Say to the Dumpee?

❏ What should you say to a friend whose wedding has been canceled? Don't quip, "Better now than later." Instead say, "I'm sorry to hear the news." Don't probe for details or criticize the other partner. Instead, focus on boosting your friend's self-esteem. Tell him he's still a great catch; compliment him on his looks or a recent achievement. If this is a fairly close friend and you feel comfortable doing so, write down a list of the person's special attributes, such as a sharp wit or sense of style—and suggest that the friend post the list on the fridge or the mirror to read often.

TIME SAVER

The 4-Step Thank-You Note

Receiving gifts is (almost) always fun. Writing thank-you notes isn't. Here are four steps to get you through the task in no time.

1. Keep each note short—three or four sentences is fine. You can express your thanks just as sincerely in a few sentences as you can in several paragraphs.

2. Start your note by thanking the giver for joining you in your celebration (a wedding, shower, or holiday gathering). Then thank the person for the gift, naming the item specifically ("Thank you so much for the beautiful set of wineglasses!").

3. State how you plan to use the gift ("We really enjoy entertaining, so the glasses will get plenty of use.").

4. Close with a cordial remark ("Hope to see you again soon!").

GIVING AND RECEIVING GIFTS

The Envelope, Please

❏ If you're looking for a way to minimize the chore of writing wedding gift thank-you notes, address envelopes as you receive responses to the invitations. Preparing envelopes is a good, mindless task that you can handle when your energy has run out and you're not up to dealing with more complicated issues. And it will save you time when you get to writing the notes themselves.

I (never) Gave at the Office

❏ How do you give one colleague a holiday gift without hurting the feelings of others? Give the gift outside the workplace. If you are good friends, you probably see each other socially, too. Do it on one of those occasions.

Does Your Date Rate?

❏ How do you know whether to give a holiday or birthday gift to someone you've been dating for only a short while? If you want to, go ahead. Just keep it simple and inexpensive, with a personal touch of humor or common interest. For instance, if you already share an inside joke about something or if you have an interest in common (such as theater or sports), give a gift that reflects this.

You're So Thoughtful! (and I'm not)

❏ What do you do when someone surprises you with a holiday gift and you have planned nothing in return? Thank the person. Later, you can attach a loaf of home-made bread or a bouquet of flowers to a thank-you note. But don't make an issue of scrambling to return a comparable gift just to even the score.

TIME SAVER

Kids Should Say Thank You, Too!

It's a great idea to get children in the habit of writing their own thank-you notes by preschool age. But even if your child can form letters, it would take forever for him to write an entire note. So ask him what he wants to say and transcribe his comments in a brief note. Then have him write his own name at the end. Recipients—whether grandparents, other family members, or friends—are guaranteed to be delighted!

THE HOLIDAYS

So Many Cards, So Little Time

❑ You have too many names on your holiday card list and not enough time to send out all the cards. Edit your list, cutting out groups of people instead of one here and one there (to avoid hurt feelings). For instance, if you see your family during the holidays, you might talk to them and propose not exchanging cards. You might decide the same thing with neighbors or coworkers. Then you can trim the list further by eliminating people with whom you no longer correspond, for whatever reason. Your editing will most likely leave you with a list of people whom you do not see regularly and to whom you really want to send holiday greetings and catch-up news.

 PROBLEM PREVENTED

Holiday Havoc

If every holiday becomes a tug-of-war between your spouse's family and yours, get around the problem by making a decision ahead of time about where you will celebrate and with whom. Then stick to it. Here are a few suggestions.

• If both sets of in-laws live near each other and get along, try combining the celebration at one house—at least for a meal, dessert, or cocktails.

• Start a new tradition, such as celebrating in your own home, then visiting family and friends at another time. Be kind but firm to family members whose noses are bent out of joint.

• If parents, in-laws, or other relatives have always insisted that you travel to see them at the holidays, invite them to your home instead.

• If it's possible, try to have children see their grandparents at some point during the holidays. If distance or cost is too great, arrange a phone call. (The phone call could become a tradition.)

• Don't split up your own family just to please your extended family.

• Try to include visiting an elderly grandparent or other relative or friend in a nursing home or hospital as part of your holiday celebration.

Sticky Social Situations

❑ You also can save time by enclosing a group letter in your cards. Keep the letter short—two or three paragraphs. Then add a brief handwritten note to each card, such as "Hope to see you soon!" or "How's the new job?" and sign your name.

Christmas Cards: Bah, Humbug!

Sending holiday cards can get pretty expensive. Here are a few ways to save.

• **Send fewer cards.**

• **Send festive postcards** (you can even buy postcards made specifically for holidays). The postage for postcards is less than it is for cards in envelopes.

• **Buy your cards the day after Christmas,** when they go on sale. (Many clearance sales offer cards and other holiday trappings for half price or less.)

• **Buy inexpensive cards.** This doesn't mean you're a Scrooge. Remember that most people throw cards away after the holidays, and the whole point of sending cards is keeping in touch with loved ones.

• **Make your own cards.** You can turn this into a real craft project or create cards on your computer with a graphics program.

❑ Alternatively, type a basic catch-up letter on your computer, then modify it slightly for each person on your list. (Remember to keep your letter brief!)

If It's Not a "Merry" Christmas

❑ You know that the holidays can be particularly rough for someone who's ill or in mourning. You want to remember that person, but it certainly doesn't seem appropriate to send a card that says "Merry Christmas!" Do send a card, but make it one that says something noncommittal such as "Season's Greetings"—or use a card that's blank inside and write your own brief note, just to let the person know you're thinking of her.

HELPING THOSE IN MOURNING

Attendance Counts

❑ When someone you know (or the loved one of a friend or acquaintance) dies, you might not be sure whether you should attend the funeral or other services. Perhaps, you think, the family will be too grief stricken to notice whether you are there. Wrong. They will notice (they may not see you at the time, but they'll read the guest book later), and they will appreciate your making the effort. So do it for them, if you possibly can.

Black to Basics

❏ Don't know what to wear to a funeral or memorial service? You probably have something appropriate in your closet. A woman should wear a dark, conservative suit, dress, skirt, or slacks. A man should wear a dark, conservative suit and tie or blazer and slacks. If you don't own a jacket, wear a sweater in a subdued color.

Keep Good Company

❏ If the member of a family to whom you are close has died, should you visit the family or stay away? Visit. Just go and sit, if necessary, to keep a widow or widower, child or parent, company. If family members feel like talking, talk with them. If they don't, don't force them to.

Send a Card

❏ If you can't decide whether it's better to phone or send a card to a grieving family, send a card. It will mean a great deal to them, even if it is belated. If possible, add a personal note to the card. Say how much the person will be missed or relate a particular memory you have of the person. The family can share the card, read it when the chaos subsides, and refer to it during lonely moments.

Make a Movable Feast

❏ If you want to take food to a grieving person or family but don't know

Good Grief

It's hard to know what to say to someone—even a close friend—who has lost a loved one. Here are a few tips to help you navigate the waters of a friend's or family member's grief.

• *Don't* say, "Is there anything I can do?" Instead offer specific help. Offer to pick up the children at school, host a child for playtime or overnight, take care of a specific errand, clean the house before funeral guests arrive, or return phone calls.

• *Don't* say to a widow or widower, "You're young; you'll find someone else." Instead say, "We'll miss [the deceased] intensely."

• *Don't* say, "I know how you feel," even if you really do. Instead say, "I survived something similar. I'll call you soon."

• *Do* say, "I'm so sorry." Mean it.

• Months, even a year or two after the person's loss, *do* say, "How are you?" Mean it. Accept whatever answer you get.

what to make, keep a few things in mind. The meal should be simple and complete. Label each dish, including directions for heating or serving. Try to make something that can be frozen; other friends may be bringing food at the same time, and the grieving family may be even more appreciative of something they can pull out of the freezer later.

❏ If you want to take a meal to those who are grieving but you aren't a cook (or time is tight), make up a gift bag containing prepared foods that go together for a meal. For instance, a package of spaghetti, a jar of good spaghetti sauce, heat-and-serve rolls or bread sticks, and perhaps a bottle of wine will be much appreciated.

When a Parent Loses a Child

❏ It's difficult to know how to respond to a parent who has lost a child. Most parents in this situation fear that the child will be forgotten as the years go by and her peers grow up. Make it a point not to forget. Share memories or photos of the child with the parents. Don't be afraid to talk about the youngster. If you know the family well, you might even send a note or flowers each year on the child's birthday or on the anniversary of her death.

❏ One way for a group of friends to keep a child's memory alive is to jointly contribute to a memorial to the youngster. You might join with other families to start a local scholarship fund in the child's memory or a fund to send young sports enthusiasts to soccer or baseball camp. Or get together and purchase, as a memorial, a flowering bush or tree for the family's yard or the school grounds. You might hold a small ceremony when the living memorial is planted. Make sure to consult with the youngster's parents before proceeding with any of these projects.

PET PEEVES
Tailgaters, Telemarketers, and Other Terrors of Daily Life

TELEPHONE ISSUES

Telemarketing Turnoffs

❑ Telephone solicitations waste your time—and the caller's—if you're not interested in the product or service being offered. As soon as you recognize that you won't be buying, tell the caller politely but firmly, "No thanks, I'm not interested." You don't need to feel any guilt about hanging up because most telemarketers will welcome the opportunity to move on to another, more lucrative call.

At the Sound of the Beep, Hang Up!

❑ Particularly during dinner or family times, telemarketers can be an annoying interruption. Those are good times to let your answering machine screen your phone calls. There's no reason to feel obligated to answer the phone every time it rings. Telemarketers usually hang up when they reach an answering machine, and if you're not interested in what they have to offer, that will save both of you wasted time.

❑ Some people hate to think that others are "screening" their calls through the answering machine. If a friend or acquaintance complains to you about this, you don't need to make excuses as to why you couldn't get to the phone before you heard the caller identify herself. Instead, be straightforward. Playfully respond that you were indeed screening and mention that, in-

We've Got Their Number

My husband and I have a way of dealing with telemarketers. We tell them we don't make purchases or donations over the phone. If they want our business or a donation, they must send us something in the mail. This gives us a chance to talk over each decision, and it discourages con artists.

If a telemarketer calls us repeatedly, we request that the company put us on its "do not call" list. By law, the telemarketer cannot call us again for a year. If someone calls within a year, the company can be fined for each offense.

—DOREEN MEANS
Greenfield, New Hampshire

stead of giving you a hard time, she should feel honored that she made the cut!

Get an Unlisted Number

❑ If you're anxious to eliminate many telemarketing calls in one fell swoop, write to the Direct Marketing Association, Telephone Preference Service, P.O. Box 9014, Farmingdale, NY 11735-9014. Include your name, address, and phone number and ask to have your name removed from the databases used by the association's members.

If He Wants to Chew the Fat

❑ No matter who's on the other end of the line, listening to someone eat over the phone is an annoyance no one should have to put up with. If you receive a call from an inconsiderate eater, make an excuse as to why you will need to call back. If you're the one who placed the call, once you realize the person you've reached is eating, simply say, "I can see I've interrupted your meal. I'll call back in 20 minutes when you're through." Even if the person protests that it's no bother, insist on being considerate and get off the line.

Don't Hold the Phone

❏ It's tough to talk on the phone when your young child is trying to grab it or is demanding attention. If this is a common problem at your house, try keeping a coloring book and crayons (or materials for some other quiet activity) near the phone. That way, your child can sit with you and stay occupied while you talk.

FRIENDS AND ACQUAINTANCES

Love 'Em and Leave 'Em

❏ Waiting for someone who is chronically late can be both frustrating and irritating—or worse, if it leads to missed appointments. Don't get angry. Explain to the person how his lateness affects you. Say something like, "I know you don't mean to make me feel as if your life is more important than mine, but that's how I feel while I'm waiting." Ask what's keeping him from being on time and offer to help solve the problem. Let him know that you won't wait the next time. If he's late the next time, don't wait—simply leave. He probably won't be late again.

❏ Friends and acquaintances who are perpetually late can be particularly frustrating for a hostess who has planned a meal for a certain time. Next time, forget the browbeating; simply tell the Johnny-

✔ PROBLEM PREVENTED

Hold All Calls!

If you like the convenience of call waiting most of the time but still want to place an occasional call without interruption, that's no problem. Most telephone companies allow you to temporarily disable the service by punching in a code before you make a call. (It's also important to disable call waiting before using a phone line for a computer modem.) Check with your phone company to find out what code will do the trick. Once you get in the habit, it's easy to remember to do this when you don't want to be interrupted.

come-latelies that dinner is one hour earlier than it really is.

Don't Wait for Wafflers

❏ Ever find it hard to make plans because one or more people in a group can't seem to commit to a date? Ever been let down by someone at the last minute? If you're planning something where a firm commitment is important, set a hard deadline for final decisions. If you can't get a commitment from someone at that time, count that person as a "no" and plan accordingly. The person might be able to join in after the deadline, but at least the group won't be depending on her.

✔ PROBLEM PREVENTED

We Interrupt This Phone Call . . .

Busy signals are annoying to callers, and if they persist, a caller may give up entirely. Call waiting is one solution, but taking a second call can be rude to the person who's already on the line. A better solution is a voice mail service. Unlike traditional answering machines, most such services accept messages even when you're on the line, so callers never get a busy signal and you get your important messages. Call your phone company to find out if it offers such a service.

Are You In or Out?

❏ Guests who do not respond to your invitation can throw your party and menu planning off—but only if you let them. If you're down to two days before the party and you haven't heard back from someone, give him a call. Say you just wanted to be certain he received the invitation and you hope he will be able to come.

The Perpetual Dinner Guest

❏ Ever have a friend who repeatedly dined at your house without once offering a return invitation? If you wish to remain friends, have a discussion about how the friendship has seemed one-sided and talk over ways to make it seem more fair. It's always possible the person is not aware of her behavior and will appreciate your honesty.

❏ If money is at the heart of the issue, the next time the friend invites himself over, say something like, "The truth is, our budget right now doesn't allow for many extra meals. But if you'd like to bring along something, we'd love to have you."

You Were Saying . . . ?

❏ Don't you just hate it when you're in the middle of a story and someone jumps in with "Oh, that reminds me . . ." or the hostess pops out of her seat and asks if anyone needs their coffee warmed up? Next time this happens, simply smile and say sweetly, "Would you mind if I just finished my thought? I'm certain to forget what I was saying if I get off track for even a minute!" Sometimes a little humor is just what it takes to defuse an awkward situation.

Pucker Up

❏ Some people are kissers; you know the type. It can be 15 years or 15 minutes since you last saw them, but they've got to kiss you hello and good-bye. Many people don't mind this; others dread it. When you're feeling less than affectionate, simply set the scene by making the first move. When you first see the kisser, give a friendly greeting and a little wave, then move out of lip range. Or extend your hand for a handshake. Once you break the person of the habit, you probably won't have to worry about it again.

Smokers: Butt Out

❏ It can be awkward to tell a friend or visitor not to light up in your house. One easy solution is not to buy ashtrays. When a guest asks if she can smoke, politely answer, "I'm sorry, but I don't have any ashtrays. Would you mind smoking outside?" You'll have to supply a trash receptacle for the butts outside, but at least the smoke will waft away harmlessly.

TIME SAVER

Here's Your Hat . . .

It's always fun to entertain—except, of course, if your guests don't know when to leave. If you've tried turning out all the lights, lowering the thermostat, and changing into your pajamas—all to no avail—next time save yourself the aggravation. Instead of having these people over to your place, suggest meeting at a restaurant. That way, you can determine how long the evening lasts. Or go to a play, movie, or concert—something that has a limited duration. Once the event is over, you're free to go home.

DRIVING

Tailgate Tease

❏ Tailgaters are annoying—and potentially dangerous. To shake them, try tapping the brakes very lightly a couple of times. The driver behind you should get the hint from the sudden flash of your brake lights. If a tailgater persists, pull over and let her pass. It's not worth the aggravation and safety hazard to try to stay ahead.

TRAVEL

Silence Is Golden

❏ When you're sitting next to a talkative person on a plane, train, or bus and you'd really rather be left alone, pull out a book. If the person keeps talking, explain that you've been looking forward to reading this book and you finally have the time now. Then bury your nose in it.

Group Travel: Fairness down the Road

❏ Traveling in a group can raise problems of finances and fairness. Even if everyone seems to be chipping in fairly for gas, food, hotel stays, and so on, keeping track of expenses can be burdensome, and splitting every bill evenly can be unwieldy. Here's a better way. At the start of the trip, have everybody throw the same amount of money—say $50 or $100 per person—into one envelope. Every time a group expense comes up, pay for it with cash from the envelope. (If the money in the envelope runs out, have everybody add more.) At the end of the trip, divide what's left in the envelope evenly among all those who contributed. It's a simple, fair method—and it frees people from second-guessing or worrying about their fellow travelers.

SHOPPING

Just Bag It

❏ Having someone bagging groceries at the supermarket is usually a great convenience; it keeps the line moving and makes your life easier. It's not so great, however, when the bagger has no regard for the contents: Bread gets mashed under canned soup; grapes are squished under the milk. The easiest way to save your food when you don't trust the bagger is simply to thank him for the offered help and tell him that you'd much rather bag for yourself. If he's hesitant, tell him you have a system that makes it easier to put the groceries away. Chances are he'll gladly hand over the task without question.

❏ Alternatively, when you unload your groceries onto the conveyor belt at the checkout counter, set out the heaviest items first so they get packed first. Save the eggs and baked goods for last.

AT THE OFFICE

Dump the Dirty Dishes

❏ A common problem in offices with kitchens is that many people leave their dirty lunch dishes in the sink with little regard for what will become of them. It's usually an office manager or department secretary who ends up cleaning up the mess. Instead of getting mad, try posting a note. Let your coworkers know that the new office policy dictates that whatever dirty dishes are left in the sink will be thrown away at the end of the day. You'll be amazed at how quickly workers clean up after themselves.

Work Those Phones

❏ Many times, especially in small offices, workers have to cover more than one job. Sometimes this means that others need to cover the phones when the switchboard operator is out to lunch. This can become a problem when the operator takes an extra-long lunch break. If you find yourself waiting for an inconsiderate coworker, plan ahead. The next time you're scheduled to cover the phones, let the operator know that you have a lunch date precisely ten minutes after she is due back. If necessary, repeat this subterfuge every time you cover the phones; the operator should pick up on the new routine before long.

AT HOME

Mommy's Office, Junior Speaking

❑ Young children love to play with office equipment such as tape, staplers, and phones. The problem is that these tools often disappear after the kids are done with them. To keep the kids happy and the paper clips handy, give the youngsters their own office tools—or, better yet, toys resembling those tools. Or keep a box of toys in the home office so that toddlers can play while you're paying the bills.

Unreliable Contractors: Build In Extra Time

❑ Wherever you live, you have probably experienced trouble scheduling a carpenter, plumber, or other contractor. A contractor who can't begin a job when he says he will can be annoying—especially if the delay causes you serious inconvenience. Although contracting work is, by nature, inexact (contractors want to have continuous work but have to rely on "best guess" estimates about the time a job will require), you can reduce the chances of frustration and bad feelings.

If the job isn't urgent, consider extending the lead time needed by the contractor. If he says, "Well, I could probably get over there on the first of the month," tell him to start on the tenth. Let him know you have built in extra time for him that way. Don't give him the chance to fall behind schedule on a job before yours. If the job is one that can wait even longer, schedule the work several months in advance, giving the contractor the option to start sooner if time permits.

Finally, make it clear to the contractor that you are counting on him to start when he says he will and that you expect to hear from him in the weeks and days leading up to the expected starting date. Often it isn't the delay that causes problems, but not being able to adjust your plans for a delay that comes unexpectedly. A lot of problems can be avoided with a phone call a week ahead of time that lets you know the contractor is running two days behind schedule. If the contractor doesn't make the call, make it yourself. You'll both be happier.

Dark Closets: Light Up

❏ If you hate stumbling around the attic or groping through a closet that has no lighting (and no wiring with which to hook up a light), here's an inexpensive solution. At a discount store or lighting store, buy a battery-powered light that has an adhesive back. Stick your purchase right to the wall or ceiling.

PERSONAL BUSINESS

Get out of the Waiting Room

❏ It's annoying to arrive on time for an appointment, only to be kept waiting. If you're tired of spending your life in waiting rooms, try scheduling appointments as early in the morning as possible. Professionals—whether they're doctors, dentists, or car mechanics—can't always tell exactly how long a particular procedure will take, and emergencies can put them behind schedule. But if you arrange your appointments for early in the morning, the odds are much better that you'll get in—and out—before these folks start running late.

The Stamp Tax

❏ Paying bills by mail costs you time and postage. To reduce the expense, try electronic payments. Most utilities, credit card companies, and other billers can arrange some form of direct withdrawal from your bank

Doctor Deaf: 3 Ways to Make Her Listen

If you have a doctor or health care provider who seems too busy or important to explain procedures or fully answer your questions, don't let her get away with it just because she is the expert. Try any of these techniques for getting straight talk.

1. Use your ignorance to your advantage. Force the expert to slow down when she answers. Demand to be told things in plain English. Insist that she repeat or rephrase sentences that don't seem clear to you. Repeat back to her what you understand to be true and make her confirm it.

2. Don't be afraid to be emotional. Doctors don't like to see patients who are upset or crying, especially in front of other patients or staff.

3. Refuse to leave the office until you are satisfied with the information you've received.

account. They automatically deduct bill payments, and you get a copy of each bill, so you can protest if necessary. Ask the companies you do business with for more information.

Petty Bureaucrats: Love Them to Death

❏ We've all run into overworked, bored, or uninterested lower-level bureaucrats who hold the key to something we need and seem determined to make it difficult for us to get it. If that happens to you, try to put yourself in their shoes and be kinder than you ever imagined you could be. Commiserate about how thankless and frustrating the bureaucrat's job must be. Keep your tone of voice warm and try to make a light joke or two. If you're visiting in person, acknowledge the person's life—ask about family photos on the desk; find something in common to talk about. If the person seems to be doing a good job—or on the verge of giving you the key you need—ask if you might write a note of appreciation to a supervisor. You'll not only feel less tense about the interaction, but you also may make things easier for the next person in line.

Index

Underscored page references indicate boxed text. **Boldface** references indicate illustrations. *Italic* references indicate tables.

Buttonholes, opening, 202, **202**

C

Cabbage, odor from cooking, 52
Cabinets
  kitchen
    for baby items, 8–9
    for children's items, 8
    saving space in, 7–8
  in long, narrow rooms, 62–63
Cabins, preventing frost damage in, 256
Cakes
  layering, 114, **114**
  stale, uses for, 118–19
  transporting, 114
Call waiting
  alternative to, 366
  disabling, 365
Cameras
  protecting, on boats, 189
  protecting film in, 218
Camping
  bears and, 183–84
  carrying water for, 185
  equipment for, care of, 185–88, 188, 189, 193
  meals for, 183, 184, 186, 187
Camps, summer. *See* Summer camps
Candlelight, for dinner parties, 340
Canned foods, donating, to charity, 25
Canoe paddles, storing, 21
Car(s)
  carrying household items in, 22
  carrying snow shovels in, 268–69
  charging systems, 176–79
  clearing snow from, 270
  dogs chasing, 209–10, **209**
  exterior of, 173
  frozen doors on, 266–67
  fuel efficiency of, 170
  in winter, 266
  getting stranded in, during blizzard, 270

heaters in, 176
ignition systems, dampness in, 180
jump-starting, 177, **177**
leaky exhaust systems in, 255
leather upholstery in, maintaining, 176
leaving dogs in, 206
lockouts from, 170–71, 267
locks on, 170–71, 267
mud on floors of, 245
overheating of, 174–75, 175
parking, 180
prewinter checkups for, 255
radiator corrosion on, 269
rear-wheel-drive, improving traction of, 269
records, how long to keep, *26*
skidding on ice, 267–68
storing, 172
stuck in mud, 246, **246**, 269
stuck in snow, 269
tires on, 170, 173
trouble starting, 176–80
  in cold, 269
wheels on, 173–74
windshields of
  cleaning, 172
  foggy, 171–72
  icy, 266
winter emergency kit for, 267
Cards
  condolence, 361
  holiday
    inexpensive, 360
    sending, 359–60
Car keys, keeping track of, 21–22
Carpeting
  cat scratching of, 215
  cleaning, 46–47
  selecting, 60, 61–62
  vehicle, mud on, 245
Car rentals, insurance for, 226

Carriers, pet, choosing, 237
Car seats, renting, 126
Car trips
  with children, 234–35, 235
  in hot weather, 229–30
  snacks for, 230
Cassette tapes, storing, 14
Castoffs, advertising to get rid of, 29
Catalogs, storing, 19
Cats
  afraid of veterinarian, 215–16
  climbing on countertops, 214
  collars as danger to, 214
  deterring scratching by, 214–15
  diarrhea in, 212
  disciplining, 210–11, 215
  doors for, 214
  for eliminating mice, 251
  falling from heights, 213
  as finicky eaters, 212
  history of, 212
  houseplants ruined by, 213–14
  litter box use by, 211, 215
  as predators, 213, 251
  sleeping in warm places, 215
Cauliflower, odor from cooking, 52
CDs, storing, 14
Cedar chests, mothball odor in, 55
Ceilings, bulging, 161–63, **161**, **163**
Cellular phones, low-cost plans for, 264
Centerpieces, for dinner parties, 337
Chemotherapy patients, eating problems of, 121–22
Chicken
  leftover, uses for, 117
  marinating, 111
  skinning, 111
  stretching to feed more people, 116
Chicken livers, low cost of, 125

Underscored page references indicate boxed text. **Boldface** references indicate illustrations. *Italic* references indicate tables.

Underscored page references indicate boxed text. **Boldface** references indicate illustrations.
Italic references indicate tables.

Underscored page references indicate boxed text. **Boldface** references indicate illustrations. *Italic* references indicate tables.

<u>Underscored</u> page references indicate boxed text. **Boldface** references indicate illustrations. *Italic* references indicate tables.

Underscored page references indicate boxed text. **Boldface** references indicate illustrations.
Italic references indicate tables.

Fish as food
marinating, 111
odor from cooking, 51–52
Fish as pets, 216
Fixtures
brass, preventing
tarnishing of, 41
chrome, cleaning, 42
Flashlights, protecting, 189
Flatware, storing, 9
Fleas
killing, 203, 204–5
preventing, 203–4
Flood damage, from burst
pipes, preventing, 259
Floor covering, selecting, 60
Floors
cleaning, 44–46
preventing tracked-in
mud on, 243–46
squeaky, 160–61
Flour
as cleaning agent, 43
freezing, 113–14
Flower gardens, 96–98
swapping plants for, 96
Flowers, cut
odor in vase from, 98
preserving, 97
Fog
driving in, 246–47
on windshields, 171–72
Food(s). See also specific
foods
for camping trips, 183,
184, 186, 187
canned, donating, to
charity, 25
cutting costs of, on
vacations, 226–27
difficulty cutting, from
arthritis, 306–7
as gift
to those in mourning,
361–62
wrapping, 122, 331,
331
marinating, 111, 125
odors from, 51–54
in microwave ovens,
54
in refrigerators, 53–54
repackaging, for space
saving, 7–8

shopping for, 123–27
without driving, 312
spicy, burning from,
119–20
storing
on open shelves, 8
in pantries, 8
Food co-ops, saving money
with, 124
Foot aches
from blisters, 233
from carrying heavy
luggage, 219
Forgetfulness, 304
Four-wheel-drive vehicles,
limitations of, 268
Framing squares, hanging,
148, **148**
Freezers, odors in, 53–54
Freezing, for storage
corn, 95
flour, 113–14
Freezing, from weather
of car doors, 266–67
of car locks, 267
of ice on windshields, 266
of outside spigots,
preventing, 255
of pipes
methods for thawing,
258–59
preventing, 257–58
Friends
chronic lateness of,
365–66
difficult social situations
with, 348–49
visiting summer camps,
253
who can't commit to
dates, 366
who don't reciprocate,
366–67
Frost
preventing damage from,
in cabins, 256
protecting vegetable
garden from, 93, **93**
Frostbite, treating, 265
Fruit
dried, rehydrating, 107
preparing, 107
stains, on clothing, 49, 49

Fuel efficiency, of vehicles,
improving, 170, 266
Funerals
dressing for, 361
preplanning, 303–4
Furnace, checking, when
buying new home,
284–85
Furniture
mixing and matching, 61
rearranging, 61
selecting, 60
shopping for, 137–38
storing, 21
upholstered
fading of, 66
urine stains on, 57
wooden
cleaning, 47
cracking of, 66
darkening of, 66
fading of, 66
scratches on, 67
warping of, 66

G

Games, computer, limiting
children's use of,
277–78
Garages
parking cars in, 180
storage in, 19–21, **21**
Garbage disposals, odors
in, 54
Garden(s)
flower, 96–98
swapping plants for, 96
herb, 95–96
indoor, 194–97
insecticide alternatives
for, 80
insulating, with snow,
254–55
jar, how to make, 326
raking, 254
rock salt damaging, 255
vegetable (see Vegetable
gardens)
watering, 94
Garden hoses, uses for, 101
Garden tools
care of, 98
selecting, 99
storing, 20, **20**

Underscored page references indicate boxed text. **Boldface** references indicate illustrations.
Italic references indicate tables.

Garlic
odor on hands from, 51
peeling, 117
Gas, sewer, 165
Gates, sagging, 104, **104**
Get-togethers, family, ideas
for, 279
Gift(s)
baby, 319, **319**
bridal, 318
for children, 324
Christmas (*see* Christmas
gifts)
for colleagues, 358
computers as, 277
for dating partners, 358
engagement, 343
for family and loved
ones, 320–23
of food, 122
to those in mourning,
361–62
wrapping, 122, 331, **331**
handmade, 326
for hospital patients, 327
housewarming, 318–19
for mail carriers, 326–27
mailing, 330
for new parents, 319–20
for nursing home
residents, 327–28
packing, on return trips,
222–23
receiving, when you have
nothing in return,
358
shower, 317
for students, 323–24
for teachers, 324–26
thank-you notes for, 357,
358, 358
of time, teaching a skill
as, 328
trims for, 325
wrapping, 122, 321, 322,
331, **331**
with homemade paper,
329
Glass
broken, disposing of, 32
cleaning, 37
Glasses
keeping track of, 23
securing screws in, 233

Gloves, baseball, breaking
in, 194
Gold jewelry, cleaning, 41
Gore-Tex garments,
restoring water
repellency of,
193–94
Government auctions, 131
Grandchildren
communicating with,
301–2
grandparents' relation-
ships with, 279
Grandparents, on-line
communication
with, 276–77
Grass. *See* Lawns
Grass clippings, benefits of,
90
Grief, helping people cope
with, 360–62, 361
Groceries, shopping for,
123–27, 124, 368–69
Guest bedrooms, freshening
air in, 56
Guest lists
dinner party, 332
wedding, 342
Guests
dinner party
food brought by, 335
greeting, 336
kitchen help from, 339
seating, 335
dogs visiting with, 348
houseguests, 344–47
at summer camps, 253
wedding, seating, 342–43,
342
who ignore invitations,
366
who won't leave, 367
Guns, moving, to new home,
291
Gym bags, deodorizing,
56–57, **57**

H
Haircuts
complimenting, 352
saving money on, 135–36
Hammers
loose heads on, 151
selecting, 149–50

Hammocks, ideas for
hanging, 249
Hands
arthritic, 306–9
cold, methods for
warming, 264–65
Hardware, storing, 144, 145,
147, 147
Hats, storing, 12
Hazardous materials,
disposing of, 29,
31–32
Health care proxy, for
making medical
decisions, 303
Hearing loss, 309–10
Heat
from hot-water radiator,
165–66
household dryness from,
257
summer
car trips in, 229–30
relief from, 247–48
sun exposure and, 285–86
with wood, 262–64
Heaters
auto, 176
hot-water, preventing
damage to, 252
Herb gardens, 95–96
Hiking
altitude sickness while,
185
carrying water while, 185
Hinges, faulty, 158
Hiring
computer consultants,
277
dinner party help, 334
home inspectors, 288
movers, 290
students
as movers, 294
for odd jobs, 135, 136
tutors, 275
Hobbies
crocheting, 198–99
embroidery, 202
indoor gardening, 194–97
knitting, 198–99
renting equipment for,
132
sewing, 199–202

Underscored page references indicate boxed text. **Boldface** references indicate illustrations.
Italic references indicate tables.

Holes
in convertible roofs, 173
in tents, 185–86
in walls, 156
Holiday cards
inexpensive, 360
sending, 359–60
Home(s). *See also*
Decorating, home
buying, 284–87
resale value and, 284
selling, 289–92
home repairs before,
289–91
making home inviting
for, 291–92
market analysis for,
289
to prequalified buyers,
291
setting price for, 291
Home inspections, before
moving, 288–89
do-it-yourself, 288
Home inspectors, hiring,
288
Home offices. *See* Offices,
home
Homeowner's insurance, for
covering move, 297
Homework
difficulty with, 275
work space for, 274–75
Hoses, garden, uses for, 101
Hospitals, gifts for patients
in, 327
Hotels
without desks, 240
inexpensive, on
vacations, 225–26
Hot-water heaters,
preventing damage
to, 252
Hot-water tanks, preventing
damage to, 252
Hot weather
car trips in, 229–30
relief from, 247–48
Houseguests
entertaining, 344–47
limiting stay of, 347
Houseplants
bugs on, 197
cats ruining, 213–14

easy-to-grow, *195*
lighting for, 196
moisture for, 196–97, **197**
watering, 194, 196, 197
House swaps, for vacations,
251, 253
Housewarmings
gifts for, 318–19
parties for, 341
Housework, children
helping with, 273
Humidity
household, in winter, 257
houseplants needing,
196–97, **197**
Hunting season, protecting
dogs during, 207
Hypothermia, treating, 265

I

Ice
melting, rock salt alternatives for, 255
stopping skidding on,
267–68
on windshield, 266
Ice dams, on roofs,
preventing, 260–62
Illness, during travel,
finding doctor for,
229
Indoor gardening, 194–97
Ink stains
on carpet, 46
on fabric, 49
on telephone, 40
Insecticides, alternatives to,
80
Insect repellents, 76, 84
Insects. *See* Pests
Inspections, home
before moving, 288–89
do-it-yourself, 288
Inspectors, home, hiring,
288
Insulation
attic, as cause of ice
dams, 261
garden, in winter, 254–55
for pipes, 257
Insurance
for car rentals, 226
on computers, 132
health, for travel, 228

homeowner's, for
covering move, 297
movers', 297
tracking claims for, 18
trip cancellation, 230
Interruptions, to conversations, 365, 367
Introductions, forgetting
names during, 349
Invitations
failure to respond to, 366
reciprocating, 354–55,
366–67
Ironing clothes, during
travel, 231–33
Isolation, aging and,
300–301
Itching, from insect bites, 79

J

Jar gardens, how to make,
326
Jewelry
gold, cleaning, 41
packing, 223, **223**
repairing, 234
storing, 9
Jobs, helping children find,
283

K

Keyholes, frozen, on cars,
267
Keys, car
extra, 170–71
storing, 21–22
Kisses, avoiding, in greetings, 367
Kitchen
disinfecting, 36
organizing, 7–9
Kitchen cabinets
for baby items, 8–9
for children's items, 8
saving space in, 7–8
Kitty litter. *See* Litter boxes
Knitting needles
organizing, 198, **198**
plastic, warping of, 199
Knives
one-handed, for arthritis
sufferers, 306–7, **307**
utility, as timesaving
tools, 151

Underscored page references indicate boxed text. **Boldface** references indicate illustrations.
Italic references indicate tables.

L

Labels
  for luggage, 221
  for moving boxes, 294–95
  for paint cans, 154
Lamps, difficulty turning on,
    for arthritis
    sufferers, 309
Lateness
  dealing with, 351, 365–66
  of office workers, 369–70
Laundry
  delicates in, 12
  drip-drying, 13, **13**
  freshening, in suitcase,
    223
  reducing, 12
Lawn mowers, care of, 88
Lawns
  browning of, 90
  crabgrass on, 88–89
  dandelions on, 89–90
  grass clippings on, 90
  moss on, 89
  mowing, 87
  watering, 87–88
Lawn tools, storing, 20, **20**
Leaks
  from burst pipes, fixing,
    259–60, **260**
  in car exhaust systems,
    255
  in copper water pipes,
    260
  in Gore-Tex garments,
    193–94
  perfume bottle, 224
  roof, 166, **166**
Leather, cleaning, 50
Leather upholstery, in cars,
    176
Leaves, raking, 254
Leftovers
  odors from, 52–53
  uses for, 117–19, 119
Lemon, as cleaning agent,
    43
Life jackets, protecting,
    from mice, 257
Lighting
  in attics, 371
  in closets, 371
  for houseplants, 196

Lilac bushes, pruning, 103
Lime deposits, removing,
    from
  chrome fixtures, 42
  coffeepots, 38
  showerheads, 43
Limousines, for weddings,
    355
Linoleum floors, cleaning,
    44
Literature, classic, studying,
    275–76
Litter boxes
  cats urinating outside of,
    211, 215
  changing litter in, 212
  cleaning, 211–12
  deodorizing, 211
Livers, chicken, low cost of,
    125
Living rooms, organizing,
    13–14
Living wills, 303
Locks
  frozen, on cars, 267
  stuck, on cars, 171
Lodging, inexpensive, on
    vacations, 225–26
Loneliness, aging and,
    300–301
Luggage
  carry-on, contents of, 220
  labeling, 221
  listing contents of, 239
  lost, 239
  packing, 218–25
  repairing, 231
  saving space in, 223
  what not to pack in, 225
Lug nuts, removing, from
    wheels, 173–74
Lumber
  preventing warping of,
    155, **155**
  saving money on, 155
  storing, 20–21
Lyme disease, diagnosing,
    86

M

Magazines
  outdated, discarding,
    28–29
  recycling, 134

Maggots, 78
Magnets, for picking up
    pins, 200
Mail
  incoming, organizing,
    18–19
  receiving and sending,
    during travel,
    239–40
Mail carriers, gifts for,
    326–27
Maintenance records, filing,
    16
Masts, sailboat, storing, 21
Mattresses, air, as guest
    beds, 10
Mauls, selecting, 151
Meals, stretching, 115–17
Meat
  marinating, 111, 125
  metallic taste of, 121
  saving money on, 125
  stretching, for meals, 116,
    116
  tenderizing, 125
Medical emergencies,
    during travel, insur-
    ance for, 228
Medications
  discarding, 25
  saving money on, 127
Memory loss, 304
Mice
  eliminating, 251
  preventing damage from,
    255, 257
Microwave ovens, odors in,
    54
Mildew, on wooden furni-
    ture, 66
Milk
  increasing nutritional
    value of, 121
  scorched, in bottom of
    pan, 110
Mineral deposits, removing
  from coffeepots, 38
  from showerheads, 43
Mint, growing, 95–96, 95
Mirrors, to make small
    rooms appear
    larger, 62
Miscarriage, consoling
    friend after, 353

Underscored page references indicate boxed text. **Boldface** references indicate illustrations.
Italic references indicate tables.

Underscored page references indicate boxed text. **Boldface** references indicate illustrations. *Italic* references indicate tables.

paint, 59
perspiration
  in clothing, 58
  in gym bags, 56–57
pet, 206, _210_, 211, 215
in refrigerators, 53–54
from sewer gas, 165
shoe, 59
skunk, on dogs, _210_
in suitcases, 55–56
tobacco smoke, in
    clothing, 58–59
from urine stains, 57
of vacuum bags, 59
Offices
  covering phones in,
    369–70
  dirty dishes in, 369
  home
    children playing in,
      370
    inexpensive desks for,
      65–66
    organizing, 15–18
Oils, cooking, storing, _7_
Olive oil, as cleaning agent,
    _43_
Olives, pitting, 107
Onions
  odor on hands from, 51,
    _52_
  preventing crying from,
    51, 109–10
On-line services
  for communicating with
    grandparents,
    276–77
  limiting children's use of,
    276
Organizing
  attics, _19_, 21
  bedrooms, 9–10, 14
  bills, 18, 19
  bobbins, 200–201, **201**
  children's rooms, 14–15
  closets, 10–12, 25
  collections, 70
  crochet supplies, 198–99
  embroidery thread, 202,
    202
  family rooms, 13–14
  garages, 19–21
  home offices, 15–18
  home workshops, 144–46

kitchens, 7–9
knitting needles, 198, **198**
laundry, 12–13
living rooms, 13–14
mail, 18–19
move to new home, _286_,
    _287_
schedules, _17_
spools of thread,
    200–201, **201**
tickler files, 16–17
yard sales, 33–35, _33_
Outdoor(s)
  fences, 103–4
  flower gardens, 96–98
  garden tools, 98, _99_
  growing fruits and
    vegetables, 90–95
  herb gardens, 95–96
  lawn care, 87–90
  parties, 343–44, _345_
  shrubs, 99, 100–102, 103
  trees, 99–100, **100**, 102–3
  trellises, _102_
Outlet shopping, 140–41
Ovens
  cleaning, 41–42
  microwave, odors in, 54

P
Packing
  boxes for moving, 293,
    294–95
  dishes, 292
  essentials, when moving,
    _293_
  for moving, 292–96
  for travel, 218–25
Paddles
  protecting, from pests,
    256–57
  storing, 21
Paint
  disposing of, 31
  odors from, 59
  saving money on, _61_
Paint brushes, cleaning,
    152–53
Paint cans, labeling, _154_
Painting
  fences, 103–4
  shingled roofs, 167
Paint thinner, stretching use
    of, 152–53

Paneling
  for finishing walls, _157_
  gaps in, _158_
Pans. _See_ Pots and pans
Pantries, _8_
Pants, hanging multiple
    pairs of, 11, **11**
Panty hose, stopping runs
    in, 233
Paperwork, filing, 15–18,
    25–27
Parents
  losing a child, 362
  moving in with grown
    children, _301_
  new, gifts for, 319–20
Parkas, fixing tears in,
    186–87
Parking car, in garage, 180
Parties
  birthday, ideas for, _274_,
    344
  dinner (_see_ Dinner
    parties)
  engagement, 343
  housewarming, _341_
  outdoor, 343–44, _345_
  talking with strangers at,
    354
Party favors, _336_
Patients, hospital, gifts for,
    327
Patterns, sewing, worn, 201
Pen stains, on telephone, _40_
Perfume, leaking, in
    suitcase, 224
Personal property
    inventory,
    establishing, _18_
Personal services, saving
    money on, 135–36,
    _135_, _136_
Perspiration odors
  in clothing, 58
  in gym bags, 56–57
Pests
  bats, 73
  bees, 73
  birds, 74, **74**
  blackflies, 74–75
  cutworms, 75, **75**
  deer, 75–76
  maggots, _78_
  mice, _251_, 255, _257_

Underscored page references indicate boxed text. **Boldface** references indicate illustrations.
Italic references indicate tables.

Underscored page references indicate boxed text. **Boldface** references indicate illustrations. *Italic* references indicate tables.

<u>Underscored</u> page references indicate boxed text. **Boldface** references indicate illustrations. *Italic* references indicate tables.

Shelves
determining strength of,
154
sagging, reinforcing, 154,
154
Shingles
leaking, 166, **166**
repainting, 167
Shoes, preventing odor in,
59
Shopping
Christmas, 139–40
without driving, for
groceries, 312
at factory outlets, 140–41
at Salvation Army, 129
strategies for, 138–40
tips for
appliances, 137, 137
books, 132, 134
clothing, 128–30
furniture, 137–38
groceries, 123–27, 124,
368–69
magazines, 134
medicines, 127
new home, 284–87
personal services,
135–37, 135, 136
secondhand items,
141–43
sports and hobby
equipment, 130–32
at yard sales, 143
Shovels, to carry in car,
268–69
Shower curtains, for
windows, 68
Showerheads, removing
deposits from, 43
Showers, bridal, gifts for,
317
Shrimp, deveining, 111
Shrubs, planting, 99,
100–101
Sick persons, feeding,
120–22
Silk, yellowing of, 50
Silver, cleaning, 38–40
Sinks, cleaning, 42
Skates, saving money on,
131–32
Skidding on ice, stopping,
267–68

Ski equipment
lubricating, 192
preventing theft of, at ski
areas, 191
saving money on, 131–32
ski poles, broken, 192
skis
cross-country, waxing,
191
fixing grooves in, 192
storing, 21
Skinning chicken, 111
Skirts, hanging multiple, 11,
11
Skunks, repelling, 79–80
dogs sprayed by, 210
Sleeping bags
cleaning, 187–88
drying, 188
fixing tears in, 186–87
liners for, 188
Slugs, repelling, 80
Smoke
from fireplace or
woodstove, 262–63
odors from, in clothing,
58–59
Smokers
smoking outside, 367
traveling with, 217
Snacks, for car trips, 230
Snow
clearing, from cars, 270
freeing cars stuck in, 269
as garden insulator,
254–55
on roofs, as cause of ice
dams, 262
Snowstorms. *See also*
Blizzards
car emergency kit for, 267
emergency plan for, 265
icy windshields in, 266
Softball gloves, breaking in,
194
Software, protecting, from
children, 276
Soups
removing excess salt
from, 115
stuck to bottom of pot,
115
Souvenirs, packing, on
return trips, 222–23

Space, saving
in bedrooms, 9–10
in children's rooms,
14–15
in closets, 10–12
for drying clothes, 13
in family rooms, 13–14
in home workshops,
146–49
in kitchens, 7–9
in living rooms, 13–14
Spicy foods, burning
sensation from,
119–20
Spiders, repelling, 80–81
Spigots, preventing winter
freezing of, 255
Spinach, removing sand
from, 109
Spirit solvents, as cleaning
products, 39
Sponges, cleaning, 37, **37**
Sporting goods
saving money on, 130–32
storing, 19–20
Spring weather, problems
during, 246–47
Squash bugs, repelling from
vegetable garden, 81
Squeaks, in floorboards,
160–61
Squirrels, repelling, 81–83,
82, 255
Staining decks, 168
Stainless steel, cleaning, 38
Stains
blood, on carpet, 46
chocolate, on clothing, 50
cola, on clothing, 50
fruit, on clothing, 49, 49
ink
on carpet, 46
on fabric, 49
on telephone, 40
rust, on boats, 189
on suede, 50
tea, on clothing, 49
urine
on carpets, 46–47
on upholstered furni-
ture, 57
wallpaper, 48
Stairs, carrying items up or
down, 22, **22**

Stereo systems, displaying, 13–14

Stews
  removing excess salt from, 115
  stuck to bottom of pot, 115

Stings, bee, 72

Stockings, stopping runs in, 233

Stone floors, cleaning, 45–46

Storage
  in attics, _19_, 21
  baby items, 8–9
  in basements, 247
  brooms, 10
  canoe paddles, 21
  cassette tapes, _14_
  CDs, _14_
  children's clothing, outgrown,15
  children's items, 8
  cleaning supplies, _12_
  closets, 10–12, 15
  clothing, 10–11, 15
  cooking oils, _7_
  dishes, _9_
  in family rooms, 13
  flatware, _9_
  furniture, 21
  in garages, 19–21
  hardware, 144, _145_, 147, _147_
  hats, 12
  incoming mail, 18–19
  jewelry, 9
  keys, 21–22
  in living rooms, 13
  lumber, 20–21
  mops, 10
  odds and ends, 13
  packaged foods, 7–8, _8_
  pantries for, _8_
  piping, 20–21
  potatoes, 112
  in refrigerators, 7
  sailboat masts, 21
  sentimental items, 23
  sheets, 12
  skis, 21
  sweaters, 9
  tools, 20, **20**, 144, 147–49
  toys, 14–15
  vehicles, _172_

Store brands, buying, 123–24

Stovepipes, preventing creosote deposits in, 262–63

Strangers
  conversing with, at parties, 354
  at wedding, _356_

Strawberry jars, watering, 90–91

Streaks, from window washing, 48–49

Students
  college, communicating with, 282
  gifts for, 323–24
  hiring
    as movers, _294_
    for odd jobs, _135_, _136_
  homework help for, 274–76

Studying
  classic literature, 275–76
  as outlet in retirement, 300
  for tests, 275
  work space for, 274–75

Suede, cleaning, 50

Suitcases
  odors in, 55–56
  packing, 218–25
  repairing, 231

Summer camps
  closing, 255–57
    checklist for, _256_
  essentials for, _252_
  hot-water heater in, 252
  tracking sand into, 252–53
  visitors to, 253

Summer heat, relief from, 247–48

Sun exposure, importance of, when buying new home, 285–86

Sunflowers, growing, 97–98

Sunglasses
  keeping track of, 23
  securing screws in, 233

Supermarkets, saving time in, 125–26

Support groups, after death of pet, 206

Swapping houses, for vacations, 251, _253_

Sweaters, storing, 9

T

Tables, work, inexpensive idea for, 65–66

Table saws, locating, 155

Tailgaters, discouraging, 368

Tarnish, removing, 38–41

Tarps, for covering woodpiles, _263_

Teachers, inexpensive gifts for, 324–26

Tears
  in parkas, 186–87
  in sleeping bags, 186–87

Tea stains, on clothing, 49

Teenagers, communicating with, 280–81

Telemarketing calls, stopping, 363, 364, _364_

Telephone calls
  to child at college, 282, 323–24
  children interrupting, 365
  eating during, 364–65
  handling, in offices, 369–70
  holding, during parties, 337–38
  screening, with answering machine, 363–64
  telemarketing, 363, 364, _364_

Telephones
  cellular, low-cost plan for, _264_
  cleaning, _40_
  expense of, in hotels, 240

Televisions
  displaying, 13–14
  limiting children's watching of, 277–78
  packing, for moving, 295–96, **295**

Tents
  cleaning, 187
  holes in, 185–86
  stuck zippers on, 187
  waterproofing, _193_

Underscored page references indicate boxed text. **Boldface** references indicate illustrations. _Italic_ references indicate tables.

Termites, 83–84, **83**
Tests, studying for, 275
Thank-you notes, _357_, 358
    from children, _358_
Thefts, in summer camps, 256
Thread
    embroidery, organizing, 202, **202**
    sewing, organizing, 200–201, **201**
Threading sewing needles, 199
Tickler files, organizing, 16–17
Ticks, 84–86, _85_
Tile walls, cleaning, 48
Tipping movers, 297
Tiredness. _See_ Fatigue
Tires
    bicycle
        locating puncture in, 191
        patching, 190–91
    improving fuel economy with, 170
    mountain bike, _191_
    repairability of, 173
    spinning, from mud, 246, **246**
Toiletries, travel-size, saving money on, _227_
Toilets, cleaning, 44
Tomatoes
    canned, cutting, _108_
    growing, 94
    ripening, 108
Tool belts, 153
Toolboxes, specialized, 145–46
Tools
    fatigue from using, 149–50
    fireplace, _262_
    garden
        care of, 98
        selecting, _99_
    power, extension cords for, _152_
    protecting and maintaining, 150–52
    saving money on, _133_, _141_

secondhand, buying, _133_, _141_
storing, 20, **20**, 144, 147–49
timesaving, _151_
top 10 recommended, _150_
Tourists, safety considerations for, 231
Towels, reducing washing of, 12
Town, new, relocating and adjusting to, _285_, 298–99
Toys
    boredom with, 273
    giving away, 273–74
    storing, 14–15
    yard sales for selling, 33–34
Traps, insect, _81_
Travel. _See also_ Vacations
    air
        best plane seats for, 230–31
        free tickets for, 227
        keeping track of carry-on possessions during, 224–25
        for pets, 236–37
    auto
        mapping route for, 217
        preventing fatigue from, 217–18
    business, 240
    dealing with talkative people during, 368
    discomfort from, 314
    disorientation from, 238–39
    emergency repairs during, 231–34
    family, 234–35, _235_, _236_
    financial considerations for, 225–28
    group, expenses during, 368
    health and comfort during, 228–31
    packing for, 218–25
    with pets, 236–38
    protecting film during, 218
    on rainy days, _236_

receiving and sending mail during, 239–40
safety and security during, 231
with smokers, 217
tracking expenses during, 227–28
Travel items, substitutions for, _232_
Travel-size toiletries, saving money on, _227_
Tree decorations, inexpensive, _66_
Trees
    planting, 99–100, **100**
    pruning, 102–3
    watering, 100, 102
Trellises, movable, _102_
Trip cancellation insurance, _230_
Trucks
    moving, loading, 297
    mud on floor of, 245
    pickup
        dogs riding in, _205_
        improving fuel economy of, 170
Turkey, leftover, uses for, 118
Tutors, hiring, 275

U

Unpacking, after moving, 297–98
Upholstery
    fading of, 66
    leather, in cars, _176_
    urine stains on, 57
Urine, cat, eliminating odor of, 211
Urine stains
    on carpeting, 46–47
    on upholstered furniture, 57
Utensils, using correctly, at dinner parties, 354
Utility knives, as timesaving tools, _151_

V

Vacation property
    renting, 250
    sharing, 248–49
    visitors to, 253

Underscored page references indicate boxed text. **Boldface** references indicate illustrations. _Italic_ references indicate tables.

Underscored page references indicate boxed text. **Boldface** references indicate illustrations. *Italic* references indicate tables.

Underscored page references indicate boxed text. **Boldface** references indicate illustrations.
Italic references indicate tables.

392
         Index